THEN COMES

MARRIAGE?

THEN COMES

MARRIAGE?

A Cultural History of the American Family

REBECCA PRICE JANNEY

MOODY PUBLISHERS
CHICAGO

All Scripture quotations, unless otherwise indicated, are taken from the *Holy Bible, New International Version*®. NIV®. Copyright © 1973, 1978, 1984 by Biblica, Inc.™ Used by permission of Zondervan Publishing House. All rights reserved.

Scripture quotations marked NLT are taken from the *Holy Bible, New Living Transla-tion,* copyright © 1996. Used by permission of Tyndale House Publishers, Inc., Wheaton, Illinois 60189, U.S.A. All rights reserved.

Scripture quotations marked NEB are taken from *The New English Bible.* Copyright © 1961 by Oxford University Press and Cambridge University Press. Used by permission.

All websites listed herein are accurate at the time of publication, but may change in the future or cease to exist. The listing of website references and resources does not imply publisher endorsement of the site's entire contents. Groups, corporations, and organiza-tions are listed for informational purposes, and listing does not imply publisher endorse-ment of their activities.

Editor: Elizabeth Newenhuyse
Interior Design: Ragont Design
Cover Design: Dog Eared Design
Cover Images: Rings, Veer; 50's couple: istockphoto; Block house: Veer;
Gable: istockphoto; Gay couple: 123 RF; Tv: 123 RF

Library of Congress Cataloging-in-Publication Data

Janney, Rebecca Price-
 Then comes marriage? : a cultural history of the American family / Rebecca Price Janney.
  p. cm.
 ISBN 978-0-8024-5494-2
 1. Families--Religious aspects--Christianity--History. 2. Families--United States--History. 3. United States--Moral conditions. I. Title.

 BR517.J36 2010
 261.8'35850973--dc22

                    2009049591

This book is printed on acid free recycled paper containing 30% PCW (Post Consumer Waste) and manufactured in the United States of America by Bethany Press.

We hope you enjoy this book from Moody Publishers. Our goal is to provide high-quality, thought-provoking books and products that connect truth to your real needs and chal-lenges. For more information on other books and products written and produced from a bib-lical perspective, go to www.moodypublishers.com or write to:

Moody Publishers
820 N. LaSalle Boulevard
Chicago, IL 60610

1 3 5 7 9 10 8 6 4 2

Printed in the United States of America

This book is for my cousin Barbara Burchfield
and her beloved husband, Quen, who demonstrated
to me at an early age how a Christian family loves,
lives, and sacrifices to the glory of God
and the good of each member, and for the family
I cherish most in the world, my husband, Scott,
and my son, David—may God make me worthy of you.

Contents

STATE OF THE UNION

Heather and Ryan sittin' in a tree,
K-i-s-s-i-n-g
First comes love,
Then comes marriage,
Then comes Heather with a baby carriage.

Not necessarily. Not anymore. Not in America.

✳ ✳ ✳ ✳ ✳

WHAT A MESS. They moved in together to begin a new life, two young people just out of college with the world open before them and the future beckoning its promise. Just after the last box was unpacked, they discovered that she was pregnant, so they began preparing to welcome a baby, although that had not been in their immediate plans. Nine months later the child came along, and disturbing questions entered the young man's mind, even as the relationship with his partner grew strained. When he brought up leaving, she reminded him that he would have to pay his fair share of the baby's upbringing, or else. The problem was, this child looked nothing like him. Nothing at all. His father and his father's girlfriend noticed it when they came for a visit to see their sort-of grandchild. "Maybe," they said, "the baby isn't really yours after all." He hated to do it, but he had a DNA test done and to his consternation, it revealed that he was not the father. He had come to love the baby, who wasn't really his, but he wanted out of the relationship with the mother. He faced a dilemma.

* * * *

Elsewhere a young woman reconnected with a man she'd known years before, who had since gotten married and had two children, then divorced. They dated for a while, then he proposed, offering her a beautiful ring and a pledge of marital faithfulness. As they prepared their wedding, she pored over brides' magazines and dreamed of her fairy-tale day in the spotlight as a glittering, if not exactly blushing, bride. How many attendants would there be? What color would she pick for their dresses and the theme of the wedding? Where would the ceremony and the reception take place? In the midst of these activities, she missed a period. Then another. She was often tired and grouchy. Her friends automatically thought she would move the date up, but she decided to wait out the pregnancy, then when she had recovered her figure and would once again look good in a bridal gown, she would walk down the aisle. Several years later, there has still not been a wedding.

* * * *

In another, Catholic family, a college sophomore was best friends with a girl she'd known since they were little. The girls had been inseparable during high school, but since they'd gone to different universities, their times together became precious and few. She excitedly told another friend about the weekend they'd just spent together and what her old pal's life was like. "It's like her family has this compound, with the parents' house in the front and two other, smaller houses in the back. She and her sister live in one of the houses, and her brother is in the other one with his girlfriend. It's so cool how they're all together."

A few months earlier in the same college girl's life, the woman who had moved in with her grandfather after her grandmother's death had died suddenly, and not long after that, her brother broke up with his live-in girlfriend. "I'll never live with someone before I get married," another young woman declared, citing statistics that say people who do so have the odds against them of getting married and staying that way. "I don't want that to happen to me," she decided. But one by one her friends started moving in together, and after she got her first teaching job and became engaged, she bought a house with her fiancé. They had a date for the wedding, after all, and everyone else was doing it, so why shouldn't it be right? Down the street, one neighbor told another, "You'll love this couple. You might not even have to put your house on the market, because they're engaged and are looking for their first home and would like to see if yours is what they want. She's a teacher in this school district, and he works a few miles from here. They're living with her parents now."

A woman a few doors up the street was discussing her new relationship with an old friend. "So, you're getting married then?" the friend asked this middle-aged widow. She shook her head. "Not for now. I want to get my kid through college first. If I get married now, I'd give up the benefits that come from being a widow."

These are all true stories, based on a typical, middle-class American neighborhood.

*   *   *   *   *

It seems that today the only Americans who are adamant about getting married are homosexual couples, people like Ellen DeGeneres and Portia de Rossi, who assert that they should have every right to be legally bound, that they should not be discriminated against. "What can I say? I'm the luckiest girl in the world," said DeGeneres after their sumptuous ceremony. "She's officially off the market. No one else gets her. And now she'll cook and clean for me."[1]

The world of celebrity buzzed a few other times that summer with news that the beautiful young actress Lindsay Lohan had forsaken men in favor of an affair with British musician/disc jockey Samantha Ronson. According to a friend:

> Sam and Lindsay are inseparable. Sam has been a really good influence on Lindsay. There is no one else special in Lindsay's life apart from Sam but it has taken her a while to feel like she can talk about their relationship. Lindsay hasn't dated any men since she started hanging around with Sam, and there has hardly been a day in the last two months when they have been apart. They have been shacked up in Lindsay's place and they spend weekends like a married couple going to the supermarket together.[2]

The tabloids also carried the story that singer Clay Aiken, who rose to fame as an "American Idol," revealed that he was a homosexual, shortly after the birth of his baby. He said, "It was the first decision I made as a father. I cannot raise a child to lie or to hide things. I wasn't raised that way, and I'm not going to raise a child to do that."[3] The child's mother is Aiken's producer, who conceived the boy through in vitro fertilization.

※ ※ ※ ※ ※

A teenage girl was born to a single mother fourteen years ago, and while the mom never married the baby's father, he was involved in the child's upbringing and stayed close to her as she grew up. The mother did marry, briefly, then continued to struggle on her own to make a living and bring her child up to love God and His Son, Jesus. She at last met another man, and they got married and had children.

One man divorced his first wife and had recently separated from his second one when a new love entered the picture. They both had young adult children, and they frequently attended church together, but they decided to move into one apartment so they weren't paying two rents. "I know the Bible says you shouldn't do it," he told a relative, "but I'm going to do it anyway."

These vignettes reflect so much of contemporary American family life.

※　※　※　※　※

In the 1998 movie *You've Got Mail*, there is a telling scene that portrays the way in which Americans do male-female relationships. In it Joe Fox, who lives with his girlfriend, has taken two small family members on an afternoon outing, and they've stopped in a bookstore for its story hour. Afterwards, Joe introduces the children to bookstore owner Kathleen Kelly (who happens to live with her boyfriend), who assumes that Joe is their father. Annabelle, the little girl, corrects Kathleen:

Annabelle Fox:	Oh, that's not my dad. That's my nephew.
Kathleen Kelly:	You know, I don't really think that *he* could be your nephew.
Joe Fox:	No, no, no, it's true. Annabelle is my aunt. Isn't that right, Aunt Annabelle?
Annabelle Fox:	Uh-huh, and Matt is his . . .
Kathleen Kelly:	No, no, let me guess. Are you his uncle? [Matt giggles, shakes his head no]
Kathleen Kelly:	His grandfather? [Matt giggles harder, still shaking his head]
Kathleen Kelly:	His great-grandfather?
Matthew Fox:	[laughing] I'm his brother!
Joe Fox:	[answering Kathleen's very confused look] Matthew is my father's son, Annabelle is my grandfather's daughter. We are . . . an American family.[4]

Robert James Waller's *The Bridges of Madison County* appeared in American bookstores in 1992 and gained the distinction of being one of the twentieth century's bestselling titles.[5] It deals with an adulterous affair between an unfulfilled Iowa wife and a traveling photographer in her area taking pictures of its famed covered bridges. The book went on to become a celebrated film starring Clint Eastwood and Meryl Streep. Of this story, Adrian Snell says, "The act of falling in love conquers all—even our promises."[6] This, he says, is a huge cultural myth of our time, that love is everything, but commitment is a non-starter.

According to the National Opinion Research Center at the University of Chicago,

> the American family experienced major changes in the last part of the twentieth century and will continue to shift away from traditional models in the twenty-first. Households will move further away from the family-structure model of a stay-at-home mother, working father, and children. . . . Because of divorce, cohabitation and single parenthood, a majority of families rearing children in the next century will probably not include the children's original two parents, said Tom W. Smith, Director of the General Social Survey and author of "The Emerging 21st-Century American Family." . . . Moreover, most households will not include children.[7]

It wasn't always like this.

Chapter 1

THE ENGLISH COLONIES

THE LIFE OF A LATE sixteenth-century English laborer and his wife followed a predictable path. Once a woman married in Elizabethan England, she passed from the protection of her father's home to that of her new husband. She mainly looked after the domestic affairs of her household while her husband became the main provider of an income. Each of them had a clearly defined role to fulfill, something that provided a measure of stability in an age when disease could suddenly claim a life, or economic or political conditions change one's fortunes with no prior warning. When Eleanor White married Ananias Dare as a young woman, she agreed to be an obedient spouse who faithfully served her husband's interests, but she never could have imagined the course that their lives would take or that she would have an impact on history as she lived out her pledge.

If her life had followed the usual blueprint, Eleanor White Dare would have lived and died in obscurity. As it turned out, however, she and her family played a starring role in America's founding.

She was part of a restless culture at a time when middle-class people were trying to break free from antique social rules and make decent livings for themselves in a more modern and adventurous milieu. Britain under Queen Elizabeth I was eager to establish supremacy in the New World as its chief rivals Spain and France also vied to establish colonies there. There was a feeling that Britain's birthright was glory, although her debtors' prisons bulged, and second sons strove to make a mark denied them by their birth order. Unemployment was high, and many families, burdened by religious convention, yearned to break free. In that place and time the dominant attitude was that religion should be observed, that it kept society well oiled, but that it had a specific place. Zeal and nonconformity were discouraged, even punished.

In 1585, Eleanor Dare's father, John White, sailed with Richard Grenville's expedition to the North Carolina coast as an artist who would capture images of the New World. He served along with 107 other men as they tried to establish a military outpost to claim that territory for Queen Elizabeth ahead of the Spanish, who were active farther to the southeast. Upon his return to England, White shared his enthusiasm for the Roanoke colony with his daughter and her husband; it is unclear who his wife was, but it would seem that she had died by this time. Some believe that White was part of a separatist movement, a dissident from the organized form of religion that ruled the day, thus vulnerable to restrictive rules and regulations.[1]

Perhaps that is why he was able to persuade his pregnant daughter and her husband to sail back with him in 1587. Whatever the primary reason, it took extraordinary courage and commitment to leave everything familiar to pursue a completely unknown and unpredictable future.

It is hard to imagine making a trip across the Atlantic Ocean in a rustic sailing vessel at all, let alone pregnant. Eleanor shared her misery with another mother-to-be, Margery Harvey, and fifteen other women, eleven children, and eight-seven men whose purpose was to recreate the best of English culture in the wilderness. Some men went without their wives and daughters, going either by themselves or with sons to prepare the way for the others to come when conditions were in a more advanced state.[2]

John White served as the governor of the new colony, but Simon Fernandez was in charge of the expedition itself, a privateer who engaged in several skirmishes with rivals, thus delaying the convoy's arrival by several weeks. Once they finally landed on Roanoke Island, the weary colonists faced sickness, food shortages, and unstable relations with the Native Americans. If they worked hard, however, the money and labor they invested would pay off in the sum of five hundred acres per family to begin a new life in a new world.

Although the colonists had little time for play, they did celebrate the birth of the first English child to be born on American soil when Eleanor Dare presented her husband with a baby girl, Virginia—after the Virgin Queen—on August 18. Shortly afterward, Margery Harvey delivered a child whose sex and name were not recorded.[3] Because of a dire need for more supplies, Governor White returned to England days after the birth of his granddaughter, but only after great duress and pleading from other leaders of the colony who believed that only he had enough clout to make their case before the Queen and her court. Because the colonists planned to move further inland during his time away, they arranged for a signal to inform White of their whereabouts. Although he intended to return as quickly as possible, he ended up being delayed by three years because of England's military campaign against the Spanish Armada.

When he arrived back in America on Virginia Dare's third birthday, White discovered that the colonists had neatly buried his armor, books, and pictures, but they themselves were gone. He found the word CROATOAN carved on a post, indicating the place where their native guide Manteo came from, along with the inscription CRO on a tree. He did not find a Maltese cross, which would have been a sign that they had been in danger. Because of problems with the ships and severe weather conditions, White's party was unable to find his countrymen, who vanished into history as "the lost colony." He lived the rest of his days in England and Ireland, no doubt grieved over the loss of his family, much more than for his vision to colonize the New World.

JAMESTOWN

The Reverend Richard Hakluyt spent fifty years of his life preaching throughout England about the necessity to establish an English colony in America. An advisor to Queen Elizabeth I, then to her successor James after 1603, the Anglican vicar steadfastly urged the British to send emissaries to the New World to introduce the Native Americans to Jesus Christ. For a time after the Roanoke debacle, his pleas fell upon mostly deaf ears. As the memory of that disaster faded, however, some began to listen, among them investors who thought an American colony would increase personal and national revenue, fend off Spanish control of America, provide opportunities for many restless young Britons, be a market for English goods, and provide much-needed lumber for the royal navy. There were others, however, men and women with a passion for Christ, who wanted to bring hope to those living in spiritual darkness.

English pastors exhorted their congregations to pray that God would send laborers into that ripe field to bring about "the salvation of countless thousands of miserable Indians."[4] The new king shared this impulse; in his royal charter for the establishment of a permanent English colony in America, James I proclaimed in language that seems offensive today because of its assessment of the Native Americans, that the settlers would bring about "the propagating of Christian religion to such people as yet live in darkness and miserable ignorance of the true knowledge and worship of God, and may in time bring the infidels and savages, living in these parts, to human civility and to a settled and quiet government."[5]

A pastor whom Richard Hakluyt greatly influenced in this

direction began to dream of going to America himself to spread the news of salvation in Christ. The vicar for Reculver, Kent, the Reverend Robert Hunt lived a settled life with his wife, Elizabeth Edwards Hunt, and their son and daughter. Some speculate that his marriage may not have been a happy one because he so strongly desired to go to America, but it seems more likely that his fervor to evangelize the first Americans was sincere. He would not be taking his family with him, as some men had done on the Roanoke venture. Rather, this expedition, which left just before Christmas 1606, would bring only men, 104 of them, to "Jamestown," most of whom were not even heads of families who would later join them.[6]

Hunt suffered badly on the interminable voyage from England, one that took five months to complete because severe weather kept the boats from venturing out into the open sea for many weeks. When the travelers at last journeyed across the Atlantic, constant bickering and depleted supplies plagued their relationships, with Hunt serving as an intermediary and peacemaker. At last they arrived on the Virginia coast in late April, but Hunt advised that they not disembark until each man had had an opportunity to reflect upon his spiritual condition and repent of his sins. At that point, he led a small band onto the shore where they planted a seven foot oak cross and claimed the land for God and the spread of the gospel.

By that fall, only fifty men had survived the brutally hot summer weather and the strange diseases that claimed many lives. When cooler temperatures prevailed and the harvest came in, hope revived. A frequent visitor to their fort was a young Indian princess named Pocahontas, the beloved daughter of the powerful chief Powhatan. Given her innocent age, she was able to serve as an intermediary between the English and her people, as well as to supply them with food and, in December, help save the life of brash Captain John Smith, who'd been slated for execution. It is possible that the impressionable young lady had a crush on the suave Englishman, but as far as romance goes, she reserved her greatest love for another, and in that was one of America's first love stories.

In spite of a devastating fire in January of 1608 in which the church, palisades, storehouse, and many cabins were lost—including most of the Reverend Hunt's valuables—the colony persisted. Shortly after the conflagration, however, the clergyman died of illness, a loss that the men mourned deeply. Back in England, his wife quickly remarried, which was entirely respectable for that era because people tended to die young; she went on to have six more children.

In October, seventy more colonists arrived, among them two women, a Mistress Forrest and her maid, Ann Burras. According to Gail Collins,

> The Jamestown that greeted them was a fort, about an acre in size, with a shopping district composed of one storehouse and a church that looked "like a barne," according to Captain John Smith. The homes were tumbledown shacks that one visitor said were inferior to the lowest cottage he had ever seen back in England. There is no record of Mrs. Forrest's first name, or what she thought when she discovered that she was marooned in what must have seemed like a long, rowdy fraternity party, minus food.[7]

It isn't clear why Forrest's husband financed this journey, but Ann quickly entered matrimony with carpenter John Laydon, who was eager for female companionship. Theirs was "the first recorded English marriage on the soil of the United States."[8] Jamestown remained a poor place to raise a family for several years; in the summer of 1609, four hundred more colonists arrived, but they were infected with diseases and bad reputations. Conditions became so poor that plans were put in place to abandon the settlement, which had gone from five hundred people all the way down to just sixty due to malnutrition, illness, and hostilities with Indians that had "destroyed morale and reduced the men to scavengers."[9] Not exactly a family-friendly place.

The leadership of Sirs Thomas Dale and Thomas Gates helped to restore order, largely through martial law. From six to ten in the morning, then again from two to four in the afternoons, everyone had to work. Another improvement came about through the marriage of colonist John Rolfe and the now marriageable Pocahontas. Rolfe fell in love with the young maiden, and he yearned to bring about her salvation; she was baptized and took the name Rebecca. Both Governor Dale and Powhatan gave their consent, each believing that the union would help to enhance the relationship between the English and the Native Americans, which it did. The two were married in April 1614. There has been speculation that had more intermarriage occurred, hostilities between the two groups might have largely been averted. The English, however, felt squeamish about interracial relationships.

In 1616, Rebecca Rolfe gave birth to a son, Thomas, and the family returned to England the following year to drum up greater support for colonization. While they were there, Rebecca became a favorite of royal society; in fact, King James was initially incensed that her husband had presumed to marry such a royal woman, who was clearly outside of his class. When he heard the entire love story, however, he relented. In 1617, while preparing to return to America, Rebecca became ill with smallpox and died in England at twenty-one. Her husband and son would go without her. John was killed in an Indian massacre in 1622, shortly after Powhatan died and the old alliances began to unravel. Thomas, it is said, became one of the founding families of Virginia.

By the time of the Pocahontas-Rolfe romance, Jamestown was in urgent need of a woman's touch if a permanent settlement was going to happen. If the men who had gone to America had family ties there, it was reasoned, they simply wouldn't make their money and return to England. Instead, they would make their homes—English homes—in America, thus strengthening the entire venture with permanence and stability. In 1619, the first "bride ships" arrived in Jamestown with single women of good character who would be available to marry the men who had been so long without (chaste) female companionship. No other arrangement would have been acceptable in that place and time, such as living together outside of wedlock.

Back in England, many more men than women had died during a plague epidemic, which meant that the prospects for marriage had tightened considerably for the females. One way to get more colonists to go to America was to advertise back in England that if they would come to Jamestown, women could easily find mates. One ad read, "If any Maid or single Woman have a desire to go over, they will think themselves in the Golden Age, when Men paid a Dowry for their Wives; for if they be but civil, and under 50 years of Age, some honest Man or other will purchase them for their Wives."[10]

Two types of females emigrated, those ready for immediate matrimony and those who signed on for seven years of indentured servitude, women of about twenty years of age who would receive their freedom in addition to some land at the end of that tenure. These women found themselves in a four-to-one ratio with the men, giving them far better prospects than they had known in England. A Jamestown colonist who ordered a bride from England through the Virginia Company could expect to pay between 120–150 pounds in tobacco for her expenses.

Women in Jamestown may have found it easy to find a mate, but a hard life awaited them overall. Their duties, whether they were married or single, involved laundry (in an age with no packaged cleansing agents or machines), cooking, cleaning, raising and harvesting food, and sewing, usually when the tools to make those jobs doable were in short supply. A single woman was also expected to be involved in tobacco farming since virtually everyone lived on farms, and labor was hard to come by. Says Gail Collins,

"The farms were almost all isolated, surrounded by endless forests, down winding waterways without any real roads to connect them. Plantation owners were forced to be away from home for long periods of time on business, and they often depended on their wives, or even daughters, to drain swamps, tend cattle, cultivate the tobacco, and otherwise manage things while they were gone."[11]

When in 1999 the remains of Mistress Forrest were exhumed, the condition of her skeleton at death bore witness to the harshness of life in Jamestown Colony. She had been only thirty-five when she died, yet she had only five teeth left.

Although divorce was practically unheard of, if a couple ended up in an unhappy union, it probably didn't last all that long anyway, the average marriage being about seven years.[12] At that point, either the husband or wife died, leaving the spouse free to remarry, which usually happened. In the early seventeenth century in the Chesapeake region, the mortality rate was around 80 percent. Collins says this created "patchwork families made up of widows, widowers, and several degrees of stepchildren. People developed new terms for their father's 'now-wife' or their 'new husband's children.'"[13]

MASSACHUSETTS BAY COLONY

As Jamestown stabilized, Christians back in England who disagreed with the official Anglican Church's resemblance to Roman Catholicism faced economic displacement and prejudice, harassment by the authorities, arrest, and sometimes imprisonment. Some highly educated believers known as Puritans believed that the Church could be reformed, and they set about to do this from within the existing framework of Anglicanism. They emphasized that faith alone, not good works, resulted in salvation of sin and the attainment of heaven, in addition to personal Bible study and a simplicity of worship. Out of their numbers a different group arose known as Pilgrims, men and women who maintained that the Anglican Church was too far gone to be renewed. Initially those "separatists" fled to Holland to pursue their faith, but after a dozen years of never being able to rise above menial employment and subsistent living, they decided to pursue a better life in America. There they could live out their simple faith as a shining city on a hill for all the world to see, even as they took the message of Christ to the Native Americans.

In the fall of 1620, ninety-eight men, women, and children sailed on the *Mayflower* to the shores of present-day Massachusetts.

Eighteen of the passengers were adult women, along with some older girls nearing marriageable age. Five husbands came ahead of their wives, while eighteen brought theirs, three of whom were pregnant. They arrived in early November, the worst time of year to establish a colony. Whereas the Roanoke and Jamestown colonists had faced tremendous heat and unusual diseases, the Pilgrims endured a brutal winter in which over half of them perished; 78 percent of the women died during that time. The first was Dorothy Bradford, who accidentally fell off the ship as it lay anchored at Provincetown Harbor; during the first four months the women remained on board while the men labored outside to build houses and storage facilities. In one especially sad instance, William Mullins died in February, followed by both his wife and son, leaving their teenaged daughter, Priscilla, to fend for herself.[14] Also dying that first winter were Captain Miles Standish's wife, Rose. By April, only five women were left, and in May the widow of John Carver, who had died of sunstroke, also passed away. Eleanor Billington, Elizabeth Hopkins, Mary Brewster, and Susanna White Winslow remained. Susanna had been married to William White, who did not survive that first winter, then she quickly wed Edward Winslow, whose wife had also passed away in the first months.

Not only were the conditions harsh, but they had few material sources of comfort. Each family had only been allowed to bring one trunk filled with their most important possessions. Gail Collins says, "It was possible they would never again see a clock or a cat or eat an apple. If their few scrawny goats died . . . they would lose their only source of milk. There were no spinning wheels . . . or other implements the women had used in Europe to make the things they could not buy at market. If they ruined a dress or broke a plate, it couldn't be replaced."[15]

It seemed especially important for those colonists to remarry as quickly as possible after the death of a spouse to ensure not only their personal survival, but that of their wilderness venture as well. Couples in that harsh state found comfort and strength with each other.

These may not have been demonstrative people as couples usually behave in the twenty-first century, but neither were they void of romantic impulses. There are, for example, lively and tender stories of the rivalry between Miles Standish and John Alden for the affections of Priscilla Mullins. According to Puritan custom, single men and women lived with married couples who served as mentors and chaperones. John Alden resided with Captain Standish, the colony's burly military protector, and his wife, Rose. The men developed a close friendship that underwent a challenge after Rose's death when they both set their caps on the pretty, vivacious Priscilla. According to the legendary account of the *Courtship of Miles Standish* by Henry Wadsworth Longfellow, there was a bloom of romance even in that rough country. He wrote that when the good captain asked Priscilla Mullins to marry him through Alden, the young lady replied, "Why don't you speak for yourself, John?"[16] Obviously she wasn't about to marry the first man to ask but had her heart set on someone for whom she had deep feelings. The Aldens got married and went on to have eleven children, but Standish did not have to wait long for his own succor. Of the five wives who had remained in England, four eventually came to America, in 1623. On that ship a woman called Barbara also sailed; she became better known as Mrs. Standish, with whom he had seven children.

Each person had a job to do in the New World, including the children. When they had lived in Holland, the young people became used to working to support their households since their immigrant fathers held low-paying positions there. In the Massachusetts Bay Colony that first winter, the children proved even more resilient than the grown-ups and ended up caring for the ailing adults, performing nursing and household responsibilities, cooking, cleaning, and keeping the fires burning.

Chapter 2

Down the Rivers, o'er the Prairies

HER TIME HAD COME. She sprang into action, preparing for her short journey away from the village and into the woods where she would deliver her child alone. Just sixteen years old, she possessed the knowledge imparted to all females by her clan, to bear whatever pain came with childbirth patiently, bravely. In the woods she fashioned a serviceable birthing shelter for herself and her child out of nature's raw materials in the time she had before she could no longer move about freely. Once the baby came, his young mother plunged him into the creek, a practice that she learned from her people would begin the long journey to a worthy manhood. Then she returned to the shelter where she guarded him fiercely, fastening him to a cradle board that would require his bones to grow straight and strong, capable of walking through difficult terrain as he learned to hunt. The device also was constructed in such a way as to catch the baby's excrement, often with wads of moss. Many European commentators observed that native women were so sturdy that childbirth barely affected them, that this might be due to their innate stoutness, or perhaps to their "ignorance of Eve's curse."[1]

Depending on her tribe's customs, the new mother would live apart in her hut for a short time or a lengthy sojourn, but like most other Native Americans, she would not have sexual relations with her husband again until she had weaned their child, around the age of two or three, but sometimes as old as four. In some tribes, it was considered acceptable if the husband had a concubine during this period, but just not in the home he shared with his wife. Likewise, toilet training went at its own natural pace, as they believed all things in life should proceed. There were, of course, North American tribes in which the birth experience was more communal, where the prospective mother enjoyed the assistance of a midwife and perhaps female relatives. Across the board, however, birth accorded new mothers with great prestige and honor.

This characterized the way in which Native American children came into the world at the time when Europeans first began arriving. There were, however, variations on the theme according to the customs and precepts of the many tribes that made North America their home. When Columbus reached the Americas, its native peoples spoke about two thousand different languages, bearing witness to the scope of their diversity.[2]

They did, however, share certain attributes in terms of their family relationships.

Historian Gary B. Nash has written of the way they depended for their survival on a precarious food supply during the earliest history of the Americas.[3] When the various tribes learned to domesticate plants, however, it revolutionized life; instead of wandering about looking for food as nomads, they were able to settle in groups where they could plant crops and hunt in one area. "With this acquisition of partial control came vast cultural changes," says Nash.[4] Those alterations include the development of villages, population growth, the increase of artistic, religious, and political activities and advancements, as well as a clear delineation of labor among the sexes with all of the implications these changes brought for interpersonal relationships.

Common among the North American tribes was a philosophy of common property, something that the Europeans found difficult to understand because they valued ownership so highly. Native Americans, however, believed that the land and its wealth were to be shared among themselves as each person labored in his or her capacity to provide for one another, beginning with one's family. Many of the societies they created were matrilineal, meaning they traced their descent through the mother's family. Although some generalizations can be made about their lives in North America, it must be understood that there were many variations along the common themes. For example, families often grouped together to form a village, and depending on its size and strength, those clans could develop into a "nation," as with the Senecas and Mohawks.[5]

Frequently political power lay in the hands of women, who ruled over most aspects of family and village life while their sons and husbands went on hunting forays. This was especially true of the many tribes that made up the Iroquois culture. Men shared political power, but they could be replaced if the leading women so desired.

The ways in which Native Americans raised their children differed categorically from the European philosophy of child rearing. Overall, the first Americans believed less in societal subordination to authority figures than to the principle of personal autonomy. This concept involved the mastery of one's self and, as a result, the individual would become a more valuable part of the tribe's life. Several Europeans who dealt with Native Americans noted with a mixture of shock, wonder, and disdain how permissive the Indians were with their children, how little discipline they meted out. The French Roman Catholic priest, Father Gabriel Sagard, worked with the Huron Indians in the early 1600s, and in his writings he commented on how their offspring ran amok:

> For this reason everybody lives in complete freedom and does what he thinks fit; and parents, for failure to punish their children,

are often compelled to suffer wrong-doing at their hands, sometimes being beaten and flouted to their face. This is conduct
too shocking and smacks of nothing less than the brute beast.
Bad example, and bad bringing up, without punishment or cor-
rection, are the causes of all this lack of decency.[6]

This differed fundamentally from the way in which John Robin-
son, a Pilgrim minister, viewed children:

And surely there is in all children . . . a stubbornness, and stoutness of mind arising from natural pride, which must, in the first
place, be broken and beaten down; that so the foundation of
their education being laid in humility and tractableness, other
virtues may, in their time, be built thereon. . . . For the beating,
and keeping down of this stubborness parents must provide
carefully . . . that the children's wills and willfulness be restrained
and repressed. . . . Children should not know, if it could be kept
from them, that they have a will of their own, but in their parents' keeping.[7]

In Pennsylvania, missionary David Zeisberger worked among
the Moravian Indians, and he recorded his observations in 1780.
He also mentioned the lack of discipline, but he didn't believe the
children were always any the worse for it. He saw that some of the
children didn't turn out so well because of it, however. Zeisberger
learned that most native parents feared some sort of payback from
their children if they were too hard on them as youngsters. When
they did sometimes resort to punishment, parents favored water as
a means of discipline, either by dropping the mischief maker into
it or by throwing it at him or her. In some clans, parents employed
fish teeth to scrape a child's skin, not so much for the discomfort
it caused but for the marks of shame they created for everyone to
see. The withdrawal of affection sometimes brought a miscreant
back into line, as did public ridicule; shaming was a powerful form
of rejection and teaching in Indian society. And sometimes a

mother would break down and sob if her little girl misbehaved, which usually did the trick.

The Indian child grew up learning to emulate the relational aspects of adulthood as well as the roles that each person was expected to fulfill. A boy's playthings were often tools of the hunt, while a girl's "toys" ushered her into home and agricultural management skills. Boys heard stories about legendary Indians known for their hunting exploits much the way in which twenty-first century American males grow up following sports stars. At puberty, a boy would go off by himself to seek a spirit guardian through various forms of physical and sensory deprivation, sometimes taking this to extremes, such as inducing hallucinations. A girl's rite of passage came when she got her first period, an event that instilled her, according to her tribe, with supernatural power, which she could use either for good or ill. Boys and girls knew their places in society and were trained not to violate them in any way. Father Sagard once commented of the Huron boys, "if a mother asks her son to go for water or wood or do some similar household service, he will reply to her that this is a girl's work and will do none of it."[8]

Children received their names at a ceremony for that purpose, names usually related to some personal characteristic or attribute, and they would keep them until adulthood when they often abandoned them because they could be unflattering. Adults usually called each other by the relationship they had with someone, thus Grandfather, Grandmother, Wife, etc.

As it was for Europeans of the same era, childhood lasted only a short time and served mainly as a preparation for adulthood, to establish one's own family, and become a useful member of society. Native American girls began to entertain suitors for marriage around fourteen to sixteen years of age, and the boys at eighteen or nineteen. Long before that time, however, both engaged in sexual activity, which their parents thought of as an instinctive physical act and nothing to be put off limits. Naturally this riled the Europeans, who considered this attitude worthy of animals who didn't know any better. What surprised the westerners even more, however, was that during courtship, couples showed no outward affection or emotion toward one another, nor were they acquainted with kissing.

The marriage relationship wasn't between two people, according to Native Americans, but a societal matter that involved everyone in the family, and by extension, the tribe or village. Today Americans often say that a man marries a woman, not her family and vice versa, but the first Americans believed that who you married had everything to do with communal life. During childhood, a girl or boy's parents might fix their eyes on someone for a marriage partner, even to the point of discussing the choice with the parents of the other party. Nevertheless, if the time came and the children disagreed, they could deny their parents' choice. Likewise, a girl might go to her parents with her first selection for a husband, and they could tell her to try again.

When a young man decided upon a partner, he often had someone act as a go-between to determine whether the feelings were mutual and whether her family approved. According to John Henry Hauberg, during the two-day festivities known as the Crane Dance, the men decided which women they wanted to marry, then had their mothers present their sons' case to the girls' mothers.

The necessary arrangements are made and the time appointed for him to come.

He goes to the lodge when all are asleep, or pretend to be, and with his flint and steel strikes a light and soon finds where his intended sleeps. He then awakens her, holds the light close to his face that she may know him, after which he places the light close to her.

If she blows it out the ceremony is ended and he appears in the lodge next morning as one of the family.

If she does not blow out the light, but leaves it burning he retires from the lodge. The next day he places himself in plain view and plays his flute. The young women go out one by one to see who he is playing for. The tune changes to let them know that he is not playing for them.

When his intended makes her appearance at the door, he continues his courting tune until she returns to the lodge. He then quits playing and makes another trial at night, which usually turns out favorably.[9]

When the young people had made their choices and received family support, presents were exchanged between the couple, followed by a feast for everyone in their village. Some wedding ceremonies were simple while those of other tribes were elaborate with most of them occurring at night. Brides and grooms usually engaged in a ceremonial washing of their hands to symbolize a break with the past and a new, clean beginning, and the Hopi Indians took the water ritual a step further, with the washing of the couples' hair in one washbasin followed by it being woven into one cord.

The husband and wife usually resided with her parents for a year, a period in which the couple might not have intercourse so that they might get to know each other as well as a brother and a sister. This was a trial period when the husband proved that he could provide for his wife and any offspring. There are conflicting reports about divorce in Native American culture, with some sources claiming it was rare, while others remarked on its frequency. Although adultery was condemned, consent was given for extramarital relations during pregnancy and nursing. David Zeisberger, who worked among the Moravians, observed that marriages often ended when couples were young, even when the union had produced children, and that it wasn't until they were older and more settled that their marriages "took."[10]

Native American relationships evolved economically, socially, and spiritually when the tribes experienced a shift from nomadic living to a settled life based on the predictable production of food. When the Europeans arrived and began interacting among them, native life underwent further changes as they began adapting to some of the white people's ways. Kissing was introduced, for example, along with a questioning of prior practices, such as the natives' view that fornication was something natural. Some Indians intermarried with Europeans, the most famous case being that of Pocahontas and John Rolfe. A widower, Rolfe asked permission of Governor Thomas Dale to take the native woman for a wife, explaining that the union would be "for the good of the plantation, for the honour of our countrie, for the glory of God, for my owne salvation, and for the converting to the true knowledge of God and Jesus Christ, an unbeleeving creature, namely Pokahuntas [sic]."[11]

Chapter 3

FOR GOD
AND GOLD

THE SPANISH REACHED America via Christopher Columbus's fabled voyage nearly a century ahead of the British; but for various reasons, England dominated the early colonization of the New World. Columbus's original, twofold purpose in crossing the ocean blue was not so much to establish a Spanish settlement as to find a "northwest passage" to the Orient and to bring the knowledge of Christ to native populations. He and his male crew, followed by other explorers, prepared the way for a series of Spanish-sponsored conquistadores to take lands previously unknown to pad the coffers of their sovereigns. They roamed Florida and the southeastern United States, journeyed to the Midwest as far as Illinois and Indiana, and explored the Pacific coast, Arizona, New Mexico, Texas, Kansas, and Oklahoma. Those conquerors were mostly established men from common backgrounds whose authority derived not so much from compelling personalities, although many possessed them, but from royal commissions. In their highly class-oriented society, their exploits enabled them to advance socially.

Once the British began to settle the New World, the Spanish, as well as the French and Dutch who followed, were unable to keep pace, and the history that most shaped the future nation is that of the English colonies. In large measure the reasons point to marriage and family life, which the British stressed while settling America. Their immigrants consisted of men, women, and children, not just single men (either unmarried or married but traveling solo) out for a romp and riches in the wilderness. The more stable a settlement's relationships, the steadier its life. The conquistadors were not known as founders of communities. The actual development of Spanish towns and villages in the United States occurred much later than the British, French, and Dutch colonies, and in most cases, not until well into the eighteenth century. For example, the first permanent European settlement on the Pacific coast, San Diego, wasn't founded until 1769.

Like the English, the Spanish sought to bring the hope of Christ to these distant shores, but while the former spread the gospel through laypeople, families, and districts oriented around the church and Christian principles, the Spanish sent Roman Catholic priests and nuns, all single, to lead the effort. In addition, Spain was in a state of economic decline during the age of exploration as the center of commerce shifted away from the Mediterranean region to Britain, Holland, and France. Religious and dynastic wars had drained Spain's capital—and other cultural factors were at work as well. While mostly Protestant northwestern Europe boasted a developing and thriving middle class built around commercial enterprise, a society that was becoming more open to economic and social mobility, the heavily traditional and Roman Catholic Spanish tended to disdain business vocations, preferring that people stay within the classes to which they were born. Spanish nobles made up just 2 percent of the population, but they controlled upwards of 97 percent of the land.[1] As a result, Spanish culture lacked the dynamism of the north, and Spain's influence as an international power began to ebb.

Spanish family life during that era was rooted in Roman Catholicism, which stressed the importance of having children who would grow up in the knowledge and service of God. Women ruled the domestic scene, including the management of servants, while they remained in a subservient position to their husbands, or fathers if unmarried. During the eras of exploration and conquest, however, Spanish females and family life were mostly absent from America. There was, says John Huxtable Elliott, "an acute gender imbalance" of men in the New World.[2]

With Spanish men away for extended periods, they sometimes intermarried with native women or African slaves, or had dalliances with them. In some cases they married others in spite of having wives at home. Children of mixed blood, *mestizos*, would be formally associated with one of the parents, unless that child was illegitimate; then he or she would forfeit that privilege or right. Elliott believes that the conquistadors "took and discarded Indian women at will."[3]

A Spanish merchant who married his native woman in 1571 wrote home to say that the rules for social and marital relations were more flexible in the New World, yet he was quick to point out the issue of status. "Here," he said, "this involves no loss of honour, for the nation of the Indians is held in high esteem."[4] Says Elliott, in the absence of available Spanish single women or already established wives, intermarriage was "a matter of course."[5] Mindful of the religious and social ramifications, the Crown intervened at one point, ordering women to join their husbands.

In the end, women never came in large enough numbers to fully correct the disparity in those early years of New World colonization.[6] Actually neither did men go en masse to America. The draw of work, so attractive to the English, was not a factor for most Spaniards because they considered labor to be the arena for slaves and natives.

In Spanish America, as in the mother country, the Church exercised authority over marriage so that, for example, if there were disagreements among marriage partners, the Church could inter-vene to solve them. Likewise, it determined degrees of consan-guinity and made judgments about premarital and extramarital relationships, abandonment, and divorce. It carried "broad juris-diction in matters of personal behavior," and women trusted deeply in the "paternal figures of the men of the cloth and in the church as a source of protection and justice."[7] That defense came in exchange for a woman's submission to the male authority in her life, as well as the Church.

Spanish women in America often turned to the Church for a different reason—to maintain a primary and overarching relation-ship through it. Nuns were highly regarded individuals to the point at which there were often waiting lists to join. In fact, Roman Catholic theologians held up the ideal life of nuns as even above the married condition, and "nuns were held in great reverence" in Spain and in America.[8]

Those who couldn't afford the dowry made to the Church, or who were held back by social or racial reasons, could form a group called a *recogimiento* where they would live corporately with other women under a priest's or friar's patronage. Others became *beatas*, who took "simple vows to live retired, devout, and chaste lives."[9]

The founding families of Los Angeles were a particularly inter-esting group of settlers. These forty-four men and women formed families of "mixed culture," establishing the City of the Angels in the latter 1700s.[10] Known as *pobladores*, these individuals and fam-ilies established permanent ranches and villages, creating a solid commercial foundation for that area. Among them were Maria Fabiana Sebastiana Quintero, who at the age of fifteen married a soldier. Pablo Rodriguez and his wife, Maria Rosalia Noriega, had ten children, only four of whom reached adulthood. One husband among the pobladores died within a year of his wife, and their par-ents raised the children. The first known mayor, or *alcalde*, of Los Angeles was a widower named Jose Maria Vanegas, who met a pregnant, unmarried woman, Victoria, and married her. Together they built a family of their own.[11] The success of the Los Angeles pueblo was in large measure due to the stability of the relationships of its people, including the town's kindhearted *alcalde*.

THE FRENCH

By 1665, 75,000 colonists of English stock lived in North America but only 3,500 French. The latter's homeland had been less stable and, therefore, had fewer resources with which to pursue colonization in the earlier part of the century. With their kings trying to maintain order and authority and their country frequently at war, peasants were reluctant to leave their farms to emigrate, even after the monarchy tried to entice them with a four-year plan to help settle four thousand farmers in America. French Protestants, who had experienced persecution and were interested in the offer, were banned from leaving the country. Nevertheless, famed explorers such as Samuel de Champlain, the Italian-born Giovanni da Verrazzano, Jacques Cartier, and Jacques Marquette and Louis Joliet, who mapped the Mississippi River, mounted significant expeditions for the French.

Initially, the French were interested in acquiring fish and furs, and those who ventured into the wilderness found themselves tightly regulated by imperial officials. According to one source, this had a "deadening effect that prevented real and constructive growth."[12]

Many settlers moved farther to the west in search of more space, and since there weren't many of them to begin with, this weakened "New France." The French worked closely with native Indians, generally treating them more humanely than other Europeans. They intermarried with them as well, and the French who did so tended to adopt the free-spirited Indian way of life. To remedy the situation, the French government sent women to the New World between 1646 and 1715. Overseeing these *Les Filles du Roi* were a missionary named Marguerite Bourgeoys and her sisters, who also created matches for them.[13] Marguerite believed her calling was to create strong French families that would form the core of a robust French colony in North America.

France was 90 percent Roman Catholic during this period and a center for the Counter-Reformation within that church. French Protestants, called Huguenots, faced serious persecution, and when they were at last permitted to leave the country, many of those hard-working, intelligent people fled to northeastern America, among them doctors and accomplished artisans, including Irenee' DuPont and Apollos Rivoire, Paul Revere's father.

French Catholicism offered single women and men opportunities to go to America as nuns and priests, whose job was to build a social order based on the Church's teachings and values. They were responsible for the lion's share of evangelism among the natives. One Mohawk girl, Kateri Tekakwitha, received her baptism from Father James de Lamberville and took the name Katherine, dedicating her life to serving Christ Jesus through the Church, ministering to her people, and spending long periods in prayer. She forsook marriage.

Not all French people or settlers were so high minded. They often clashed with natives, and one of their major centers, New Orleans, got off to a notorious start. Three years after the city's founding in 1718, a priest described it as "a place of a hundred wretched hovels in a malarious wet thicket of willows and dwarf palmettos, infested by serpents and alligators."[14]

Some of the roughest characters who inhabited New Orleans included "deported galley-slaves, trappers, gold hunters and city scourings." Governors tried, often in vain, to maintain order, but frequently had little assistance from soldiers sent by the Crown, men they described as "riffraff."[15] It was not a family-minded zone.

The instability of the French city was reflected in the life of Marie-Therese Bourgeois Chouteau, the daughter of a French father and Spanish mother. (Control of New Orleans shifted between the two countries.) At fifteen she entered into an arranged marriage with a tavern owner and baker, Rene Auguste Chouteau, who ended up deserting her and their baby son a year later. After he went back to France, the teenage mother fended for herself and her child on her own in that decadent place where people were often laws unto themselves. She seemed destined to be alone and forgotten. According to most accounts, Marie-Therese began a relationship with a native Frenchman Pierre Laclede, a businessman with an urge to explore. Marie-Therese was twenty-three at the time, and although she was still married, her condition was a hollow shell. Laclede took her and her son into his home, and together they had four more children. When Laclede ventured up the Mississippi and established the city of St. Louis, Marie-Therese was with him, acting as his wife. They built their family life, unconventionally, as they dominated the social and commercial scene of nascent St. Louis. Apparently, Chouteau was not impressed when he at long last returned from France in 1767.

The deadbeat dad and husband made loud gestures to the civil and Church authorities about getting his wife back. Although their relationship was paper thin, that paper was legally binding. According to the laws of the Church and the French, Marie-Therese was still married to Chouteau. The authorities, however, didn't want to upset the first family of St. Louis and dragged their feet for years. In 1774, however, an official governor's order decreed that Marie-Therese return to New Orleans and her husband. Because no one backed up the order, the issue wasn't resolved until 1776 when Rene Chouteau died suddenly, "in an apoplectic fit," likely alcohol induced.[16]

She lived out her days in St. Louis with her children and Laclede, who died two years after Chouteau, wielding significant clout in business and society in spite of her unconventional relationships. Defenders of her reputation maintain that she and Laclede had a common-law marriage, the best they could have done given the circumstances, that divorcing Chouteau had not been an option for her, and she was so young when he deserted her that she couldn't have been expected to remain single. In the free-wheeling atmosphere of that time and place, this was an acceptable, albeit confusing arrangement, say her advocates. Interestingly, Chouteau herself seemed intent about maintaining her reputation by going along with some conventions. For example, baptismal records at New

Orleans's St. Louis Cathedral reveal that Laclede's children with her were actually baptized under the last name Chouteau, as if they were Rene's offspring. Not only did they not bear Laclede's name, the Chouteau children also did not inherit his assets upon his death. Even in a rough place like New Orleans and in frontier St. Louis, it was important for many people to keep up appearances where relationships were concerned.

THE DUTCH

Among the European nations that founded major American settlements, the Dutch moved into the mid-Atlantic region in the early seventeenth century. Primarily interested in the fur trade, Holland initially sponsored Henry Hudson's voyage through the river valley that bears his name with the hope that he'd discover the fabled "northwest passage" to India. Although the Dutch West India Company sent a group of colonists to the Hudson district in 1624, the Protestant Dutch people themselves were largely uninterested in the New World. With heavy-handed officials, *patroons*, in charge, the Dutch chafed at the thought of relinquishing the economic and religious autonomy they enjoyed at home. With few families settling in Hudson's valley, and still fewer of them pursuing farming, the outpost got off to a slow start and never progressed beyond part of Manhattan and southeastern New York state. Less than a hundred colonists coped with hostile Indians—the Dutch administrators gained a reputation for treating them brutally to be rid of any potential threats—while constructing a fortified village known as *Wiltwyck*. Women and children remained inside the stronghold while the men worked outside on their farms, in case of attack.

In less than ten years, New Amsterdam had mushroomed from two thousand people to nearly nine thousand—but only half were Dutch by that time. In large measure, this growth can be attributed to the presence of some established families who had superseded an earlier generation of single men out to earn a quick fortune in furs. In September 1664, Director General Peter Stuyvesant handed over

"New Netherland" to the English, who renamed it "New York."

* * * * *

As we have seen, the British were able to dominate the early settlement of North America because their families provided "a solid core for a racially well-knit people, who early indicated that they had come to stay."[17]

Furthermore, while the Spanish and French "ranged over vast stretches of land, unhampered by any family ties, except momentary domesticity with occasional native women," the English created permanent and secure homes, schools, and churches, influenced heavily by their women, who "encouraged a cultural uplift (that) broke down some of the rough-house tendencies of the masculine frontier."[18]

Chapter 4

WITH THE GIRLS
BE HANDY

HUMAN NEEDS ARE pretty much universal, even across abundant stretches of place and time. Customs and beliefs, however, fluctuate, sometimes dramatically, so that norms in one era shock to the core people from other times. When we consider the childhood of our second president, John Adams, we may marvel that he, or any other young colonists, ever made it to adulthood. Back then children were initiated into adulthood at a tender age, although most parents desired to give their offspring carefree periods of play, knowing how short the time was before duty called. By three, most children already had to perform simple tasks as their contribution to the household, out of necessity. Nor did they enjoy much parental oversight; mothers and fathers were about their own pressing work, and if it didn't get done, the consequences could be dire—starvation, nakedness, the prospect of freezing to death. David Freeman Hawke says

that children in colonial America were trusted "early with responsibilities that would horrify a modern parent."[1]

When John Adams was just eight years old, his mother and
father presented him with a gun, not a toy, but the real shooting
deal. He could just about lift it, and without guidance, he daily
traipsed through the woods and bogs "bringing down birds, or
trying to."[2] His experience typified early eighteenth-century American childhood. Children were out of necessity initiated into an
adult arena early on.

Although variations need to be accounted for due to regional,
religious, economic, class, and cultural differences, life and relationships for men, women, and children from the early colonial period to
the Revolution shared many characteristics. In fact, "the rude
upbringing of Abraham Lincoln nearly two centuries later on a frontier nearly a thousand miles inland from the Atlantic differed little
from what the early settlers endured."[3] Life was hard for those people,
and the way they related to each other needs to be viewed with that
ever-present reality in mind. For example, one ten-year-old girl took
charge of her parents' household for a week while they were away,
caring for twins and a grandfather. That included preparing all the
meals, keeping the fire going, lugging water, and cleaning. "As her
reward, she received enough money to buy a new apron."[4]

Kids were particularly at risk from accidents—fires, scalding
water, and disease presented constant peril. In 1740, a diphtheria
outbreak swept away large numbers of young people, up to half in
some communities.[5] Gail Collins reports that women generally
were more involved with their household tasks because they simply
had to be, often leaving their children to fend for themselves. Some
women also referred to their babies as "it," probably because death
was always so close. Rather than be attached to their infants, mothers demonstrated a more "generalized concern."[6] Families usually
had large numbers of children, an average of seven to nine.[7]

Benjamin Franklin was one of seventeen, seven by his father's
first wife and ten by the second, who was his mother. He remembered "13 sitting at one time at His Table."[8] At ten, he learned his

father's soap and candle-making trade because that's what children did—work.

Colonial life centered around the hearth and the churches, which were the hub of communities and provided "the most intimate, lasting tie beyond the farm."[9] This was, says Hawke, "a fairly stable world of isolated farms with only occasional excursions beyond them."[10] In that environment, people were pretty safe from personal crimes. In fact, Hawke tells the surprising story of a 1704 journey made by a thirty-eight-year-old woman from Boston to New York. Sarah Kemble Knight said she never felt afraid of being accosted or threatened in any way as she trekked along mostly by herself but sometimes in the company of postmen. Hawke writes, "It did not disconcert her to wake up one night and find she was sharing the room with two men in a nearby bed."[11] Honor was central to the social code between the sexes, and it would not have been right to compromise someone in Miss Knight's vulnerable position.

One thing that she could count on in her travels was a lack of personal hygiene. Cleanliness was not next to godliness for colonial Americans; it was, instead, a mostly foreign concept. On the occasion of her first shower, Philadelphia's Elizabeth Drinker reported, "I bore it better than I expected, not having been wett (sic) all over att (sic) once, for 28 years past."[12] This lack of sanitation may have resulted in the notoriously bad teeth displayed by Americans, especially the females. One observer noted that they were "pitifully tooth-shaken."[13] Benjamin Franklin attributed this unfortunate condition to the consumption of frozen apples and soup.[14] However hygienically challenged the colonials were, it did not prevent them from marrying and being given in marriage, though we may wonder how they endured, rather than enjoyed, their bodies. Men in their midtwenties usually wed, while women went to the altar slightly earlier. Nor was it unusual for a woman to be in her teens and/or pregnant at the time; Hawke believes that some 20 percent of later seventeenth-century colonial women were expecting when they got married.[15] New England law banned its couples from having premarital intercourse, and if a child appeared less than nine months after the wedding ceremony, husband and wife might be compelled to go to court and face a fine or nine lashes.[16] Nevertheless, as the eighteenth century proceeded, fornication became almost routine in New England, while in other regions it was "taken for granted."[17]

Adultery, on the other hand, was not tolerated but instead regarded as a violation of a sacred trust made by a couple, usually before God by a minister, or by civil authorities. (Quakers could marry without a minister or magistrate because of their convictions about egalitarianism of class and rank.) In New England, three women actually were hanged for their indiscretion, and the notorious Mary Latham faced severe punishment after she grew tired of her much older husband and had sex instead with a dozen other men.[18] There is a common stereotype today of prudish colonial men and women coming together simply to procreate, but they regarded sex as an enjoyable part of their lives. They also believed that if people took the right amount of pleasure in one's spouse, conception would be more likely to occur.[19]

Couples may have had premarital sex more often than we imagine, but, with the usual exceptions, they did not live together outside of marriage unless they wanted to bring the wrath of the community upon themselves. According to a tale related by David Hawke, an unmarried, cohabitating duo in Connecticut encountered a magistrate while they were out one day. The following conversation is said to have taken place:

"John Rogers," he said, "do you persist in calling this woman, a servant younger than yourself, your wife?"

"Yes, I do."

"And do you, Mary, wish such an old man as this to be your husband?"

"Indeed, I do."

"Then by the laws of God and this commonwealth, I, as a magistrate, pronounce you man and wife."[20]

Usually, the coming together of young people just prior to the

Revolution involved deliberations between parents or guardians over a suitable dowry. A brief period of betrothal or engagement followed, and it became more fashionable for women to abstain from having sex before marriage. According to a new standard, "the woman was supposed to play a passive, virtually hostile role," writes Gail Collins. "A true ladylike female rejected a suitor on first proposal, even if she intended to accept him eventually. And she never felt the surges of something as tawdry as sexual attraction, or even romantic love." She quotes eighteenth-century author Dr. John Gregory as saying, "A woman of equal taste and delicacy marries (a man) because she esteems him and because he gives her that preference."[21]

The same man cautioned intelligent females to keep a tight lid on their brains: "If you happen to have any learning, keep it a profound secret, especially from the men, who generally look with a jealous and malignant eye on a woman of great parts, and a cultivated understanding."[22] He didn't think that was necessarily a good trait in a man, and he thought there were some who could "rise above such meanness. But he added that it was unlikely such a paragon would appear."[23]

In the post-Revolutionary era, as the colonies began to chafe against an overreaching monarchy, some forward-thinking women rebelled against what they considered to be old-fashioned mores about clothes that only revealed one's head and hands. One Boston commentator stated that "if current trends continued, women would soon be completely nude."[24] In addition, men and women had actually begun to dance with each other, and not just in the same room at a respectable distance, prompting the Rev. Cotton Mather to write, referring to Isaiah 3:16–17:

> Because the daughters of Zion are haughty,
> and walk with outstretched necks,
> Glancing wantonly with their eyes,
> Mincing along as they go,
> tinkling with their feet,
> The Lord will smite with a scab

the heads of the daughters of Zion
and the Lord will lay bare their private parts.[25]

Abigail Adams agreed with the importance of female modesty. When she saw a Paris stage production in which the women cavorted in skimpy skirts, she remarked, "I can never look upon a Woman in such Situations without conceiving all that adorns and beautifies the female Character, delicacy, modesty and difference, as wholly laid aside, and nothing of the Woman but Sex left."[26] When she became First Lady, Mrs. Adams took it upon herself to elevate American womanhood, and part of that process involved her commenting on the way in which they presented themselves. She cautioned them not to follow the current fashion in which they "wear their Cloaths (sic) too scant upon the body and too full upon the Bosom for my fancy" and ended up, she said, looking "like Nursing Mothers."[27]

COLONIAL FAMILIES

In colonial America, most people married only those from their own religious background, a pattern that David Freeman Hawke believes remained in place "until well into the twentieth century."[28] Parents educated their own children, for the most part, and book learning was regarded as secondary to the more important work at hand that kept the family going. Likewise, their educations, such as they were, were mostly practical, oriented around the needs of farming or running a business. Reading was for understanding the Bible or conducting trade, mostly the former. Girls learned to run homes, boys to follow in their father's work; there was no "generation gap"; men handed down their trades from one generation to the next.[29] When families worked mostly on a subsistence level, women and men worked side by side, especially on farms. Although this meant a certain equality for females, they mostly desired to be in the home.[30] Men at that time had legal control of all property, as well as of the children. Divorce was extremely rare. People expected life to be hard and relationships to need time to work out, and most of them would have rather died than have born the intense shame and scrutiny of divorce.

Relationships among women were important in that society of spread-out farms with northern females enjoying greater opportunities to drop in on each other than their southern counterparts.[31] Childbirth was a time when many women (if they were available) came together over the event, taking charge of the situation in a celebratory mood while men hovered around the periphery. Southerners lived farther apart and had less time for female companionship, and as a result, they were, says Gail Collins, "desperately lonely."[32] A North Carolina circuit judge told about a newlywed couple living eighteen miles from anyone else. He said, "When a male visitor told the young bride he would bring his own wife to visit her, she wept with gratitude."[33] In her own studies, Collins reached the conclusion that southern women suffered the additional disadvantage of being frequently ignored by their husbands, who lorded it over the family, regarding them as "submissive . . . frail and chaste," and not a force to be reckoned with.[34]

FAMOUS SPOUSES AND FAMILIES

Not all northern men were model husbands either, of course. Human beings are, after all, afflicted with the sin of self-centeredness. Writer/commentator Cokie Roberts offers personal insights about that era based on her assessment as a contemporary journalist. She tells the story of one of our leading Founding Fathers:

Benjamin Franklin set off from his hometown of Boston at the age of seventeen to make a new life for himself in Philadelphia. While boarding at the Read family's home, he became taken with their daughter, Deborah, who was fifteen. He proposed at one point, but then he needed to go to London to buy a new printing press, and while he was there, he neglected her badly. She ended up marrying a rogue named John Rogers, who went through a good deal of money before ending up, presumably dead, in the West Indies. Two years after he left Philadelphia, Franklin returned and, unable to find a girl with a good dowry who would marry him, he wed Deborah. They couldn't legally marry, however, because she couldn't prove that her first husband was actually dead.[35]

Instead, they engaged in a common-law marriage to which Franklin brought a bright future as a famous inventor, businessman, patriot, and statesman. He also presented Deborah with an illegitimate son, whom she raised. Together they had a daughter and another son. Deborah had a sharp mind and worked hard at their various enterprises, but her husband was not often at home and didn't heed her pleas to return, even after one five-year foreign stint. In defense of Ben, he wanted her to be with him, but she had a terror of seafaring and refused to budge from Philadelphia. Deborah was aware that her spouse had difficulty staying away from other women, but she remained faithful to the marriage and still wouldn't go with him.

In 1765, he went to London where he stayed for an entire decade in a political capacity, not even returning for his daughter Sally's wedding. However, he wrote often, sometimes tenderly, to Deborah, who became ill during his sojourn. He never saw her again. In her last letter to him she said, "Sally will write. I can't write anymore. I am your affectionate wife D Franklin."[36] She died in December 1774, and at last, Franklin returned to take charge of the many affairs he had entrusted to his dedicated wife over the long years. Although theirs was not an exemplary marriage, they stayed together in a manner of speaking and made the best of it while making allowances for each other's weaknesses. Franklin referred to his grief over the death of his "old and faithful companion, and everyday [I] become more sensible of the greatness of that loss that cannot be repaired."[37] Cokie Roberts writes that many years after Deborah's death, Franklin said he dreamed that he went to heaven to get her back. She wouldn't return, however, telling him, "I have been your good wife . . . almost half a century. Be content with that."[38]

In the twenty-first century, commuter marriages are not uncommon. Sometimes two career couples end up working in separate cities for short or long periods with one of them flying home for weekends. That was not an option three centuries ago. One marriage that bore lengthy separations out of necessity, which often happens during a time of war, was that of John and Abigail Adams, whose love for each other has inspired generations. Unlike Ben Franklin's sometimes-disengaged relationship with his wife, the Adamses were fiercely devoted to each other. During the first part of their marriage, John practiced law on the road to make enough money for their needs since their farm wasn't providing sufficient income. Once they were in the black, they answered the call of patriotism, becoming key figures in the fight for independence, and John was away for lengthy periods in his role as a leader from Massachusetts. Abigail said at that time, "I find I am obligated to summon all my patriotism to feel willing to part with him again. . . . I make no small sacrifice to the public."[39]

They were to endure nine years of living mostly apart, and it tore at their hearts, especially when he was abroad, and they had to censor their own letters to each other in case they fell into enemy hands. While Abigail ran the farm, raised their five children, cared for sick and needy relatives, and suffered a miscarriage on her own, she said she considered it her patriotic and Christian responsibility to bear it well. "I feel," she once said, "a pleasure in being able to sacrifice my selfish passions to the general good. . . ."[40]

Abigail Adams's example is true of countless other women as well—their roles expanded out of necessity while their men were off fighting. Whereas Benjamin Franklin once remarked that the only political task suitable for women was to help men keep their heads when discussing current affairs, Revolutionary-era females were being called on to be very political indeed. They not only boycotted tea and British goods that made their lives a little easier, they also ran farms and businesses and sometimes suffered the torments of living under armies of occupation. Some were raped by enemy soldiers. Others followed their husbands to battlefields and army camps to be with them and contribute in any possible way. There's the story of the legendary Molly Pitcher, for example, a "camp follower" who took over her husband's position at a cannon after he fell from heat exhaustion. The British General Cornwallis once said, "even if [he] destroyed all the men in America, [he'd] still have the women to contend with."[41] Of those long-suffering women Abigail Adams said, "We possess a spirit that will not be conquered. If our men are all drawn off and we should be attacked, you would find a Race of Amazons in America."

Both she and her husband endorsed the model of "Republican Womanhood"— that if females were properly educated, they would make better mothers who could raise their children to rise to the responsibilities of democratic living. They maintained that the new country would only be as strong as its homes and families. When John Adams became the nation's second president, he lived out his respect for his wife and American women by often consulting with Abigail about important decisions because she was "the one person in whom he felt he could really confide."[42] They were happily married for fifty-four years, a union that Paul Boller calls "one of America's great love stories."[43]

A glimpse into the lives of two other famous founders reveals the patterns, expectations, and troubles that husbands, wives, and their children faced during that era. Thomas Jefferson was a southern gentleman of the first order, as well as a keen intellectual with a passionate sensitivity toward life and relationships. He married a young widow, Martha Wayles Skelton, in 1772, a woman who shared his courtly manner and love of books. They had three girls before her death in 1782; in the years before, she had suffered from poor health, which prompted Jefferson to decline foreign government assignments. His daughter Patsy remarked, "As a nurse, no female ever had more tenderness or anxiety" than her father.[44] When Martha died shortly after their daughter Lucy's birth, Jefferson fell into despondency for several weeks in what has been described as a "violent burst of grief."[45] He destroyed all of her portraits and their correspondence.

Two years later, he went to France to represent the new nation, taking with him his eldest daughter, Martha. That October, little Lucy, who remained behind with her sister Mary at their aunt and uncle's home, died of whooping cough. Due to the slowness of communication, however, Jefferson didn't find out about this until the following May.[46]

He sent for Mary right away, but when she finally arrived in France, she barely recognized him. Yet he was a perceptive and involved father who did everything he could to help her adjust. When grandchildren were born years later, he rejoiced over the events with exceeding joy, calling this the "arch of matrimonial happiness."[47] When Mary got married, he advised her to "consider the love of the other as of more value than any object whatever on which a wish has been fixed."[48] Martha remained so close to Jefferson that "her husband never completely displaced her father, and the dearest wish of her heart was to be with (him) under any and all circumstances."[49]

Jefferson experienced deep, sharp anguish when his wife passed away, and he never remarried, which was a frequent practice in an age when spouses often died unexpectedly. He was the first president not to have a First Lady by his side. However, accusations and speculation regarding his relationship with the enslaved Sally Hemings dogged him over the years and have persisted to our own time. One of the first instances of open conjecture about this arose in 1802—the relationship had been quietly gossiped about before then—when a reporter charged that Jefferson had fathered children by one of his slaves. The third president did not respond to personal attacks and said nothing; naturally, as a political figure, Jefferson was a prime target for rumors. His daughter Martha's children said "such a liaison was not possible, on both moral and practical grounds."[50]

However, it was not uncommon then for masters to engage with female slaves. Today, in an era when many presidents have been reputed to be involved in extramarital affairs, many Americans are likely to believe that Jefferson, who lost his wife at a young age, did have a relationship with Hemings. To settle the matter, DNA tests were conducted in 1998, and they concluded that "an individual carrying the male Jefferson chromosome fathered" Sally Hemings's last known child. Those eager to maintain Jefferson's reputation say it wasn't necessarily Thomas Jefferson's baby: "There were approximately twenty-five adult male Jeffersons who carried the chromosome living in Virginia at that time, and a few of them are known to have visited Monticello."[51] In other words, researchers have arrived at conflicting positions on this matter.

Today, blended families are as common as those composed of a husband, wife, and the children they conceived together, but colonial and revolutionary America also had their versions of stepfamilies, with a different twist. In contemporary America, families normally come together out of divorces, but two to three hundred years ago they did so mainly due to death. For example, in the late seventeenth century, southern families were what Gail Collins calls a "collection of offspring from widows' and widowers' former marriages."[52] In fact, our nation's first "first family" was blended. At eighteen, the high-born Martha Dandridge married Daniel Parke Custis, who was more than twice her age. Of their four children, two died as babies, and eight years later Custis passed away, leaving his wealthy wife with three-year-old Jacky and one-year-old Patsy. Less than two years later at a Williamsburg cotillion she met a debonair colonel in the King's army, and she became smitten. Although George Washington had initially hoped to marry Sally Fairfax, someone else had gotten there first, and when he saw Martha Custis, he began to turn his affections toward her.

A few months before their January 1759 wedding, George Washington expressed his deep love for her in a letter: "Since that happy hour . . . when we made our pledges to each other, my thoughts have been continually going to you as another Self. That an all-powerful Providence may keep us both in safety is the prayer of your ever faithful and affectionate friend."[53]

They shared a mutual faith in Jesus Christ, and Washington raised Martha's children as if they were his own. It hurt him profoundly when Patsy died of complications from epilepsy as a teenager, and he showered fatherly attention on his stepson, Jacky.

When Washington abandoned his own position in the King's forces to lead the patriot cause, both he and Martha became hostage targets, but she maintained a strong sense of duty to her husband and country. While she could have stayed comfortably at Mount Vernon during the war, Martha traveled to various battle zones to be with her husband and to lend support to his troops. In that respect, she was very much like countless other women who became camp followers of their military men.

Women from various social stations and backgrounds accompanied their husbands as they went to war, and many took their children as well. It wasn't unheard of for a pregnant woman to give birth, only to have to rally enough to keep up with the forward march of her husband's unit. They performed necessary work for the troops, including the washing and mending of clothes, food preparation, and water collection. Those with a higher educational or social background often acted as secretaries, and nursing the wounded was a major activity among the women. At times, they were even pressed into battle, the most famous example being that of Molly Pitcher, who, as we have seen, took over her husband's position at a cannon after he fell victim to heat exhaustion. If a female camp follower became widowed, it wasn't uncommon for her to marry one of the other men in the regiment, which provided a certain, if small, amount of social security.

In his book *The Road Less Traveled*, M. Scott Peck famously, succinctly stated that life is difficult. The people of Colonial and Revolutionary America, whether they were well known or obscure, knew and accepted this simple but profound truth. Because of it, they were better able to adapt to their circumstances, and their relationships were better for it. Like Thomas Jefferson at the death of his beloved wife or Abigail Adams when she miscarried, they felt their losses deeply, but they moved on, living, loving, adjusting.

Chapter 5

JUMPING THE BROOM

ARAMINTA'S EARLY years as a slave epitomized the life and relationships of people living in bondage in America. No one knows in what year she was born because almost no slave owners bothered to keep such records, but in her case, it was around 1820. She lived on a Dorchester County, Maryland, plantation with her parents, Harriet and Ben Ross, and seven siblings, a close family that nurtured each other and worshiped the Lord God. Araminta learned early in life that slaves were meant for work, and when she was seven, her owner hired her out to other whites in the area because he was in need of the money. One of her first jobs involved caring for an infant, but every time the child cried, the mother whipped Araminta for not doing a good enough job. Another "surrogate master" forced her to do outside labor when she was sick with measles, then complained that "she wasn't worth the food she ate."[1]

She began to dream of escaping to the north, and the

stories she heard around the fires at night spoke of an "underground railroad" that helped slaves reach freedom. Her desire for liberty intensified after an incident in which she almost lost her life. When Araminta was thirteen, she tried to distract an overseer when she spotted a slave attempting to run away. She ended up getting hit in the head with a two-pound lead weight and nearly dying from the blow. The attack left her prone to fall asleep in all times and places, unpredictably, for the rest of her life.

When she got older, Araminta began using her mother's name, Harriet, and she continued to get hired out to various owners. She had exceptional strength, in spite of her affliction, and she resented it whenever a boss demanded that she put on a sideshow-type exhibition of it. One bit of attention that she did welcome, though, came from a free black man who worked for the same owner. John Tubman's parents had been slaves whose master set them free before he was born, and in 1844 he proposed to Harriet.

Nowhere in the South could slaves legally marry, nor could they reside with a spouse who didn't work on the same farm or plantation, whether he was free or not. She shared her longing with him to be free, to achieve it by running away, feeling sure that he would understand, but he didn't. He was resigned to their condition and even threatened to turn her in if she ever tried to escape. Five years later, Harriet heard rumors that she and two of her brothers were going to be sold to an owner in Georgia, and she decided the time had come to flee. John refused to cooperate. If she had to leave him, she concluded, so be it; she could always try to be reunited later, after he had time to miss her. The night before Harriet's escape, her master saw her walking along, looking calm and untroubled, little knowing that, in the words of Charles Blockson, "She was . . . quitting home, husband, father, mother, friends, to go out alone, friendless and penniless into the world."[2]

In December 1850 she began making the first of what would be nineteen incursions into the south to rescue her family and others from slavery. On her third trip, in 1851, Harriet determined to get John so they could live truly free once and for all. Hearing of a militia patrolling the area near her old plantation, Harriet sent word to John that she had returned for him and told him where they could safely rendezvous. He responded through an intermediary that he didn't want to see her, that he was married to someone else. Stunned, she considered risking everything to confront him personally, but she concluded that she would go on without him. He had, after all, made another bed and was sleeping in it.

Although Harriet Tubman went on to become the Moses of her people, the Underground Railroad's most celebrated conductor who led three hundred slaves to freedom without ever losing a "passenger," her story reflects the unsettled dynamics of slave families and their relationships in the years before emancipation (1863). Those people, brought to America against their will and destined to work for masters who would probably never set them free, still managed to carve "out their own worlds as best they could."[3] Eugene Genovese has observed,

> The wonder is . . . that possibly a commanding majority fought for human ground on which to live even as slaves. From black and white sources we learn of the tenderness, gentleness, charm, and modesty that often marked the love lives of ordinary field hands as well as of more privileged house slaves.[4]

CHILDHOOD IN SLAVERY

Gail Collins tells of a little slave girl who grew up on an isolated farm with virtually no outside contacts in the first years of her life. She didn't even realize "she was a child until her mistress's granddaughter visited." She said, "I thought I was just littler, but as old as grown-ups" because of her heavy, adult responsibilities. She added, "I didn't know people had grown up from children."[5] Life for enslaved children was hard and too often short. Although they usually survived birth, perhaps because their mothers were physically strong, didn't wear restricting corsets, and didn't use substandard doctors, they had a more difficult time navigating infancy.[6] The harsh conditions to which they were subjected caused them to die at "twice the rate of white babies. . . . More than a third died before age ten." Poor prenatal care and inadequate nutrition were contributing factors.[7]

Slave mothers had to go right on working after delivering a baby—there was no maternity leave—so they weaned their infants too quickly. Fieldwork kept them apart from their newborns for long periods, and caretakers were often too young or too old to do a good job. "Mothers sometimes came back to find their babies left lying in the sun," Gail Collins says, "covered with flies or ants. The older children were cared for like a herd of livestock."[8]

Slave children were able to play with white girls and boys until their free companions left them to pursue their educations. The slaves were not allowed to read or write, and they went off to work in the manner of adults many times their size, but child slaves were often hurt on the job, usually from fires or from using knives in the kitchen. They could expect beatings for not performing their tasks well enough, and sometimes even horrific abuse, like Harriet Tubman had experienced when she was hired out as a little girl. One master heard that a slave girl had fallen down the steps with his baby, so he took a board and smashed it against her head, killing her.[9]

A parent never knew when his or her child might be sold away from them, which created another source of acute tension. There were countless, heart-wrenching scenes of children being torn away from mothers and fathers, knowing they would never see each other again. In spite of the losses and threats of losses, slaves forged strong relationships among themselves. Indeed, some authorities such as Gary Nash state that many planters encouraged those ties because they made slaves better workers, that in spite of the obstacles, slaves "established with remarkable success . . . a relatively stable family life" in situations that "made family life almost impossible to maintain."[10]

He says, "It was at the level of the family—the close intimate connections between man and woman, parents and child, and brother and sister—that slaves developed the most important bastion of defense against the hardships of slavery."[11]

There are stories of benevolent relationships between owners and slaves, of white women who had strong associations with their "mammies," and masters and mistresses who cared for their slaves as well as their own children. (Of course, there was always the baleful reality of bondage hanging over them.) The case of a Boston couple who purchased a slave to be a companion for the wife is especially extraordinary, at least initially. We tend to think of slavery as a southern phenomenon, but in the mid-1700s, it was practiced throughout the American colonies, and at that time a seven-year-old Gambian slave went to live in the home of tailor John Wheatley and his wife, Susannah. She was given the name of Phillis after the slave ship she had traveled on, and early on she demonstrated a keen intelligence. The Wheatleys began to educate the girl, including instruction in Latin, while their son Nathaniel taught her other subjects, including history and the Bible. She became a faithful follower of Christ and was baptized, and at thirteen, Phillis Wheatley started writing poetry, often about current events. Her poem "On Messrs. Hussey and Coffin" was published in 1770, the first time a black female's work had appeared in print in America. Her eulogy of George Whitefield that year brought fame.

Three years later she went back across the ocean, this time to England to stay with the renowned Countess of Huntingdon, a great Christian lady who served as patron and advisor to many preachers and leaders of the faith. She helped cultivate Phillis's spirituality while introducing her to many celebrated people; over the years Phillis came to know a variety of eighteenth-century notables, including George Washington. After she achieved her own fame, Phillis was granted her freedom, but she chose to remain with the Wheatleys until John passed away, and then she married John Peters, a free black man. They had three children, only one of whom survived, and John ended up deserting her. She went to work as a servant and lived in a boarding house, coming to an unsung end in 1784 when she and her baby both died within hours of each other.

She had started life in American as a commonplace house slave, became an accomplished poet, and earned her freedom, yet she ended up dying in a condition that came far closer to the normal experience of so many of her fellow African American slaves.

SLAVE MARRIAGE

Eugene Genovese studied the lives of slaves extensively and concluded that "nowhere did slave marriages win legal sanction, and therefore families could be separated with impunity."[12] Most slave owners encouraged the unions of slave men and women because they wanted to keep up the morale of their workers; it was a way to maintain control over them. The best age, according to the owners, for them to get married was around twenty because when slaves were younger, they tended not to stay together. Slave parents, on the other hand, pushed for teenage unions, believing that "early marriages cut down the chances of their 'going wrong'" morally.[13] Genovese's studies suggest that the earlier the wedding, the more likely a divorce.

Masters could, but didn't usually, force unions, preferring to let nature have its way with the couples. They did, however, discourage marriages between slaves who lived on different plantations. Such relationships created economic complexity for the owners, but they occurred frequently anyway. When slavery ended, Andy Marion, who had lived in bondage in South Carolina before emancipation, gave his viewpoint. "If you didn't see (a prospective wife) on the place to suit you," he said, "and chances was you didn't suit them, why what could you do?"[14] The term "broad marriage" was used to describe the joining together of slaves from separate masters. When they happened, the couple most often lived apart during the week, then got permission from both owners to visit on weekends. The wife's master did better than those of the husband in such instances because "children followed the condition of the mother."[15] The husband worked hard to get consent to see his family, knowing that his master would often feel irritated by the slave's mobility. Another difficulty for broad marriages was the increased risk that a spouse or child from a different plantation could be sold. In addition, suspicion found fertile ground because "living apart during the week generated tensions and fed jealousies."[16]

On some big plantations fieldworkers wouldn't marry house slaves because they represented different stations in their community, but more typically, those lines did cross. It was much harder for slaves on small, isolated farms to find mates. In addition, in the early years of American slavery, men outnumbered women. When a male and female became attracted to each other, they often did their "courting" in the presence of others, mostly in the evening after work. There is an especially sweet story of Violet Guntharpe, who, as an old woman, remembered meeting her future husband in a pig pen when she was fifteen.

> I glance at him one day in the pigpen when I was slopping the hogs. I say, "Mr. Guntharpe, you follows me night and morning to this pigpen; do you happen to be in love with one of those pigs?" . . . Thad didn't say nothing but just grin. Him took the slop bucket out of my hand and look at it, all round it, put it upside down on the ground, and set me on it. . . Us carry on foolishness about the little boar shoat pig and the little sow pig, then I squeal with laughter. The slop bucket tipple over and I lost my seat. That ever remain the happiest minute of my eighty-two years.[17]

Marital faithfulness was very important to enslaved people. They highly valued fidelity as "a personal and social responsibility, but [one] which was often a challenge to maintain."[18]

WEDDINGS

Enslaved men and women engaged in a variety of wedding styles depending on their and their masters' situations. Surprisingly, some slave owners went all out to celebrate a slave union, with Christmas being a popular time, when most family members were home and

could participate. White ladies could get as wrapped up in prepa-
rations for a slave's nuptials as they would for their own offspring,
and other whites often attended. Sometimes planters performed
the rites and other times, white ministers or black preachers offici-
ated. Genovese says, "Many of the white ladies enjoyed the fuss and
filled days with writing invitations to their own relatives and friends,
as well as to neighboring planters, who were invited to bring their
slaves."[19] He provided a description of a Mississippi slave wedding
from the 1830s:

> The negroes are usually married by the planter, who reads the
> service from the gallery (of the Big House)—the couple with
> their attendants standing upon the steps or the green in front.
> These marriages, in the eyes of the slaves, are binding. The cler-
> gymen are sometimes invited to officiate by those planters who
> feel that respect for the marriage covenant, which leads them to
> desire its strict observance, where human legislation has not
> provided for it.[20]

In another account, a woman named Tempie Herndon told the
story of her "broad marriage" wedding. She recalled the master killing
a "shoat" and the cook creating a large, white iced cake with bride
and groom figurines, and a huge feast on the lawn of the big house.
She wore a beautiful white dress with many accessories, but perhaps
most touching was the way she cherished the ring that her man
Exeter had fashioned for her "out of a big red button" with his pocket
knife. She said it reminded her of a red satin ribbon, and she wore it
for fifty years until she lost it in the washtub doing laundry.[21]

Most of these affairs were far simpler. If whites were uninvolved
with the vows, the couple would often, according to Gail Collins,
employ "a wise elder, usually a woman" to do the honors.[22] Caroline
Johnson Harris told an interviewer about her own such wedding.
She didn't even tell her master it was going to happen because she
maintained he wouldn't have cared, so she consulted with "Aunt
Sue," who advised her to consider the matter carefully first. Two

days later, the bride-to-be and her intended, Mose, returned to tell Aunt Sue they were ready.

> Then she called all the slaves after tasks to pray for the union that God was gonna make. Pray we stay together and have lots of children and none of them get sold away from the parents. Then she lay a broomstick across the sill of the house we gonna live in and join our hands together. Before we step over it she say, "In the eyes of Jesus step into the Holy Land of matrimony." When we step across the broomstick, we was married.[23]

Whether the wedding was formal or more casual, the conventional practice of jumping over the broomstick sealed the matter in the absence of formal recognition by civil authorities. There isn't consensus, however, about where or how the custom originated, with some saying it was imported from Africa, while others claim that couldn't be the case. Genovese says that "the wedding ceremony served the vital function of lifting the couple out of their private relationship and reminding them that the bond between them also bound them to their community and entailed wider responsibilities," its purpose down through the ages.[24]

He also commented on the one thing lacking in all slave weddings, the "climax" of the occasion when a couple is legally bound until death parts them. He calls this "the inevitable collapse of the essential Christian message during the exchange of vows . . . they were bound to react grimly to the absence of such words. . . . Not many blacks could have thought it clever when a white minister offered 'until death or distance do you part.'"[25] He quoted Matthew Jarrett, who had lived in slavery in Virginia: "We slaves knowed that them words wasn't bindin'. Don't mean nothin' lessen you say, 'What God has jined, cain't no man pull assunder.' But dey never would say dat. Jus' say, 'Now you married.'"[26]

Unions between slaves were especially poignant in light of all that threatened them, including the way in which couples from different plantations went on living apart. Mothers tended to hold families together in those cases because children usually followed their condition. Fathers did their best to stay connected on their weekend visits, to guide their children morally and spiritually, and to teach them various skills. While masters were supposed to see to a family's provisions, slave fathers would also supplement the family's needs. Some of them showed fierce dedication to their wives and children, including one man who walked twenty miles one way to visit after his spouse's owner moved.[27]

Another obstacle to relational stability and happiness was the threat of being sold, never to see family members again. The example of what happened in the life of Sojourner Truth unfortunately rang true for numerous other slaves. One morning her parents were horror-stricken to see their owners "bundling their five-year-old son and three-year-old daughter into a sleigh and driving them off to sale."[28] The boy resisted, but he had to give in to the master's superior position as the parents stood by feeling powerless to stop the wretched scene. Gail Collins says, "The episode haunted Truth's childhood."[29] She also related the appalling story of Laura Clark who "remembered being taken off to the frontier by her master when she was a small girl and seeing her mother run after the wagon, fall down, and 'roll over on the ground, just acryin.'"[30] There can be no doubt, but much admiration, that in spite of the terrible circumstances in which they lived, slaves still managed to bond with their children.

Some authorities point to other reasons for the high number of slave marriages between men and women living on separate plantations:

> As John Anderson explained: "I did not want to marry a girl belonging to my own place, because I knew I could not bear to see her ill-treated." Moses Grandy agreed. He wrote, "No colored man wishes to live at the house where his wife lives, for he has to endure the continual misery of seeing her flogged and abused without daring to say a word in her defence." As Henry Bibb pointed out, "If my wife must be exposed to the insults

and licentious passions of wicked slave-drivers and overseers, heaven forbid that I should be compelled to witness the sight."

A study of slave records by the Freedmen's Bureau of 2,888 slave marriages in Mississippi (1,225), Tennessee (1,123) and Louisiana (540) revealed that over 32 percent of marriages were dissolved by masters as a result of slaves being sold away from the family home.[31]

Slave men and women experienced vulnerability in other wrenching ways. When they got sold away from each other, they were free to remarry, but the emotional turmoil of the earlier partings exacted a heavy payment. So did the defenselessness they suffered when particularly cruel masters found it "necessary" to beat slave women for the smallest infractions, knowing their husbands had no legal right to stand up for them. One pregnant slave nearing her time accidentally cut down some of the wrong cotton, and the overseer brutally beat her while, according to one source, her spouse "just stood there hearing his wife scream and staring at the sky, not daring to look at her or even say a word."[32]

That unnatural situation proved injurious to those marriages as the violence desecrated every standard of decency, even as it diminished the basic role of the husband as protector. Although rare, some husbands did take action when their wives were about to be thrashed, risking everything to do so. One man hid his wife in a cave for seven years, bringing her and the three children she bore there provisions from the plantation he worked on.[33]

Gary B. Nash maintains that "probably the most destructive and socially disruptive weapon" that white owners used against their slaves was miscegenation, the coupling of female slaves with their masters.[34] Again, it rendered "the male head of the family . . . powerless to defend those closest to him from the most intimate and painful form of attack."[35] Most of the time this practice involved rape and seduction and tended to be "more violent and cruel" on plantations, where it happened more frequently than in towns and cities."[36] Occasionally, affection was involved, but the couple was, says Genovese, "not free to love each other without considerable emotional confusion."[37] Likewise, the mulatto children of those unions enjoyed "no special consideration or privileges."[38] He adds that miscegenation "poisoned southern race relations," and it brought about "psychological devastation."[39] South Carolina author Mary Boykin Chesnut wrote of the personal anguish it brought her:

> I hate slavery. You say there are no more fallen women on a plantation than in London, in proportion to numbers, but what do you say to this? A magnate who runs a hideous black harem with its consequences under the same roof with his lovely wife and daughters? . . . Fancy such a man finding his daughter reading "Don Juan." "You with that immoral book!" And he orders her out of his sight. You see, Mrs. Stowe [author of *Uncle Tom's Cabin*] did not hit the sorest spot. She makes Legree [the horrible overseer] a bachelor.[40]

A former slave's perspective came from the pen of W. E. B. DuBois:

> I shall forgive the white South much in its final judgement day; I shall forgive its slavery, for slavery is a world-old habit; I shall forgive its fighting for a well-lost cause, and for remembering the struggle with tender tears; I shall forgive its so-called pride of race, the passion of its hot blood, and even its dear, old, laughable strutting and posing; but one thing I shall never forgive, neither in this world nor the world to come: its wanton and continued and persistent insulting of the black womanhood which it sought and seeks to prostitute to its lust."[41]

To try to protect their daughters from that brutal reality, slave mothers did not tend to teach them about sex. One little girl was told, instead, that a train had delivered her. This is representative of the creative ways that slaves employed to maintain family life in the

center of bondage. They were able to fashion relationships and customs unique to their African backgrounds and American environment, holding on to them, and each other, to their credit, for dear life.

Chapter 6

THE VICTORIAN IDEAL

THE VICTORIAN ERA is full of irony. In that period, men dominated commerce, politics, the arts, education, and religion, and a woman's job was to serve her husband and family, but it was a traditionally oriented woman who defined and shaped most the of the nineteenth century, an age known by her name. During Queen Victoria's sixty-three-year reign, it was commonly said, "The sun never sets on the British Empire" because its colonies spanned every time zone. Even those lands not under its control did not escape the Victorian influence, including its former dependent, the United States.

Queen Victoria was born in 1819, the daughter of the Duke of Kent, who died when she was eight months old, "leaving . . . nothing but an inheritance of debt."[1] She lived as modestly as a princess could, and in 1830 when childless William IV became king, Victoria stood next in the succession. A month after her eighteenth birthday, when she officially reached the age at which she could rule, William died. Before that time, she and Prince Albert of Saxe-Coburg had fallen for each other, but it wouldn't be until she'd served as queen for three years that they decided to marry. Their marriage would set the tone for countless relationships in the Western world, although it differed in at least one important respect—as the reigning sovereign, she had to propose to him. Victoria ruled over millions of subjects, but she insisted on pledging to Albert her obedience, according to the time-honored vows of Christendom. In turn, the Prince Consort did his best to serve the Queen as his main task in life, trying to lighten her many burdens, once saying, "I endeavor to be of as much use to Victoria in her position as I can."[2] She chose to behave as many middle class wives of her era regarding the roles of husbands and wives. One source said, "When the queen was urged to assert her authority as head of the house and nation, since her husband was but one of her subjects . . . She would reply, that she had solemnly promised at the altar to *obey* her husband."[3]

After nine children and twenty-two years of happiness that has eluded most contemporary British royal marriages, Albert died unexpectedly of typhoid fever at forty-two, and his widow never fully recovered from the shock of his passing. Nevertheless, she followed her strong sense of duty and obligation to lead her nation in spite of her heavy grief, and she remained on the job until her own death in 1901. In her eponymous age, Victorian morality stressed the importance of the way in which people behaved toward one another.

Modern Americans have tended to roll their eyes at the elaborateness of Victorian manners and morals, especially those concerning male-female relationships and the family. According to one source, the principles of that age were characterized by "sexual repression," and hypocrisy lurked beneath the surface of the culture's "strict set of moral standards" and its "outward appearance of dignity and restraint."[4] The prevailing contemporary image of Victorians is one of buttoned-up prudes who went to laughable lengths to avoid mentioning body parts around members of the opposite sex and who wore so many layers at the beach that it's a wonder they didn't drown. While morals were much stricter in Victorian America than at many other times in our nation's history, there is more to the story. Few people realize that the "myth of Victorian repression" actually can be traced back to the early twentieth century, to the "Bloomsbury Group's" Lytton Strachey, author of *Eminent Victorians*.[5] In fact, Victoria herself had her little secrets, including her skill as an artist who just happened to draw male nudes. In addition, there was an entire subset of literature devoted to erotica in that period. Because of their individual family histories, both Victoria and Albert knew much about the way in which stray expressions of sexuality could hurt people and society, and they sought to elevate that God-created function. Both of them had "knowledge of the corrosive effect of the loose morals of the aristocracy in earlier reigns upon the public's respect for the nobility and the Crown."[6] Prince Albert's own parents had been "involved in public sexual scandals" that resulted in their divorce and his mother's early death when he was young.[7]

Eugene Genovese commented on the nineteenth century Victorian standard that "nice people did not engage in extracurricular activity." He concluded,

> Although the upper classes violated their own precepts, which like most precepts were intended to guide the masses rather than their betters, the new sentiments made steady progress . . . playing around in the pantry no longer amused Society in the old way; husbands and wives were expected to observe their marriage vows, or rather, to exercise discretion and respect each other's sensibilities.[8]

The Victorian influence on American life became especially strong in the aftermath of the Civil War, which ended in 1865. The ill will that had clouded the cross-Atlantic relationship since the fight for independence and the War of 1812 had dissipated. Now it was more of a bond between close family members who had reconciled after a falling out. Particularly the wealthy in the northeastern region of America, those with old money as well as the ones making it hand-over-fist in the industrial boom, imitated British styles and manners, then set the mood for the rest of the country. Their homes have been described as "elaborate fantastical affairs" that "evoked romantic fairy-tale images."[9] They featured towers and gargoyles as well as a panoply of color, contrasted with a much heavier interior consisting of dark wood, carpets, drapes, and wallpaper, leading some commentators to conclude that they were like whitewashed tombs containing darkness on the inside.

VICTORIAN RELATIONSHIPS

Although the word "Victorian" can evoke images of elaborate homes and clothing styles, the hallmark of the era was how people related to one another; if a person got that wrong, he or she couldn't expect to get far in life. Men and women alike took pains to use correct etiquette in their private and personal dealings with each other, using as their chief guide Jesus' Golden Rule to "do to others what you would have them do to you" (Matthew 7:12). One expositor of Victorian manners, which drew heavily from the Bible and traditional Judeo-Christian teachings, was the renowned writer and editor Sarah Josepha Hale, who presided over the day's major women's magazine, *Godey's Lady's Book*. That publication exerted major influence in American homes from 1830 to 1898, and Hale strategically marketed it to men so they would buy subscriptions for the females in their lives. The chief end would be the elevation of American womanhood, which had its advantages for their sons, husbands, and fathers.

Hale and her magazine advocated the education of women to "reign on the domestic front, also known as the 'woman's sphere.'"[10] Within the home, women were to find completion and contentment, she maintained, believing "that women were the champions of the spiritual, domestic realm."[11] Today we tend to judge Victorians harshly for confining women, for putting them "in their place," without understanding their belief that a woman gained an exalted status in the home. The American Victorian ideal was for women to rule over "the empire of the home," and if they did so well, society itself would function smoothly, and its highest aspirations would be met. Hale believed that the only times women should focus on other, outside, work was when it became economically necessary or when they were engaged in foreign medical missions.

In that era one other respectable outlet for work among middle-class women was teaching, but only if they were single. Until well into the twentieth century, actually, a female teacher of children could not be married because of the possibility of her becoming pregnant—a condition seen as requiring privacy and discretion, particularly if one was working among unsullied boys and girls.

Hale retired from forty years at *Godey's* in December 1877, and in a letter to her readers, she reiterated her message about women and their role in society, in the face of suffragettes and feminists who cried out for more opportunities. She said she left:

> with the hope that this work of half a century may be blessed to the furtherance of their happiness and usefulness in their Divinely appointed sphere. New avenues of higher culture and for good works are opening before them, which fifty years ago were unknown. That they may improve these opportunities and be faithful to their higher vocation, is my heartfelt prayer.[12]

VICTORIAN MARRIAGE

Writer Melissa Moore has said that Victorian women "were born, raised and educated to become wives and nothing else," as if being a wife were the lowest of possible conditions.[13] Little did she comprehend that in that period, a woman's role in marriage was more high-ranking than most of us have been aware. It was a woman's job to advance goodness and decency in her marriage and her home, and then the rest of the social order would fall into place. More than a way for a woman to avoid the "embarrassment" of being a "spinster," or a means to attain financial and/or social security, marriage was a path to her destiny. In general, Victorian America regarded women as being spiritually superior to men, that theirs was an innate purity somehow missing in the male chromosome. The wildly popular author of *Uncle Tom's Cabin*, Harriet Beecher Stowe, had strong feelings about male/female relationships and once stated that if women acted like men, they would "destroy the feeling of chivalry and delicacy on the part of men."[14]

Arbiters of public mores encouraged the husband, on the other hand, to be virtuous in his relationship with his wife, to treat her with respect, love, and kindness, as well as to share all that he was and had with her. Domestic happiness was the pinnacle of human gratification, and he could do much to promote it. Nancy Rosin writes that men and women of that era may have been stiff and corseted, but they were romantics underneath all the layers of clothes and rules of etiquette. "Expressions of love from that period clearly demonstrate that Victorians were often exceptionally sentimental and romantic—and that they were fond of showing it in numerous special ways."[15] They may have acted formally toward each other publicly, but couples employed elaborately decorated Valentines and gift booklets "full of gleeful cherubs and romantic imagery."[16] Rosin says that Esther Howland, who was known for her Valentine designs, nevertheless believed that the greetings should be discreet, choosing to put "motto cards" on the inside.[17] Likewise, men and women often used flowers to communicate their feelings, and *The Language of Flowers* acted as a guide to help them understand the "symbolism and poetry" behind various types of flora. Rosin says, "Flowers became a means of hidden declaration, ardor, rendezvous, or any other sentiment difficult to verbalize—unbridled by general rules of refinement."[18]

If a suitor could not demonstrate adequate assurance of his ability to provide a good home, steady income, social respectability, and faithfulness to the marriage vows, he could a expect a woman's rejection. In true Victorian form, there were even books that helped women accept and refuse proposals in writing, a prime example being *The Worcester Letter Writer*, published in 1879. In fact,

Heather Palmer says, "The rules and suggestions for courtship and romance occupy most of the space in Victorian etiquette and letter writing books."[19] While a woman had to wait, according to firm social custom, for an offer of marriage, she was free to accept it or to turn it down. Not only would she base her decision on her emotions, but she would also analyze his promise as a husband. Victorians may have wed for love, but they weren't mass subscribers to the "love-is-blind" school of thought.

In one letter to a man who had proposed, the young woman rejected him "on the grounds of unsteadiness." She wrote:

> Sir—There was a time when your addresses would have flattered and pleased me, but that time has long since passed away. Your conduct during the last two years has been made known to me, and viewing you in the light of a dangerous man, I do not desire any more intimate acquaintance. I could not reasonably expect happiness from a union with an individual who has destroyed the mental quiet of more than one young person, by his total disregard for what is due to the weaker by the stronger sex. . . .[20]

Her letter demonstrated not only her skills as a judge of character, but also one aspect of the nature of Victorian American male-female relationships; the man was viewed as the stronger of the sexes, an attribute that enabled him to function as his wife and family's primary source of protection from bodily and emotional harm. Victorians embraced the ideals of chivalry and gallantry that enlivened associations in the Middle Ages, with images of brave knights rescuing fair maidens abounding. The man was to be the woman's "head" morally as well as physically and intellectually.[21]

How men behaved toward women occupied considerable time and attention among the style gurus of Victorian manners. An 1860 article in *Peterson's Magazine*, for example, discussed whether it was appropriate for male relatives to kiss female family members "on the plea of consanguinity."[22] We may think that Victorians were a prim bunch, but it is amusing to consider that one woman who was concerned about such kissing was "pronounced prudish" by some of her friends.[23] The article concluded that the practice was "ill-bred," that "whatever hurts the feelings of a wife, or secretly angers a lover, or annoys a young lady, cannot be well-bred." Furthermore, it concluded,

> Everywhere in the United States—and very properly—kissing is regarded as more or less sacred . . . in modern time, and in this country, kissing between sexes has become proof of special endearment, rather than a mode of ordinary salutation; and being as such, it is, strictly speaking, not proper except between husband and wife, [24]

An article in *Godey's Lady's Book* from December 1860 admonished newly minted husbands to protect their wives and children financially as well as physically and emotionally. Entitled "A Whisper to a Newly Married Pair: A Whisper to the Husband on Expenditure," it advised the man to be generous in providing for his family:

> When once a husband has entered the marriage state, he should look on his property as belonging to his family, and act and economize accordingly. I remember being acquainted with a gentleman who was constantly saying, "It is true, my property is large, but then it belongs not to myself alone, but also to my children; and I must act as a frugal agent for them. To my wife, as well as these children, I feel accountable either for economy or extravagance." Another . . . who was in stinted circumstances, was constantly debarring himself of a thousand little comforts, even a glass of wine after dinner, sooner than infringe on what he used to call his children's birthright.[25]

CHALLENGES

There was a burgeoning women's rights movement during this era that pitted itself against Victorian middle-class mores and instead promoted an equality of the sexes that would provide women with a greater public voice. Elizabeth Cady Stanton was a major feminist spokeswoman, and while she wasn't always appreciated, her sense of moderation and decorum gained her a measure of respect, as well as a significant following. Hers was not the only voice of the movement, however. When Victoria Woodhull compared marriage to slavery, a national uproar ensued—"There was never a servitude in the world like this one of marriage."[26] Melissa Moore found this comparison illogical saying, "If marriage were truly like slavery, there would be no more point in reforming it than there would be in reforming slavery."[27] If an institution is that bad, it ought to be abolished.

Harriet Beecher Stowe had no time for the likes of Hull, saying that one of the happiest times of her life was when she was at home raising her children and enjoying the intimate company of other mothers. Her biographer, Joan D. Hedrick, commented about "the richness of (Stowe's) relationships with other women. Informal bonds of 'kinship' developed among women engaged in the common task of tending children: they delivered one another's babies, suckled them, sewed for them, and passed on clothes that their children had outgrown."[28]

VICTORIAN CHILDHOOD AND LITERATURE

It has been said that "The Victorians are sometimes credited with 'inventing childhood.' "[29] From art and literature we get an idyllic picture of middle-class boys and girls in adorable clothes cavorting outside among flowers, followed by docile bunnies, or sitting primly at pint-sized tables having tea parties. For those living on farms, the image contains some dirt smudges, but there remains a sense of purity and fun in the midst of milking cows and gathering eggs. Children of the cities' grittier lives escaped many of those pleasures, but for most, their "parents took (them) seriously, sparing neither rod nor love. Rules were clear-cut, infractions punished swiftly, but Victorian children were also doted on by an entire world of nannies and nursemaids, a retinue of aunties, cousins, and grannies."[30]

Children learned early on never to speak disrespectfully or argue with their elders because "they know best."[31] In addition, they were to show deference to them by rising to greet visitors, for example. Their literature reinforced lessons from home about how to treat others, with some of the leading era's authors writing for young audiences, among them Rudyard Kipling, Lewis Carroll, Anna Sewell, Louisa May Alcott, and Charles Dickens. Stories of that period "tended to be of an improving nature with a central moral lesson at heart."[32] They contained "idealized portraits of difficult lives in which hard work, perseverance, love, and luck won out in the end; virtue would be rewarded (think of Bob Cratchit and Tiny Tim in Dickens's *A Christmas Carol* or the March girls in *Little Women*) and wrongdoers are suitably punished."[33] King Arthur, *Ivanhoe*, and other tales of chivalry found a ready audience among Victorian children, as well as adventures by Robert Louis Stevenson and Mark Twain.

Victorian adults and children took every opportunity to improve themselves so that they would know how to behave around others, at home and in public. Their manners and rules of style and etiquette were oriented toward demonstrating the utmost consideration for other people. One of their highest ideals was that of sacrificial service; they did not live for their own gratification. Rather, showing concern and civility toward each other came out of a culture influenced not only by an English Queen, but by the Scriptures.

Chapter 7

EXTREME
MAKEOVERS

IN 1774, ANN LEE declared her personal state of independence from the British Crown and came to America. She was tired of being kicked around for her maverick ways, and as far as the English were concerned, she and the rebellious colonies deserved each other. Lee had begun her eccentric life as a Quaker, then shifted into a more animated form of religious expression after claiming to have received personal revelations from the Almighty. Dubbed the Shaking Quakers—shaking was a means of casting off sin—her followers had scandalized polite society in Britain. There also was something about Ann Lee, the way she insisted that Christ had returned, this time as a woman. Oh, and by the way, she was that woman.

In the sanguine era following America's underdog victory in the Revolutionary War, the promising country provided fertile ground for many communitarian efforts to spring up. It was yet another series of attempts to be the shining city on a hill first envisioned by John Winthrop on his ship to the New World in the early seventeenth century. This time, charismatic, sometimes eccentric, figures led the charge, often clashing with the strict manners and mores of the era. In nineteenth-century America, men, women, and children were expected to live by certain customs, including male headship of the family and female rule of the domestic sphere. Children were cherished, as well as expected to emulate their elders, and breaking codes of conduct brought fast, sometimes physically painful, consequences. Those who began, and joined, Utopian experimental associations marched to the proverbial different drummer—they were the nineteenth-century version of those ancient monastics who set themselves apart from the rest of the world to reach a higher state of being. Ralph Waldo Emerson, himself an innovative Transcendentalist, once remarked on the proliferation of perfectionist communities, saying that there wasn't "a reading man but has a draft for a new community in his waistcoat pocket."[1]

Sydney Ahlstrom estimates that some sixty experimental societies began in the early decades of the century, most of them finding their inspiration in "Christian perfection," the idea that a person could, with unusual effort, reach a state of sinlessness.[2] Those who got caught up in the fervor "almost by definition . . . rejected codes and statutes, traditions and customs—and this they did with more than usual abandon in the open society of the young American republic."[3] Only one of those groups actually made it into the twentieth century in anything resembling its original form, while most of the rest had meteoric histories, short-lived but intense. All of them stood cultural values regarding relationships on their heads. As J. C. Furnas puts it, "Hopes of revising relations between the sexes were strong in the days of stovepipe hats."[4]

THE SHAKERS

Ann Lee Stanley brought eight disciples with her from England in 1774, calling themselves, rather grandly, "The United Society of

Believers in Christ's Second Coming." By 1850, some six thousand "Shakers" covered nineteen communities. At the heart of Stanley's teachings was the conviction that sex had been a pervasive evil since Adam and Eve sinned in the garden, and she turned around Jesus' saying about money, promoting instead that sex was the root of all sin.[5] She believed that with God's kingdom "literally at hand, procreation was unnecessary."[6] In fact, she used rather harsh language when referring to "consummated marriage," calling it "a covenant with death and an agreement with hell."[7] She might have been describing her own marital state. As a young woman she had decided to remain single, but her father wouldn't hear of it and arranged a marriage. Eight pregnancies followed, all of them ending in heartache: four babies were stillborn, and none of the other children made it past their sixth birthdays. It is unclear whether Mother Ann left her husband or he abandoned her, but she lived without him for a significant part of her life. At any rate, the experience completely soured her toward physical intimacy. It is interesting that in spite of her severe opinion of marriage and sex, Ann Lee taught that if a person had difficulty controlling himself sexually, marriage would be an appropriate outlet for passion, outside the perfected state of a Shaker community. She wrote to an adherent, "Unless you are able to take up a full cross, and part with every gratification of the flesh, for the Kingdom of God, I would counsel you, and all such, to take wives in a lawful manner, and cleave to them only; and raise up a lawful posterity, and be perpetual servants to your families; for of all lustful gratifications that is the least sin."[8]

Mother Ann crafted a religious community centered around orderly, regulated, and separate living quarters for men and women, and her followers spread out into New England, Kentucky, Ohio, and Indiana. J. C. Furnas says, "Their buildings, tools, livestock and orderly methods were the wonders of a rural America that badly needed examples of improvements in such respects."[9] As innovative as they were, as lovely as their buildings and elegantly unadorned furniture, the Shakers were backward in the arena of human relations. Colonel T. W. Higgonson observed that they existed in a state of "pallid joylessness," and Furnas believes that theirs was "a world of emotional anemia."[10] It was as if they had never grown up to be completed men and women who knew how to relate to one another in the joy that God reserved for husbands and wives. They lived parallel, rather than intersecting, lives. Their "mass dances" were "close-order drills of separate bodies of each sex marching, jumping, hand clapping and singing."[11] If everyone had gone Shaker, there would be no one left, but they were so certain that the end was near anyway, that were wasn't any reason to procreate.

The world, of course, continued, seedtime and harvest, but the Shakers, alas, did not. (There are only a handful of practicing Shakers in the United States today.) Their communities remain, as they were in the nineteenth century, a matter of curiosity, and a source of high-quality furniture and style.

Two other communitarian societies followed the celibate ways of Mother Ann Lee, including the "Universal Friends," which was the creation of Jemima Wilkinson. Hers was another derivative of Quakerism, and she referred to herself, along those lines, as the "Universal Friend," who in the late 1780s gathered two to three hundred supporters in New England and eastern Pennsylvania, as well as an "entourage of a dozen or more celibate women."[12] She maintained that marriage was not important and became deeply upset when any of her devotees became pregnant. According to Raymond Lee Muncy, "On one occasion, she suggested that the baby be named 'Abomination.'"[13] The last of Wilkinson's unsullied supporters died about ten years after the Civil War.

Similarly, followers of George Rapp in eastern Pennsylvania also considered reproduction to be unnecessary given the imminence of God's coming kingdom. Like his female counterparts, Rapp considered sex for pleasure to be a foreign concept.

Another flamboyant woman brought her own experimental community on the American scene in the 1820s near Memphis, Tennessee. Fanny Wright's Nashoba Colony also envisioned a new era in human relationships, but not just of those between men and women. Rather, the native Scot proposed a community for slaves in which they could become educated and earn enough money to pay for their freedom. Hers was an eyebrow-raising interracial experiment consisting of white abolitionists and slaves. She further ruffled feathers by suggesting that in addition to eliminating slavery, people would be better off without the nuclear family, organized religion, or private property.[14] In fact, she often viewed marriage as a means of enslaving the woman and maintaining order in society. It was, she said, "an invention of religionists to assist them in maintaining a hold on every relationship in society."[15] Rumors abounded that Wright endorsed interracial relationships, as well as free love, which may have been difficult to disprove given her aversion to conventional society. She was, after all, an advocate for birth control long before it was acceptable to speak of such intimate matters. Her own public speaking was a scandal in a society that considered such activity inappropriate for a woman.

A deeply committed feminist, Fanny Wright married a French physician and, according to one source, the wedding occurred after she became pregnant with their child.[16] The union ended in divorce in 1852, the year of Wright's death. After contracting malaria, she went to Europe to recover, and the community fell apart in her absence some four years after its inception.

MORMONS

As a young man in western New York State, Joseph Smith set off to ask God what church he should attend, which one best promoted God's truth. Smith claimed that God made it clear he shouldn't bother with any of them, that they had all become twisted wrecks of apostasy. Instead, Smith should prepare himself for a series of relationships that would usher wandering humanity back to the right path as His latter day prophet. For ten years, from the time he was fourteen to the age of twenty-four, Smith entertained "other heavenly messengers." He was known in his community as a "seer," a man who engaged in magical practices and divination to find lost artifacts, and Smith claimed that he had discovered golden plates that revealed accounts of "God's dealings with ancient Israelite inhabitants of the Americas," which became the Book of Mormon, translated by his heavenly envoys.[17] He also claimed that John the Baptist had ordained him. For the rest of his life, Smith experienced a breathtaking ride as he gathered supporters and went in search of an ideal place to build a community based on his principles. He had a knack for inciting the ire of local officials as he developed his own little theocracies, and ended up dying at the hands of a mob at thirty-eight.

One concept that especially disturbed Victorian Americans about Smith was his belief that God had told him polygamy was legitimate. (He didn't seem to find it coincidental that he experienced difficulty keeping his own marriage vows.) Smith maintained that while men could have many wives, however, women could not follow suit. Raymond Lee Muncy calls Smith's religion "one of the unique experiments among the nineteenth century American utopians to alter the marriage system of the Christian world."[18]

In that system, "celestial marriage" was the ideal for men and women to attain, and "a fullness of salvation depended on the quantity of family members sealed to a person in this life."[19] A Mormon marriage was seen as "divine in its origin and potential" and was "intended to last beyond the grave and through eternity."[20] The blessed state could only be attained if the couple was "sealed" or married in a Mormon temple, followed Jesus fervently, and was confirmed as a marriage by God's Holy Spirit. Otherwise, a marriage would end when the partners died. If, however, a couple did not do these things in the beginning, they could backtrack and start again with a proper ceremony.

Smith taught that "eternal marriages are a work in progress," and spouses had to prove their commitment to it "through persistent actions."[21] Then the Holy Spirit would confirm the sealing "through a revelation from God directly" to the couple, an event that might occur here, or hereafter.[22] In addition, a husband and wife could include their children in the sealing process so that the family could prosper on earth and live on into eternity. If children came after the couple was sealed, this could still occur by means of an additional ceremony.

By 1844, Smith had attracted many followers and enjoyed a sizeable fiefdom in Nauvoo, Illinois. The Nauvoo *Expositor* produced an issue that was derogatory to Smith and his aberrant ways. His response was to order his followers to destroy the newspaper's printing press, which led to Joseph Smith's arrest on the grounds of violating the First Amendment.

What the authorities did not realize was that Smith was guilty of far greater trespasses. Starting in the 1830s, he had covertly married at least thirty-three women, a third of them between the ages of fourteen and twenty, and a third were already married. Todd Compton wrote about the terrible condition of those women's relationships with Smith. "For all of Smith's wives," he says, "the experience of being secretly married was socially isolating, emotionally draining, and sexually frustrating . . . they found their faith tested to the limit of its endurance."[23] While those women looked forward to a blissful afterlife, they endured "acute neglect" and a life of solitude in the meantime.[24] Compton says that in Smith's scheme, "a fullness of salvation depended on the quantity"—not just the quality—"of family members sealed to a person in this life."[25]

Smith followed his recipe for marriage until shortly before he died, taking a nineteen-year-old after telling her that God had instructed him to marry her. The arrangement was so hush-hush that she didn't know Smith had married her twenty-two-year-old sister just four days earlier. Both marriages were short-lived, however; Smith died at the hands of a mob less than a year later.

In spite of Smith's ignominious end, Mormons persevered under the leadership of Brigham Young and remain the only one of the nineteenth century communitarian experiments to have persisted to the present in much its original form—minus polygyny.

THE ONEIDA COMMUNITY

In the mid-nineteenth century a spiritual revival known as the Second Great Awakening shook the nation as thousands came to terms with their sin nature before Almighty God. Those who repented felt inspired to confront societal evils as well, in the strength and grace of Jesus Christ, setting out to reduce alcohol consumption (which was shockingly high in those days), help those in poverty, improve poor working conditions, reform prisons and hospitals, and abolish the institution of slavery. In such a climate, it wasn't unusual for a young Vermonter named John Humphrey Noyes to try his hand at making the world a better place, albeit in his own strength. His approach, however, was so unconventional that he faced not only raised eyebrows, but the long arm of the law. Like many young men of his time, Noyes went to seminary to become a minister, but while he was studying at Yale, he had a revelation that led him to believe that a state of perfection was possible—that a person could become sinless. He told his overseers that he had, indeed, become perfect, which did not go over well. Noyes ended up starting his own seminary where he could freely promote his own teachings.

He once stated, "Whoever has well studied the causes of human maladies will be sure that Christ, in undertaking to restore men to Paradise and immortality, will set up his Kingdom first of all in the bedchamber and the nursery."[26] Noyes wanted to revolutionize the way men and women related to one another. Raymond Lee Muncy says that Noyes's concept of "complex marriage" "was the most revolutionary of all social experiments associated with the communitarian movements of the nineteenth century in America."[27] As he gathered disciples and fashioned the Oneida Community, Noyes initially promoted celibacy because he believed that the fulfillment of God's kingdom was close at hand. At that time, he fell in love with one of his devotees, but she left the community and married someone else. He then reached the conclusion that there was a better kind of relationship to be had, a deeper kind of "spiritual affinity" and although the young woman had given herself to another, according to his new system, "spiritually she belonged to Noyes."[28]

Furthermore, he came to believe that monogamous marriage was a characteristic of the Church apostate, that sharing spouses, like sharing one's property, was "the social state of heaven."[29] Once again, Noyes had managed to shake up established mores. Sydney Ahlstrom says, "The Oneida Community . . . crashed head on into the most sacred institution in Victorian America; the monogamous family."[30] In 1847, he was arrested for adultery, and he remained unrepentant because he was, after all, perfect. He commented at the time, "If this is the unpardonable sin in the world, we are sure it is the beauty and glory of heaven."[31] Still, he soldiered on, setting up various rules and regulations to make his social and religious experiment work.

One social custom that he overturned was courtship, saying that dating might lead to an exclusive relationship, something that was unacceptable because at Oneida, every man was married to every woman. In addition, no one needed to date in order to determine whether they were well matched; if they were Oneidans, the thinking was, they would naturally get along. A man, however, had to secure permission to approach a certain woman to be with her, then she had to consent. Noyes also endorsed strict methods of birth control; even having babies had to be approved. The birthrate there was low, needless to say, averaging just two infants a year in a twenty-year period.[32]

It is especially sad to note that mothers were not allowed to know their children in any special way because those little ones, according to Noyes, belonged to everyone in the community. The identity of their fathers was almost impossible to determine. Children lived in a nursery with caregivers other than their mothers looking after them, and "mothers were not permitted to show special affection to their own children."[33] If a mother crossed that line, as frequently happened, her visits would be shortened, or curtailed altogether. One visitor remarked that the Oneida children seemed "a little subdued and desolate."[34]

Noyes had an especially strong aversion to and fear of his people developing strong feelings for a particular lover or child because, in his mind, it struck at the core of communal sharing. According to Muncy, this extended into their "marriages": "Rarely did the Oneida male spend the entire night with a lady as this might lead to an exclusive attachment, the worst of all Oneida sins."[35] It is difficult to imagine how that could occur when most of the adult members had relations with four or five people a week.

Critics of Noyes charged that his "seedbed of free love" was a "nursery of anarchic doctrines," and it is a matter of historical curiosity that the assassins of Presidents Garfield and McKinley each spent time at the Oneida Community.[36] Another detractor found that "'Noyesism' was most dangerous because it had embraced the human passions in all their vigor."[37]

The experiment came to a sorry end when Noyes, about to face arrest for statutory rape, fled to Canada where he spent the rest of his life. (Noyes had also faced growing internal pressure along the way to reinstate traditional marriage, especially so among his younger followers.) He did reverse his earlier teachings about marriage, advising members to abandon its complex version in favor of exclusive relationships. Marital partners normalized their status with the lovers they had taken at the time of the community's reorganization as a joint-stock company. (The community was also known for manufacturing several products, including animal traps and silverware.)

Although the Utopian leaders and their followers had hoped to reshape the pattern for marriage and family, either to abandon or revolutionize them, traditional ways overcame each of those attempts.

Chapter 8

OF BLOOMERS
AND REVIVALISTS

THEY CALLED HER "The Undisputed Queen of American Womanhood," and as such, Frances Willard reigned in the post–Civil War era, with women following her life as closely in the papers and magazines as they would Jackie Kennedy or Princess Diana a hundred years and more later. They copied her fashions, considered her thoughts and opinions their own, and joined her influential organization, "The Women's Christian Temperance Union," by the tens of thousands. While Willard served at its helm, the WCTU boasted a half million members across ten thousand local offices. She was as dominant with the women of her time as Oprah Winfrey is today.

Willard came from the Midwest, the proverbial "girl next door," who received an education in Milwaukee at Catherine Beecher's renowned school. She became an educator herself, as well as a writer, a woman who believed that femininity must take precedence over feminism. She came close to marrying twice, only to conclude that her prospects were not well suited to her temperamentally, but she nevertheless championed the American family and home life with all her considerable energy and creativity.

Her parents raised her as a Christian, but when she was in school, Willard came to terms with grave doubts about the faith of her father and mother. She wrestled with its claims and emerged from that period with renewed vigor and conviction about her Lord, Jesus Christ. This occurred during the Second Great Awakening, the lengthy revival characterized by lay participation, emotional zeal, an emphasis on free will versus predestination, and a call for social reform. At its hub was a New York lawyer named Charles Grandison Finney, who gave up his practice to become an itinerant evangelist after his 1821 conversion. He strongly believed that people whom Christ had changed should, as an outgrowth of their faith and the power of God at work in them, go out and change a suffering world. Many who came under his influence, including Willard, Theodore Weld, and Phoebe Palmer, became the greatest leaders of the antebellum reform movements.

Finney was a passionate speaker who taught that the lack of a theological education need not deter people filled with the Holy Spirit from preaching or teaching. He also encouraged "mixed meetings" in which women were free to speak with men present, something that shocked Victorian Americans, who considered it scandalous for a woman to present herself like that publicly. Finney told his female supporters that they should confront sin in the world, that it was necessary for them to reach beyond their personal homes and concerns. A huge dispute arose within churches and among their leaders over this issue, and in 1827, a conference made up of evangelicals addressed it head-on. Those who believed that women should keep silent appealed to various New Testament passages written by the apostle Paul, while those who championed a larger public role for women pointed to the second chapter of the book of Acts, which spoke of God's Spirit being poured out on "all flesh" on the day of Pentecost. They argued that women need not abandon their femininity in doing so, or compromise their relationships with their husbands, children, or communities. Rather than reach a consensus, however, the conference ended in a stalemate with the two sides parting ways.

CHRISTIAN FEMALE LEADERS

Among Finney's converts was Phoebe Palmer, a dynamic woman who, along with her husband, Dr. Walter C. Palmer, became a familiar leader in the holiness revivals of the 1830s at the height of the Awakening. She exercised great influence as a prolific writer of books and as editor of a major holiness magazine. In addition, for more than sixty years, she and her sister held a Tuesday Bible study in which they discipled many Christian leaders, including two Methodist bishops. Palmer used to ask how the Church could hope to carry out its mission "while the gifts of three-fourths of her membership are sepulchred in her midst."[1]

Christian women who desired to speak publicly in those days did so not in order to draw attention to themselves but to address social ills that threatened families. Initially this involved the fight to abolish slavery, in which human beings had no right to call even their spouses or their children their own. Among those female abolitionists were sisters Sarah and Angelina Grimké of South Carolina and the distinguished Harriet Beecher Stowe, whose father and brothers were distinguished preachers and antislavery activists. Although Stowe had her own contribution to make, she did so from behind the scenes, believing it was not her place to lecture in public. Then she took up her pen, and everything changed, including her life and even, some say, the course of the nation's history.

One Sunday at church, she experienced a vivid daydream in which she pictured the brutal beating of a slave, something that she had heard about many times through her contacts on the Underground Railroad. Her daydream became a detailed story, and while her family sat down to lunch that day, she excused herself to write it all down, page after page. The account got published as a magazine serial, then in novel form as *Uncle Tom's Cabin*, a book that Americans both lauded and condemned, just as they came to laud and condemn her. Southern authorities banned the sale and distribution of the book. A few years later, during the Civil War, she went to the White House to meet President Lincoln, who is reported to have greeted her with, "So, this is the little lady who made this big war."[2] In spite of her fame and the public voice she used to help others, some of Stowe's happiest times were spent in the sweet fellowship of women and children. She once told her friend Sarah Allen, "Do you know what I count the happiest years of my married life—those just after you came to the hills when our children were all babies and we raised flowers together and discoursed of roses callas and geraniums and babies between whiles—that was the Indian Summer of my life."[3]

During the Civil War, which lasted from 1861 to 1865, American families once again faced tests that arose when their fields and byways became battlegrounds, their homes were sequestered by enemy troops, and their men marched off to war leaving their wives completely in charge. In addition to expanded duties on the home front, women also organized relief societies to promote the physical and spiritual well-being of men in uniform, and they threw benefit plays, concerts, and dances to raise money for the cause, whether that of the North or the South. Once the war ended, bringing with it the abolition of slavery, many women continued to beat their drums for other, pressing causes, including temperance.

At that time, Americans drank enormous amounts of alcohol, often beginning at breakfast with hard cider.[4] Men under the influence all too often beat their wives and children, and terrible accidents occurred when men didn't have their wits about them while operating machines in the escalating industrial age. Those women who had rallied for abolition now turned toward ridding America of the scourge of alcohol. Women who championed that cause also tended to promote other ones as well, including schools for the blind, deaf, and newly free slaves, better working conditions, child labor laws, prison reform, and the creation of hospitals for the mentally ill. Their hero was Frances Willard.

One reason for her widespread appeal, not only among women but men as well, was her femininity, which she carefully cultivated. She supported a wider role for women not so that females could exalt themselves, or neglect their most important relationships, but to improve social conditions so that all American homes would be strengthened and reach their potential. "She was convinced that by making women more active in public life, society would become purer."[5] She passionately opposed saloons because countless American men drank themselves into drunken rages there, only to return to their homes where they tormented their women and children. She led many "women's crusades" to shut them down, and outdoor prayer meetings where there was no holding back. During one such occasion on a bitterly cold Chicago night, she and about thirty other women chanted Psalm 146 over and over again outside a disreputable establishment. They had gone to the saloon the day before and returned at dawn to take up their cause, having managed to close fifteen other bars that week alone. Then Willard began to pray aloud for the owner:

O God, in the name of our desolate homes, blasted hopes, ruined lives, for the honor of our community, for our happiness, for the good name of our town in the name of Jesus Christ sweating out the passion of the cross, for the sake of this soul which will be lost, make this man cleanse himself from his heinous sin. O God, open his ears that we may beg, may implore him . . .

O God, pity women! Jesus Christ, help the mothers of sons when their husbands betray them. O God, pity women, help them to end this curse! O, tender Christ, torn in Thine consuming agony, give us of Thy tomorrow and tomorrow, endless tomorrows until this man's heart shall melt. We are here, O dying, deathless Christ . . .[6]

The man for whom she prayed could stand it no longer, openly begging her to stop praying his soul into hell, and he would gladly shut the place down. She finally stopped when "whiskey and beer ran like rain over the pavement and into the gutter where she knelt."[7]

In spite of Frances Willard's enormous popularity and the noble activism of like-minded women, most Americans frowned on a woman venturing too far from the domestic arena. Willard herself believed that they should primarily occupy the special sphere, that their greatest fulfillment would be among their friends and families, in their homes. New Jersey senator Peter Frelinghuysen said that women had a "higher and holier" function than engaging in the turmoil of public life. [8] It is fascinating to consider that some zealous, evangelical Christians led the charge for women to enlarge their tents for the purpose of remaking society in the image of Christ. Nancy Hardesty writes, "While 'feminism' grew as a movement in the nineteenth century, the first women involved were largely Christians coming out of the revivals. Their purpose was to gain a voice to reform society, to make it more Christian. Those women were motivated by a faith and a fervor that sustained them in the face of difficulty and oppression."[9]

The first national women's rights conference was held in a Methodist church in Seneca Falls, New York, in 1848. Gail Collins says that "out of deference to the sensibilities of the time, (the leaders) asked (Lucretia) Mott's husband, James, to preside."[10] When Elizabeth Cady Stanton called for woman's suffrage, Lucretia Mott cautioned her to "go slowly," saying, "If thou demands that, thou will make us ridiculous."[11] Stanton's father later threatened to disinherit her. The nation's newspapers covered the event with a scornful tone, which echoed popular opinion of it.[12]

That initial conference had been based on fundamental Christian principles and rose out of that faith community. However, the leadership quickly tired of ongoing arguments among themselves about scriptural interpretation of the role of women; the fact was that not all evangelicals agreed about the public role of women. Four years later at a Syracuse, New York convention, a Polish Jew named Ernestine Rose told the audience:

> For my part, I see no need to appeal to any written authority, particularly when it is so obscure and indefinite as to admit of different interpretations. When the inhabitants of Boston converted their harbor into a teapot rather than submit to unjust taxes, they did not go to the Bible for their authority; for if they had, they would have been told from the same authority to "give unto Caesar what belonged to Caesar."[13]

The members concluded that the equality of women and their right to speak publicly should be based on the self-evidence of basic human rights and freedom. From then on, the women's movement broke with evangelical Christianity.[14]

YOU GO YOUR WAY, I'LL GO MINE

From that time, "feminism" became more of a secular word than one associated with evangelical women and men who labored together on the "sawdust trail" in revival tents, camp meetings, and the speaker's circuit. Many denominations arising out of the spiritual resurgence supported women in leadership roles, among them the Church of God, Church of the Nazarene, and the Pilgrim Holiness Church, whose first president, Seth Rees, said:

> Nothing but jealousy, bigotry, and a stingy love for bossing in men have prevented woman's public recognition by the church. No church that is acquainted with the Holy Ghost will object to the public ministry of women. We know scores of women who can preach the Gospel with a clearness, a power, and an efficiency seldom equaled by men. Sister, let the Holy Ghost fill, call and anoint you to preach the glorious Gospel of our Lord.[15]

Rees's own wife, Hulda, had been preaching since the age of sixteen, and her stepson said of her, "Like Catherine Booth, she was a balanced soul in whom domestic virtues and platform gifts developed apace."[16]

Fredrik Franson, who helped to establish the Evangelical Free Church, also contributed his own thoughts about the matter, coming out in favor of women preaching based on a passage in Acts.

> Acts 21:9 states that the evangelist Philip had four daughters who prophesied and it even says they were unmarried. The word "prophesy" is from Greek and "preach" is from Latin but they mean the same. In order to prophesy or preach one must be before an assembly not just with one person; otherwise it would be conversing. If it was acceptable for a woman to preach in those days it should also be so in our time.[17]

Oh, but how it flew in the face of convention! Americans worried that if women were publicly active, their families would suffer for it. The historian Timothy Smith investigated the lives of many of those women to see how their relationships fared, and he discovered that "between revivals they maintained a normal and apparently stable family life, if the few surviving letters may be taken at Face value." He says, "Their husbands joined happily in their meetings when they were near home and accepted periods of separation without much protest."[18] For those couples, there was a higher calling from everyday life to spread the news that salvation was available through the life, death, and resurrection of Jesus Christ. Somehow they seemed to find a way to provide balance between the two.

Christian women who spoke publicly carried Bibles and generally dressed in a modest, feminine style as they worked first and foremost to promote Christ and His kingdom while their secular counterparts, conversely, were advancing the rights of women. For them, there was a different emblem to wear, what J. C. Furnas calls a "symbolic uniform," known as Bloomers.[19] The harem-style pants were named for feminist Amelia Bloomer, although she didn't actually create them. Rather, she advocated for their use in her newspaper, *The Lily*, and she wore them herself. The public considered them a nuisance and an eyesore, as one Bloomer-sporting feminist attested:

> . . . however modestly . . . you may pass about your business, base rowdies congregated round the street corners, hotel steps, and lager beer saloons will look at you . . . in a manner that will cause every drop of blood to run cold within your veins. . . . Lost women, pointing . . . their polluted fingers, will follow you . . . (children) hooting, and shouting, and yelling . . . [20]

Clearly, wearing Bloomers in public wasn't for the fainthearted as doing so invited scorn and painted one with the uncomplimentary shade of the outcast.

Many Americans feared that what secular feminists pushed for most—woman's suffrage—would lead to the demise of the family. It is difficult to make such a connection in the twenty-first century, but at the time, the public forged a mental link between a woman's right to vote and those radical feminists who did not consider marriage and raising children to be as sacred as the majority of Americans maintained. For example, although there was scope for disagreement among early nineteenth-century feminists, many spoke out in favor of more lenient divorce laws, which was a scandal to middle America. Then there were the women's rights promoters like Victoria Claffin Woodhull, a rebel spirit who regularly flaunted convention.

She came from a poor Midwestern family that roamed about like gypsies, telling fortunes and putting on medicine shows. She dabbled in "spiritualism, faith healing, cancer quackery, blackmail and (very probably) prostitution."[21] Woodhull gained notoriety after ministering to the ailing magnate Cornelious Vanderbilt, who rewarded her and her sister-partner Tennessee handsomely for their efforts. Woodhull was no less than charmingly bombastic; she supported—and engaged in—free love, wrote for newspapers, then created her own, and decided at one point to make a bid for president. Furnas describes her as having possessed "pure-brass effrontery."[22] As far as "possession" was concerned, Woodhull stated that the Greek orator Demosthenes was her spirit guide, who helped her make career decisions.[23] She once tried her own hand at conventional marriage, taking a husband at fifteen, but she divorced him eleven years later. Two years after that, she took up with another man, but probably not in marriage. At one point, she lived with both men under the same roof. Furthermore, it was no secret that she considered marriage in the same way that she despised slavery.

With her avant-garde lifestyle, Woodhull's radicalism, which included sympathy for Marxism, anarchism, and legalized prostitution, damaged the early women's movement. She was so beyond the norm that more traditionally minded feminists tried to distance themselves and their causes from the likes of radical elements like her. In the public mind, however, there was a fear, however unrealistic, that allowing women to vote and to participate more broadly in public life would lead to the destruction of the traditional family. Besides, they maintained, women already occupied a lofty position, as on a pedestal, and to give them the vote would only make them lesser, not equals to men, and certainly not more feminine. Once reason that Frances Willard and (Godey's woman) were so popular was that they maintained their womanliness and taught by word and example what it meant to have a thriving marriage and obedient, happy children. It was okay to have women like them speaking around the country because they represented and encouraged what was best in American womanhood.

THE IDEAL WOMAN

For some twenty years, from the 1890s until about World War I (1914–1918), another curious woman charged onto the American scene, the fictional "Gibson Girl," named after illustrator Charles Dana Gibson. The public revered her as the personification of the ideal American female—tall, slender, young, and a bit mysterious, with abundant hair. She was, according to one source, "spunky and sentimental, down-to-earth and aristocratic," as Gibson wove story lines into the pictures he created.[24] He held women in the highest regard, weaving an interesting blend of the traditional Victorian ideal and a woman who was clearly at home in the world, beautiful and with a certain, independent spirit. She went to college, married well, and sometimes dominated the men in her life, but with all of her strength, the Gibson Girl never attended a suffrage rally, which might have put Americans off of her altogether, and she was, after all, a big business at the time.[25]

Gibson's girl began to fall out of fashion during World War I, and by the time the 20s started roaring, and after women had secured the vote (they did not end up voting as a unified bloc the way many feminists believed would happen[26]), a new-style American took over the national imagination, the free-spirited flapper.

Chapter 9

BESIDE THE GOLDEN DOOR

IN 1874, MICHAEL PUPIN left Serbia with five cents in his pocket and a willingness to do whatever it took to make it in the land of the free. Within twenty-four dizzying hours after arriving in the United States, immigration authorities had examined him, judged him fit to enter the country, and finding him a good candidate for the American dream, served him breakfast and sent him on his way to Delaware with instructions to report for work on a farm. Pupin eventually worked his way into the world of academia and became a renowned physicist at Columbia University. This was, indeed, a place of opportunity that many believe was unparalleled in human history.[1]

Steamships made oceanic travel financially possible for more people, and they made the trip to America from Europe faster than ever before, resulting in boatloads of immigrants making the trek with high hopes for the future.

In addition, political, religious, ethnic, and natural difficulties in their homelands prompted many to try their hands in a place where they could build better lives for themselves and their families. While some desired to stay only for a season, long enough to earn money that would improve their situations back home, most felt that they were home once they made it through the customs process and found places to live and work. Between 1790 and 1820, in the years following the creation of the United States, just a quarter of a million people left their nations to settle in the new country, but once the republic had stabilized, and then the Industrial Revolution got under way with its insatiable need for laborers, large numbers began arriving. By 1850, fully one-tenth of the population came from abroad.[2] Initially they were from northwestern Europe, including Great Britain, Germany, and Scandinavia, but as the century progressed, waves of newcomers from eastern and southern Europe formed the bulk of the teaming masses. Between the Civil War and World War I, 25 million foreigners journeyed across the ocean, lured by the abundance of land and work. Some financed their own trips, while others obtained the means to get to America from their families. Still others were recruited by various companies and agencies that didn't always live up to their promises, but who operated in such a way as to fill their own coffers.

Among the first to come in significant numbers were the Irish, who fled from their country in the aftermath of a devastating potato blight and a famine that resulted in the 1840s. By the time the "exodus" ended, there were more Irish living in the United States than in their homeland.[3] They initially fared poorly in America, coming as they did in an emergency situation with little cash and, therefore, the inability to buy land and develop their own farms in the up-and-coming West. It had taken all they had, and then some, to get to America at all. Rather, they congregated in northeastern cities, throngs of Irish who, as one priest said, were "the poorest and most wretched population that can be found in the world."[4] They stirred up antiforeign feelings among some Americans who resented their working for lower wages than those born in this country would find acceptable, a situation that affected black Americans in particular; they frequently lost their positions to the light-skinned Irish. In New England, they also had a way of displacing young farm women who once went to work in textile mills to save money for marriage and family.[5] In those respects, John Garraty and Robert McCaughey say they "strained the social fabric" of American city life.[6]

With little money to their names, the Irish inhabited slums "that would make the most noisome modern ghetto seem a paradise."[7] Their state of affairs in Boston resembled, say Garraty and McCaughey, "a perfect hive of human beings . . . huddled together like brutes," while in New York City, they populated basements and tenements resembling "great gloomy prisons" that more often than not were without running water, heat, or even windows.[8] Refuse and children filled the streets, the little ones scavenging for food and begging for pennies, some of them homeless drifters who slept in coal bins and empty barrels.[9] Unskilled female and minor laborers could work backbreaking jobs for long hours and not receive wages that were in any way commensurate with their performances; it wasn't unusual for them to earn twelve cents a day for as much as a ten- or eleven-hour shift in dangerous conditions. In the decades that followed their first, desperate, foray into American life, the Irish fared steadily better, although not easily.

ROMAN CATHOLICS AND
EASTERN EUROPEAN IMMIGRATION

In the last part of the nineteenth century, immigrants in great numbers began to come from the eastern regions of Europe, the "old country" that consisted of Russia and Poland, the Balkan countries, Italy, Greece, and Syria—people very different from those who had preceded them. Still mostly poor and lacking in education, they were "more than ordinarily clannish." For example, southern Italians typically believed that those who weren't part of their family were foreigners.[10] Initially, the single Italian men who went to America did so to earn enough money to return to Italy and set themselves up there with farms; they weren't interested in assimilating. However, the more typical immigrant, including the Italians, was part of a family that normally included a couple's younger brothers and sisters and who intended to build their lives in America.[11]

For the most part, there were common denominators among the eastern and southern European émigrés with a "high proportion" of them being unaccompanied males who wanted to save enough money to send for other family members.[12] In addition, although their early living conditions tended to be meager, J. C. Furnas believes that their new situations were a vast improvement over "the slums of Naples," and that by comparison, "a peasant hovel in Galicia or Macedonia made the shacks of a mining-company town in western Pennsylvania look good."[13] They also came to America to work in industries hungry for laborers since they didn't have enough money to purchase land and establish farms, like the early waves of Irish immigrants. Virtually all of them who weren't Jewish were Roman Catholic.

In the 1850s, Catholics made up just 5 percent of the U.S. population, but by the height of the immigration boom in 1906, their numbers had swelled to 17 percent, or 14 million out of 82 million.[14] While most of them came from Eastern Europe, significant numbers also arrived from French Canada and Mexico, For all of them, religion provided sources of "comfort and group identity" in an often harsh and suspicious culture.[15] Furnas believes, rather cynically, that Catholic priests in America encouraged the immigrants to keep the old ways in order to hold on to their loyalty, support, and submission.[16] However, those newcomers didn't need a lot of encouragement to stay close to their roots; they naturally clung to their family, religious, and cultural traditions, even to the point in which some chose to live in micro-communities, those made up of people from their villages and provinces more so than simply from their countries of origin. This was especially true of the Italians.[17] Furthermore, the church wasn't just a place to pay homage to the parish priest, the pope, or even God, although those were important, but, says Julie

Byrne, "the neighborhood Catholic church . . . was the focal point of a whole community, a whole way of life."[18] It was "local parishes (that) provided millions of heartbroken, homesick immigrant men and women the familiar comforts of ritual and belief that gave their world meaning."[19]

FACING PREJUDICE

Their hard lives and living situations often wore on them, yet through the support of their relatives and churches, they found ways to thrive in America. On the way to better things, however, they encountered a good deal of prejudice. Protestant America didn't always take to them, especially to the Catholics, whom they regarded with a combination of scorn, fear, and suspicion. Their seemingly strange practices and rituals—"smells and bells"— smacked of the Old World where priests and governing authorities, many believed, kept those from lesser stations in spiritual and socioeconomic ignorance in order to keep their own positions and fortunes safe. Byrne notes that "neighbors called Catholics names, employers refused to promote them, landlords rented them their worst apartments, newspapers blamed them for rising crime rates, and banks refused them loans."[20] A lot of Americans believed that Roman Catholic immigrants were straining national resources and contributing to social decay, and called for limits upon the number of immigrants they could send, especially since they tended to have large families. In the 1920s, restrictions were put into place that set quotas from foreign countries, and Catholic-dominated nations were allowed so few arrivals to America that not many came after the middle of that decade.

THE LIVES OF IMMIGRANT CHILDREN

A tragic aspect of the immigrant experience was the widespread child labor that occurred among the poorest of them, including the employment of ten- to fifteen-year-old males who worked in coal

mines, glass factories, and textile mills, as well as those who rolled
cigars. Messengers and newsboys often stayed out late into the
night doing the bidding of scoundrels who exploited them remorse-
lessly. There were men known as *padrones* who sent for boys from
the old country under the subterfuge that they were the children's
uncle or other relative, when all they really wanted was a source of
cut-rate labor. J. C. Furnas pictures the scrappy newsboys "fighting
rivals for rights to street corners, doing odd errands for shady characters as occasion served, and, when he lacked a family to absorb his
earnings, living in loose colonies of other such derelicts, in flop-
houses or patched-together shanties."[21]

Likewise, young immigrant girls who worked in textile mills,
department stores, and in domestic labor had to work long shifts to
supplement their parents' wages. Mexican children, who poured
into America with their families after the 1911 revolution in their
country, had to help their migrant farm parents go from place to
place with the seasons in order to make a livelihood.

It may seem difficult for contemporary middle class Americans
to imagine putting young children to work in order to pay for basic
necessities, but Furnas points out that for most of American history,
children had been wage earners. It wasn't until the modern era that
the majority of young Americans stopped working primarily to contribute to the family income, so it wasn't unusual for immigrant
youths to be employed outside their homes.[22] At least in America
they had opportunities to get ahead that were virtually unknown in
their homelands.

Nearly all newcomers, whatever their country of origin or religion, believed that with hard work and scholarship, their children
could achieve a great deal in the land of opportunity. It might not
come easily, of course, but they didn't expect it to. Roman Catholics
set up a parochial educational system to instruct immigrant children, while families from many other faith traditions sent their sons
and daughters to public schools.

Immigrant life for children didn't just consist of gritty work and
no play, fear and deprivation; it was also hopeful. Parents dreamed

that their children would do better than they ever had in all aspects of life, and that their children's children would follow on down the line with still better opportunities for education, jobs, homes, and better health. The story of Solly Saranoff typifies the immigrant experience of so many children in the early twentieth century.

The lad emigrated from Russia to Chicago in 1902 with his parents and sister when he was eight years old, moving into a four-room apartment that a relative had secured for them and which they filled with used furniture. Jacob Saranoff found work in a rag shop that paid eight dollars a week, a poorly ventilated and perpetually dusty place, but he didn't complain, not when he was able to enroll his children in an American public school. That was the realization of one his and his wife's greatest dreams.[23] Solly had his own ambition for what he would do in America; he wanted to play the piano. Although there wasn't any money for such a grand instrument, this was America, so there had to be a way. One day Solly's new friends took him to the famed community center, Hull House, where they could play and participate in various programs, and it was there that the young Russian caught sight of a piano just standing there waiting to be played. He gingerly approached it and began to touch the keys, wondering if someone would slap his hands for being so bold. No one minded, in fact, they encouraged him to play.

His parents eventually arranged for him to take lessons, and the staff at Hull House allowed Solly to use their piano to practice. Mr. and Mrs. Saranoff decided to purchase their own instrument for Solly on an installment plan, and they got the money by taking in boarders. After all, they had *four* rooms, didn't they? Solly had discovered how true it was that "all sorts of miracles happen in America."[24]

Betty Smith's endearing novel *A Tree Grows in Brooklyn* tells a fictional story based on her own experiences as an immigrant child of Irish and Austrian parents. In it, Francie Nolan's family exemplified life for many families in the 1890s and early 1900s, a tale of survival and determination amidst crushing burdens. In the account Mrs. Nolan worked as a janitor in their New York apartment building while

Francie's father earned a not-so-steady income as a singing waiter, a jolly man who unfortunately had a weakness for the bottle. To help their family, Francie and her brother would comb through the trash for scrap metal that they sold for a few pennies, some which would go to their parents, the rest that they would save or spend.

By current standards, the things Francie took pleasure in seem so small; how on Saturdays her parents gave her permission to go to the library, drink a cup of coffee, and spend the night in the front room so she could wait up for her father to return from work. Like other immigrant children, she had inner reserves of strength to help her through the hard times; when her father suddenly died while her mother was pregnant, a kindhearted official amended the death certificate to read that he died of pneumonia, rather than alcoholism. Although she had to quit day school to go to work, nevertheless, the determined young woman found other ways to get her education so that she could realize her future ambitions. The story concluded with Mrs. Nolan's marriage to a police officer and their moving out of the substandard apartment building into a much better, though still humble, home. Their own, modest, America dream had come true amidst heartache and setbacks.

THE IMPORTANCE OF FAMILY LIFE

Those immigrants who fared best in America tended to be the ones who maintained the strongest family ties, whose tenacious spirits bore a multitude of hardships for the sake of those they loved and for whom they wanted a better life than they had ever known. Among them were the Jews who fled to the United States from Russia and other parts of Eastern Europe in the aftermath of anti-Semitic *pogroms*, or riots, that destroyed their homes and businesses and took many lives. Discrimination and "lesser" varieties of persecution were, of course, part of the social fabric in those countries, and coming to America gave these weary people reason to hope for the future, in fact, for *a* future. In large measure because they had been singled out for harassment, many Jews had a strong desire to associate themselves as fully as possible with the American way of life while maintaining their cultural and religious identities. They came to the United States full of anticipation about their prospects in the land which, they heard, had streets paved with gold. Perhaps those avenues were made of asphalt after all, but as a metaphor, the promise of life here was very real to them.

Irving Howe tells the story of a boy growing up on New York's East Side who said he came home from school each day afraid that "his cot in the dining room would again be occupied by a relative just off the boat from Europe and given shelter by his parents."[25] Although their own space was at a premium, a lot of Jews took in boarders so that "privacy in the home was practically unknown."[26] The kitchen was the hub of Jewish family life, a place in which they not only cooked but also did the laundry—not just their own but often what they took in to make money—where they studied, entertained, and gave shelter to each other. Entertainer Zero Mostel recalled the kitchen of his youth as a place full of commotion, "my own private Coney Island."[27] It was also where "the Jewish mother was sovereign."[28]

In the old country, Howe points out that the father was the undisputed head of the house, a venerated figure who expected his wife and children's deference. A rabbi's daughter recalled, "One did not speak to him, nor of him, lightly. He represented an ancient civilization."[29] Although kids knew their subsidiary place in the home, Howe says that the discipline they received was "softened by parental indulgences."[30] Men were also the acknowledged spiritual authorities in the home, but women were expected to have a good command of the Hebrew Scriptures even though most of them were not formally educated. Those women were generally literate and intelligent, and according to one immigrant, "The name of God was always on her lips."[31] She may have been her husband's subordinate, but she was, nevertheless, a strong figure, "a loving despot" to her children, a woman who administered corporal punishment whenever necessary, and "the emotional center of the family," who mixed "practical sense and emotional abundance."[32]

The transition to life in democratic America proved far more difficult for male Jews than for their wives and mothers mainly because men could not long hold on to the kind of absolute authority they had maintained in a place that was used to powerful male leaders, kindly or otherwise. Women were accustomed to occupying the low rung of the totem pole, so being poor and subordinate in America was no big deal, but their men experienced a "wrenching . . . drop in status and self-regard."[33] A mother's dominant consideration was that she had a family to provide for, and she would do so, whatever form, however humble, it might take.[34] Nevertheless, very few mothers worked outside the home. They might have taken in work to do at the kitchen table, but "to spend sixty hours a week in a shop would have made family life all but impossible,"[35] says Howe. The Jewish wife and mother believed, furthermore, that her job was to provide a safe haven for her husband and children, that while the world might try to wear them down, "she alone could create an oasis of order." [36]

Another group of immigrants who had particularly strong family relationships were the Chinese, who began coming to America with the advent of the California Gold Rush in the late 1840s. Eloise Paananen and George Tsui believe that out of all the immigrant groups, they faced the most difficulty, perhaps because their ways were so inscrutable to the West.[37] During the craze for gold prospecting, Chinese families, devastated by floods followed by drought in their country, in addition to political and social rebellion, sent their strongest men to California. They were under obligation to send money home to the family, which included the elders, who enjoyed an elevated status in the home. The Chinese didn't particularly want to go to America—but times being what they were, they were desperate for relief. The hope was that the men who emigrated would make enough money to help their families, then return to China.

As they searched for gold and helped build transcontinental railroads, the Chinese faced great prejudice, dubbed "long-tailed, cloven-footed inhabitants of the infernal regions," "Chinks," and

"Coolies." Initially there were twenty-seven men to each Chinese woman, and, as a result, they endured tremendous loneliness. When they had the means, they sent for male relatives because prospective wives were back home where tradition obligated them to care for their elders.[38] With time, they began to settle in America, having summoned their wives, or for young women whom they would marry, according to their family's wishes. As family units, they built Chinatowns, operated laundries, and worked in agriculture. When they lived in cities, they often worked in one part of a building and resided in the back, each person carrying his or her weight in the businesses they maintained.

ON A PERSONAL NOTE

Natale Pellerite emigrated to America from Sicily in 1913, leaving behind his young wife and baby girl, planning to bring them over as soon as he made enough money. Along came World War I, and it wasn't until 1919 that they were able to rejoin him, with the little girl initially afraid of the father she had never really known. They lived in the Hoboken area of New Jersey for a time before taking up permanent residence along the Delaware River, in Phillipsburg, where Natale—now called Christopher Perio—and his wife Antoinette raised eight children. While she kept the home, he worked in a factory. Her lifeline was the neighborhood Catholic church; she walked to mass every day and became a familiar, and beloved figure—the priests often asked her to pray for them.

Their lives were simple, but they were closely knit together, enduring many hardships along the way, including the confiscation of their radio during World War II; authorities feared they might use the device to send subversive messages back to Italy. They didn't complain or demand their rights, however. As their youngest daughter, Dorothy, recalled, they were just happy to be in this great country and would do whatever they could to ensure its freedom. They had already sent three sons to the army; one participated in the D-Day Invasion, the Battle of the Bulge, and the liberation of a concentration camp, while another was almost mortally wounded but survived.

Most of their children established middle class homes and had families in the post-war years, including one who worked for the film industry in Hollywood, with one of his sisters living nearby. To the family back East, they had really made it. Their experience was echoed by millions of others like them, leaving their children and their children's children a proud legacy. I am their grateful grand-daughter.

Chapter 10

SEE THE USA

BEFORE THE ADVENT of major developments in transportation, most Americans lived, worked, and died close to home. It wasn't unusual for a person never to have ventured more than fifty miles beyond his or her birthplace over the course of an entire lifetime. Except for those who dwelt in the small cities and towns of the preindustrial era, people lived with their extended families on farms where they worked together to make a mostly subsistent income. One's closest neighbors could be a mile or more away, sometimes much more, and although they weren't in close proximity, they often cherished and looked out for one another. The outside world truly was "outside" of the experience of great numbers of American families, both for better and for worse, better in that parents and their children and grandchildren developed tight-knit bonds, including their values and ethics, for worse whenever an authority figure was particularly harsh or abusive.

In those days, travel was impractical, as well as a frightening proposition. There was no uniform system of roads; those that did exist were poorly built and full of obstacles, according to one source, "quagmires in wet weather, rutted and pitted with potholes a good part of the year."[1] Horses and carriages served as the primary means of conveyance for people who navigated bone-jarring and otherwise hazardous conditions. Many of the first "paved" roads, such as the turnpike that connected Philadelphia to Lancaster, Pennsylvania, were privately constructed and maintained so there was no uniformity. Still, those roads beckoned some easterners to pursue commerce and westward movement beyond the "frontier line" that separated the developed world from the wilderness. That line progressed slowly beyond the eastern seaboard, into western New York and Pennsylvania, then picked up speed as improvements were made, though primitive by contemporary standards. Homesteaders who struck out to the west often used America's waterways for transport.

In their research about the history of American transportation, Janet Davidson and Michael Sweeney discovered that "water—the lifeblood of American trade and travel for centuries—remained a profoundly important link between regions."[2] A steamboat along the Mississippi River, someone wrote in 1827 with more than a touch of wonder, "brings to the remotest villages of our streams, and the very doors of our cabins, a little Paris, a section of Broadway, or a slice of Philadelphia, to ferment in the minds of our young people, the innate propensity for fashions and finery."[3]

Once the stagecoach came on the scene, it also carried Americans who thirsted for adventure and new beginnings off to the wilds of the West, although not so comfortably as its water counterparts. Riders dubbed one route "the Shake Gut Line," but Robert G. Athearn says, "Despite such discomforts, passengers were delighted that they could bump across the land at an average speed of close to six miles an hour and that the Ohio River was now only $17.25 away from Baltimore."[4] In the early 1800s, those people who dared move west also traveled in Conestoga wagons, and later, prairie schooners, transporting all their worldly goods on those primeval U-Hauls.

Given the rigorous conditions of travel, it didn't make much sense to sell consumer goods at great distances, not to mention the time and cost of transport that entailed. Most products were locally produced by family units in the days before the transportation revolution. According to one historian, "Merchants in Boston and New York had more contact with their counterparts in London and the West Indies than with farmers a few miles away."[5] In the early 1800s, factories that produced textiles began operating in the northeastern part of the country, followed by those manufacturing, on a small scale initially, paper, glass, cotton, wool, iron, and shoes. This had a profound effect on family life as men began to leave home to go to work, where they spent most of their days. Garraty and McCaughey believe that "the factory system and the growth of cities (around those industries) undermined the importance of home and family as the unit of economic production."[6]

As far as society was concerned, there were "enormous" consequences.[7] "Because he was away so much," they say, "the husband had to surrender much of the power and authority he had formerly possessed to his wife . . . she was always there."[8] Whereas she once partnered with him, "she now left earning a living entirely to her husband."[9] In addition, husbands and wives, no longer in need of their children's manual labor on the family farm, went on to have fewer offspring.

This did not happen all at once, but was a gradual and relentless shift away from an agrarian-based lifestyle and economy toward one centered around industry and cities. Initially, factories had a bad name in America because their negative reputations in England had been made known across the ocean. Operators of those plants did their best to overcome that dishonor by winning the trust of parents, who sent their daughters to work in the textile mills where they lived in well-chaperoned boarding houses and received an education in books and manners after hours. Eventually, men and women followed their girls into those factories as well.

RAILROADS

England birthed the first railroads in the 1830s, and at first, Americans considered trains to be an impractical oddity. By 1840, however, the United States had begun to use, with some degree of efficiency, the new method of transporting people and goods. By 1850, railroads connected many northeastern districts. By the 1850s, says Robert Athearn, "In the West, the fastest growing part of the nation, it was the railroad that was of prime importance in (American growth). It helped to populate the new country, particularly its more remote parts."[10] The use of railroads stimulated agricultural production and expansion as a means of marketing, and trains lured native-born and foreign immigrants to western homesteading so that, by 1860, half the population had moved to the west of the Appalachian Mountains.[11] Trips that used to take two or three weeks now averaged less than two days, and meats butchered in Chicago could be served at a New Yorker's table.[12]

Before the Civil War those developments were in the preliminary stages, but they proliferated afterward as the railroad became a major feature of American life. Emily Dickinson sometimes waxed poetic about the romance of trains, but she also was known to call attention to their underside, especially how they brought unwanted strangers to her town of Amherst, Massachusetts. She once wrote, "Our house is crowded daily with the members of this world, the high and the low, the bond and the free. . . . But I hope they will pass away."[13] Local merchants also complained about the competition they now faced from distant purveyors of consumer goods. Railroads profoundly shaped American culture as well, as "they strengthened the connections among regions, states, and territories, making the vast continent into one nation."[14] Furthermore, "the growth of the railroad system set economic, social, and cultural changes into motion. Whether small and local or large and transcontinental, railroads connected people and places. Transportation networks made distance matter less."[15]

While trains had captured the American imagination and

changed a way of life, transforming it from a series of small towns and farms to an interconnected hub, another development was about to change the nation and its people even more.

THE HORSELESS CARRIAGE

Prior to the Civil War, Americans who lived in cities resided close enough to their places of employment so that they could walk to work. Afterward, the growth of the streetcar and trolley systems meant that people could live farther away from congested cities and still work there. The commuter was born. Chicago became famous, or infamous at it were, for its dynamic "Loop," the city's commercial center that churned with streetcars, elevated trains, horses, carriages, and the people who rode them. According to Bonnie Lilienfeld, "The wealthiest commuters lived a comfortable carriage . . . ride away from the heart of downtown, the expanding streetcar and elevated lines offered mobility to many more. Those who could afford to opted for living in lower-density areas" away from the "maelstrom" of the Loop.[16]

If trains, streetcars, trolleys, and the el provided a communal travel experience, the newly minted automobile offered a more individualistic approach to getting around, one that Americans responded to tepidly at first, then with great gusto. Autos first appeared in the United States in the 1880s to a public that regarded "horseless carriages" as "playthings for the rich."[17] Some towns banned them from their streets altogether while others restricted their use.[18] When one broke down, which happened with great frequency, the driver could expect some wise guy to advise, "Git a hoss, mister, git a hoss!"[19] A big debate ensued as to whether cars powered by electric outperformed those with internal combustion engines, so popular in Europe. Today there is a big push for electric cars, but it is far from a new phenomenon. Early vehicles ran on batteries that enabled speeds up to ten miles per hour, which was fast compared with horse speed, and that needed to be recharged every forty or fifty miles. Inventors dreamed of and worked toward the day when filling stations would be a common occurrence, and drivers could stop by to exchange their worn down batteries for fully charged ones. While the electric car drew some devotees, historian J. C. Furnas likened it to a "well-oiled roller skate" and pronounced it a "bore" to drive.[20]

In 1900, there were just eight thousand registered motor vehicles in the United States, and they were mainly owned by the wealthy.[21] About that time, people began to change their opinions about the car's usefulness, warming up to the idea that it might have some practical benefits after all. An automobile could transport people to medical help in an emergency, carry hoses to put out fires, or take goods to market, for example. In 1910, 187,000 autos roamed the nation's inadequate roadways, and the push was on civic authorities to provide a better, more uniform system of streets and highways. When Henry Ford introduced his Model T in 1909, he made it possible for the middle classes to own a car, and they embraced the idea enthusiastically. By 1920, more than nine million cars had been manufactured, and five years later, an average American worker could purchase a Model T for $300, or about three month's pay.[22]

In 1930, there were 26 ½ million cars, and the transportation revolution had helped create what James Kirby Martin calls a "consumer culture" that "blunted regional differences and imposed similar tastes and life-styles."[23] Subsequent developments in advertising, mass communication, and popular entertainment also contributed closely to that "consumer culture."[24] Martin adds, "No previous form of transportation (except walking) had been so widely available. The great American love affair with the automobile had begun."[25]

Around the same time, other creations were transforming American relationships and behavior. Telephones made it possible for people to communicate across many miles, but they also "reduced household visiting among neighbors as friends picked up the phone instead of dropping in."[26] In addition, the explosive popularity and proliferation of radios brought the nation's regions together through a mass culture that also began to erode local variations. Many new consumer goods came into American homes after Henry Ford "loaned" his methods of mass production to other industries, making products more uniform and affordable, say Davidson and Sweeney. "Radios, vacuum cleaners, and other home appliances soon appeared in large numbers, each one exactly like the next. Mass production, a term Ford popularized, helped create a culture of mass consumption. It made Americans not only want more things, but also want them again and again, in new models and new colors."[27] Naturally, in such an environment, uniformity of thought, belief, and manners followed, dictated in lesser degrees by the former nucleus of American life, Protestant churches.

Observers had mixed opinions about the effect of these new ways on American life. Some believed that cars, for example, "promoted family togetherness through evening rides, picnics, and weekend excursions," while others charged that the same vehicles created tension between parents and children regarding their usage. They also maintained that those family excursions were prompting too many people to skip church on Sundays.[28] Some critics went so far as to say that automobiles were little more than "portable bedrooms."[29] Cars changed American life, for better and for worse, including the way in which people bought them on credit, rather than saving for their purchase. "In the past," says Martin, "people had paid cash for consumer goods or done without," but now buying vehicles in this fashion was "undermining the public's devotion to thrift."[30]

In addition, Henry Ford's critics accused him of "turning men into robots" on his assembly lines as they performed repetitive, mindless tasks for hours on end. He responded that while he could never see himself doing such jobs, "to other minds, perhaps I might say to the majority of minds, repetitive operations hold no terrors. . . . The average worker, I am sorry to say, wants a job in which he does not have to put forth much physical exertion—above all, he wants a job in which he does not have to think."[31] Cold as that statement comes across, Ford believed that his mass-produced cars would enhance life for most people, that his vehicles would make it possible for a man to "enjoy with his family the blessing of hours of pleasure in God's great open spaces."[32]

THE SUBURBS

The United States was in fast-forward mode in the early decades of the twentieth century. Once a nation of farmers, America had done an about-face, with cities becoming the center of the country's life and identity; Davidson and Sweeney say "the urban experience became the American experience." By 1920, for the first time in U.S. history, more people lived in urban than in rural areas.[33] Because of the new means of getting around, America also witnessed the rise of suburbs that flanked the outskirts of metropolitan areas. According to James Kirby Martin, cars "opened up vast new regions for housing, giving workers numerous options about where to live. Though suburbs had once been the exclusive domain of the well-to-do, the automobile enabled working-class families to move there, too."[34]

A spark that appeared before World War II ignited in the postwar "Baby Boom" years between 1946 and 1964 was the trend of the husband working in the city and returning to his "bedroom community" in the suburbs after hours. FHA loans, cars, and mass transit made such a lifestyle possible, and the Levittown communities that sprang up embodied it. Vast suburban areas spread out with their mass produced houses and automobiles, appliances, clothes, and furniture, the fulfillment of the American dream, which was available to great numbers of Americans on an unprecedented level. At the heart of that goal was the importance of family life, to be married and have children who grew up to be responsible, law-abiding citizens who could hand down a strong nation to their own kids when the time came.

The car of choice for suburban families of that era was the station wagon, which many regarded as an "extension of the suburban home."[35] At drive-in movie theaters, it served as "a mobile living room," and at carhop restaurants, it functioned as "a mobile dining room." During family camping trips, it became "a home on wheels."[36] Cars had become over the years a means to a certain lifestyle that exerted a great influence on domestic life.

Many commentators have portrayed the post-war suburb as a place of dull conformity, including Inga Saffron who referred to "the cookie-cutter blandness of a bedroom community."[37] In the 1960s, The Monkees, a pop group, had a hit song, "Pleasant Valley Sunday" in which they commented wryly on suburban life in "status symbol land" where there were "rows of houses that are all the same" and where "no one seems to care." Samuel Eliot Morison and Henry Steele Commager provide the following analysis of that time and place:

> They displayed the same "ranch houses" on single or split levels, with picture windows, television antennae, and a two-car garage; the same well-manicured back gardens with little swimming pools; the same country clubs and shopping centers and supermarkets, all built to a pattern. Almost all the men commuted to near-by cities, society was matriarchal, and the well-protected young gravitated from the local high or country-day school to the state university or the Ivy League College of the East. For many Americans suburbia represented a new way of life—one that contrasted sharply with the older habits of the countryside or the city.[38]

Cars, better roads, and suburban living had put an end to the remoteness of country living, even as the farm receded in importance socially, politically, and economically.[39] (Those factors had also made it possible for large numbers of people to escape the clamor and crime of city life—where a certain conformity also held sway among residents—for a more tranquil life among like-minded neighbors.)

Americans had always worked "from sun-up to sun-down" on the farm, but generally suburban men put in eight-hour days, five days a week, leading to a new emphasis on recreation.[40] A "mania for relaxation" ensued in which Americans spent their disposable incomes on travel, golf, skiing, movies, camping, tennis, and swimming pools, and their free time listening to the radio, watching television, and going to baseball and football games. Advertising created a demand for products that promised Americans everything from better breath to more suitable spouses if they just used the right brands. Sociologists of the immediate post-war era noted a "frenetic quest for status" that "pervaded the whole of American society, but particularly suburbia."[41] Prior to that era, the country was more class conscious, but afterward, "class" became a much more fluid category. Anyone who worked hard enough to go to, and graduate from, college and then got a well-paying job could move up from the lower to the middle and upper middle classes. Such "boy-makes-good" success stories pervaded the American mind-set; post-war presidents Truman, Kennedy, Johnson, and Nixon all were products of social "climbing." According to Morison and Commager, "fluidity and mobility" described American society at that time:

> Almost everyone went to the same schools, dressed in the same ready-made clothes, shopped in the same supermarkets, listened to the same radio and television programs, read the same mass-produced magazines, drove the same cars, vacationed on the same beaches . . . Differences in wealth remained very great, but differences in what money could buy were negligible.[42]

RESULTS OF THE TRANSPORTATION REVOLUTION

The greater mobility of Americans that began in the late nineteenth century removed fathers from the majority of homes, leaving mothers more attached to the domestic arena and on their own, for most of every weekday. After World War II, the country experienced the rise of suburbia, along with greater class mobility. In many cases, people moved out of their old city neighborhoods, away from extended family members, and became more connected to their neighbors. While some critics maintain that the suburbs promoted isolation, it paled in comparison to the loneliness that a previous generation of farmers and homesteaders had experienced. The conformity that suburban life yielded—and make no mistake, wherever groups of people live, work, worship, play, and otherwise congregate, they always tend to conform to a certain standard or ideal—was along the lines of dominant, though fading, Protestant manners and mores. As a result, middle-class Americans put a high value on marriage, children, civic, and church responsibilities.

Chapter 11

THROUGH THE DARKNESS OF THE NIGHT

THE "GILDED AGE" of the latter nineteenth century gave way to the "Progressive Era" of the early twentieth, and those terms say so much about the national mood; a gilded time of promise, an era of unprecedented human progress and optimism. Many observers believed that the twentieth century would turn out to be the most prosperous and peaceful one the world had ever known, that advances in technology, science, education, and psychology would eventually eliminate poverty, disease, injustice, ignorance, and war. When Americans read the newspaper headlines in June 1914, therefore, about the assassination of the Hapsburg Empire's Archduke Franz Ferdinand and his wife by a Serbian nationalist, the tragic event seemed far removed from their own lives. By the end of August, one European country had declared war against other European countries as alliances sprang into action, and Americans shook their heads. Those Europeans were at it again. Why did they fight so much? The heads of their nations were intermarried and interrelated so deeply that this conflict seemed to be like the latest continental version of *Family Feud*.

Initially, America stayed out of the fray as President Woodrow Wilson assured the nation that the fighting had nothing to do with them. Gradually, however, as the war intensified, the United States got more and more involved. In the spring of 1915, a German submarine sank a British ship, resulting in 128 American deaths. Other belligerent actions followed on the seas, with further loss of life, but Wilson stayed on the sidelines until April 1917. By that time, Europe was on the eve of complete destruction; Russia alone had sacrificed two and a half million soldiers and witnessed the deaths of 20 percent of its civilian population. For each day of the war, six thousand Europeans died; material losses were catastrophic.[1] Sydney Ahlstrom said, "The Great War" signaled "the death march of the old order in Europe."[2] Conversely, America was becoming a world power. In his speech before Congress asking for a declaration of war, President Wilson remarked, "It is a fearful thing to lead this great peaceful people into war, into the most terrible and disastrous of all wars. . . . But the right is more precious than peace, and we shall fight . . . for a universal dominion of right by such a concert of free people as shall bring peace and safety to all nations and make the world itself at last free."[3]

This required great sacrifice from its people, and churches rallied the public to support this noble effort. All able-bodied men between twenty-one and thirty had to register with the newly created Selective Service; later in the conflict, the age range increased to between eighteen and forty-five. Nearly three million men, mostly single and with no dependents, got drafted; by war's end, a total of 4.8 million had served.[4]

With so many men fighting "over there," as the popular song put it, a number of women went to work in various war industries. About thirty thousand of them joined the military services, mostly as nurses, and several of them lost their lives, while others were wounded. When he urged the Senate to pass the Nineteenth Amendment in September 1918, President Wilson made reference to them as he helped usher in a new epoch for American women: "We have made partners of the women in this war; shall we admit them only to a partnership of suffering and sacrifice and toil and not to a partnership of privilege and right?"[5]

Across the nation, posters stirred Americans with messages that appealed to their emotions, such as "Civilization vs. Barbarism!" and "Wake Up, America! Civilization Calls Every Man Woman and Child!" Teachers encouraged their pupils to collect various items for the war effort, scrap metal, food, and bandages. They taught patriotic songs to the children and helped them sell war bonds. Young Americans learned from their instructors, churches, and parents how superior their democratic nation was to every other country in the world and that it was their responsibility to keep the torch of freedom lit.

Before the war, advertisers had encouraged American housewives to spend money on the vast array of new products available to make their lives easier, but they did an about-face during the conflict. Now, the conservation of food and various goods mattered much more than having mere wants met if civilization was to be saved from modern barbarians. Single women often worked so they could free up the men to fight; married women did as well, but it was considered more of a patriotic duty for the unmarried females to take those jobs because they didn't have families who relied on them. Virtually all men, women, and children knew they each had a role to play, and motivated by a noble theme, they readily made many sacrifices. "Expressions of patriotism often framed the war in traditional terms of masculinity and femininity and romantic love," according to one source. "Boys were stirred by the appeals to masculine heroism, as illustrated by recruiting posters . . . Posters such as the 'Spirit of America' presented Lady Liberty in a highly feminized, even sexualized form, while 'Home Hospitality' depicted an idealized matronly figure tending to her 'boys.'"[6]An address to the female students at St. Mary's College in North Carolina by Judge Robert Winston seems over-the-top today, but in that era, at that emotional time, he was well received. He told his impressionable audience that the American boys they had seen off to war on trains and ships were fighting in large measure to save and protect them from "worse than hell." He said:

> These young men will die, if need be, to save you young women from worse than hell. True, they are fighting for their country and are every inch patriots; but after all, dear young women, it is for you, and you, and you, that they fight. Behind every bayonet, as it flashes in the sunshine of France and buries itself in the bowels of some savage German, is the stimulating memory of you, the girl he left behind. And the honor and glory of being thought worthy of you—the thought that you love and honor him—will nerve and sustain him to the end. But one flutter of your handkerchief, and he will storm the ramparts of hell.[7]

The families of fighting Americans proudly exhibited the honor and pride they felt by displaying banners in their windows, a white, foot-long flag that hung vertically, set off by a red border. Those "Sons in Service" decorations contained a blue star for each son or husband on active duty, and in the event of death, a gold star replaced it. Employers and civic organizations demonstrated their own patriotism with larger versions that contained stars for each employee or member in the military.

By the end of World War I, 48,000 Americans had died in action, 2,900 were missing in action, and 56,000 had died from diseases related to the fighting. The conflict in Europe resulted in the loss of almost an entire generation of men from Great Britain and the Continent; Germany lost 1.8 million men, France, nearly 1.4 million, Britain, close to a million, and Austria-Hungary, 1.2 million men.[8] While Europeans staggered through the aftermath, America emerged as a new world power, and its women, now able to vote, stood poised at the beginning of a new era of challenges and opportunities for themselves and their families. One married woman from Muncie, Indiana, with two high school aged sons had gone to work during the war and decided not to leave her job when the conflict ended. Although she was in a minority, she represented a developing trend of women leaving their traditional domestic sphere. She remarked,

> The mister objected at first, but now he don't mind. I'd rather keep on working so my boys can play football and basketball and have spending money their father can't give them. We've built our own home . . . by a building and loan like everyone else does. We have it almost all paid off and it's worth about $6,000. No, I don't lose out with my neighbors because I work; some of them have jobs and those who don't envy us who do. I have felt better since I worked than ever before in my life. I get up at five-thirty. My husband takes his dinner and the boys buy theirs uptown and I cook supper. We have an electric washing machine, electric iron, and vacuum sweeper. I don't even have to ask my husband anymore because I buy these things with my own money.[9]

THE GREAT DEPRESSION

After the war to end all wars, America passed through the Roaring 20s, an age that boasted Charles Lindbergh, female "flappers," who defied conventional mores, speakeasies, and gangsters. Following a robust period built on the sinking sand of easy credit, the stock market began "a steep downward slide" that resulted in the "Black Tuesday" crash on October 29, 1929.[10] One group of historians has put it well, saying that while the crash didn't cause the Great Depression of the 1930s, "like a person who catches a chill, the economy after the crash became less resistant to existing sources of decline."[11] By 1933, fully one-fourth of the American labor force was unemployed, with some sources going so far as to say it was 16 million people, or one-third of the nation's workers.[12]

Profound and unwelcome changes occurred in many homes in

which male heads of households lost their factory jobs, one of the hardest hit sectors of the working world. Conversely, women's employment tended to be steadier since it didn't cost employers as much to keep them, so wives waitressed, did secretarial work, and served as domestics to keep their families going. Sometimes husbands left town in pursuit of work in other places, only to find themselves in competition with a thousand other men for the same handful of jobs. Women took in boarders, kept hens for eggs to eat and to sell, and raised vegetables to feed their families.

Sydney Ahlstrom observed that the Depression affected Americans "across class lines. . . . Men stood on bread lines, selling apples on street corners, sleeping in subways and parks and city incinerators. Armies of homeless youth roamed the land . . . Violence erupted in some communities, as men chose to steal rather than watch their children starve.[13] As a result, "unemployment upset the psychological balance in many families by undermining the traditional authority of the male breadwinner."[14] It wasn't uncommon for sullen men to withdraw emotionally or drink to excess; some resorted to suicide. One Chicago social worker found, "Fathers feel they have lost their prestige in the home; there is much nagging, mothers nag at the fathers, parents nag at the children. Children of working age who earn meager salaries find it hard to turn over all their earnings and deny themselves even the greatest necessities and as a result leave home."[15]

It is important to keep in mind that people also showed tremendous strength and courage during that adverse time, pulling together in admirable ways. In Pittsburgh, a mechanic's wife who had eight children regularly sent them about the neighborhood to make sure no one was going hungry before they sat down to eat their own supper of beans. One of the sons recalled years later that his best Christmas present as a child was the year he got twenty-six cents. Across the state, a little girl whose father worked whenever his fragile health allowed and there was work to be had, watched her mother go off to work in the cafeteria of a local industrial plant. She remembered the Christmas when her older sister got a doll, and she received an outfit for it. Another year their father made them a desk that they were expected to share. One of the most popular novels of the Depression was Margaret Mitchell's *Gone with the Wind* that portrayed the hardships of heroine Scarlett O'Hara during the Civil War. Readers connected with her because her own pliability and renewed character gave them hope as well.

People needed all the encouragement they could get at a time when three-quarters of American workers were on a part-time basis, when the average family income was $1,500, down from $2,300 just before the Crash.[16] People sometimes resorted to extreme measures for survival. In one Pennsylvania coal town some desperate families lived together in one-room shacks, while others in Oakland, California, inhabited sewer pipes. Families hung on to their homes as long as they could avoid foreclosure, taking every penny, every effort they could make, leaving nothing for extras, even for doctors and dentists. Wives bought stale bread, and children foraged through piles of rejected toys and snack foods at local factories to get a treat. When one's shoes wore down, cardboard and cotton filled in the soles, and although few people starved, there was widespread hunger, and little variety in the daily diet.

In the 1930s, the family as a social entity faced hard times. Many couples delayed marriage, resulting in the birth of fewer children in America. When people did marry, they tended to keep the ceremonies simple, and if there even was a honeymoon, that was low-key as well. The divorce rate may also have slowed, but the rate of desertion rose. Vagrant children roamed the nation.[17] According to one source, teenagers sometimes found themselves in an unfamiliar, and uncomfortable, situation when they got work and their parents were unemployed, "reversing the normal rules of provider and dependent. Sometimes children had to comfort their despairing parents."[18]

It was difficult for men to come to terms with all of this, especially not being the sole breadwinners of their families. Research suggests that those who were able to adjust regarded their situations as part of a national ordeal, rather than a personal failure.

Some of the hardest hit people were Midwestern farmers,

especially those living in Oklahoma where a proclivity for drought added to the instability of land that badly needed to lay fallow periodically. The result was a dust bowl, "great clouds of blowing silt," or "black blizzards of dust a mile and a half high."[19] People experienced respiratory difficulties, as well as trouble getting around as day became like the night.[20] Oscar Heline, an Iowa farmer, remarked,

> The struggles people had to go through are almost unbelievable. A man lived all his life on a given farm, it was taken away from him. One after the other . . . Not only did he lose the farm, but it was impossible for him to get out of debt. . . . First, they'd take your farm, then they took your livestock, then your farm machinery. Even your household goods. And they'd move you off. [21]

Tens of thousands fled to California where they became hapless migrant workers, entire families picking crops, living in terrible conditions, moving along with the seasons as they experienced deprivation, displacement, and a lack of worldly security. One migrant farmer said, "What bothers us travellin' people most is we cain't get no place to stay still."[22]

Although Depression-era living was typical for much of the world, it was unprecedented in the American experience. The hardships that families endured caused significant distress, and yet, as John Steinbeck vividly portrayed in his novel *The Grapes of Wrath* that showcased migrant workers, "the 'people' are indestructible no matter what tragedies they must surmount."[23] The popular films of Frank Capra and the poignant art of Norman Rockwell portrayed the "common man" similarly, as innately dignified and able, as God-fearing Americans, to surmount any obstacles.

WORLD WAR II

Like the First World War, the second began in Europe, after Germany's brutal dictator Adolf Hitler had violated statute after statute of the Treaty of Versailles in an effort to lift his nation's collective bent knees to the pinnacle of a glorious new era when it would boast a master race. Similarly, Italy's Benito Mussolini was engaging in his own empire building at Ethiopia's expense, while in the Far East, Japan was seizing a vast territory to rule and subdue. Appeasement, compromise, and diplomacy failed to bring about peaceful resolutions to multiple conflicts, and when Hitler invaded Poland on September 1, 1939, Europe once again plunged into war. Although America supported Great Britain in its effort to stave off the German threat of conquest, it stayed out of the fighting until the Japanese launched a surprise attack against the U.S. Pacific Fleet at Pearl Harbor on December 7, 1941.

Over two thousand Americans died in the assault, with nearly twelve hundred wounded. On December 8, President Franklin Roosevelt went before Congress to ask for a declaration of war against Japan, using the famous phrase "a day which will live in infamy" to describe the strike. On December 11, Japan's allies, Germany and Italy, declared war on the United States. Editor Jonathan Daniels assessed where the country stood at the time saying, "The twenties are gone with self-indulgence. The thirties have disappeared with self-pity. The forties are here in which Americans stand on a continent as men—men against fighting in the crudest man terms."[24]

As the nation mobilized its natural and human resources, families became an important component in securing a victory over heinous cruelty and totalitarianism. There was a surge of patriotism and a desire to do whatever one could to help, which often came in surprising forms. Housewives, for example, learned to save certain kinds of refuse that proved useful for wartime needs, things like cooking fats, old metal shovels, tin cans, bottles, paper, even empty lipstick tubes. Rubber was in especially short supply since Japan had taken control of the nations that had supplied most of the raw rubber to the American market. As a result, gas rationing occurred, not because there was a shortage of it, but because people had to conserve the use of tires on their automobiles. Families turned in old tires, rubber hoses, boots, raincoats, even bathing caps for recycling.[25] Since nylon was being used exclusively for war purposes, women had to go without stockings, learning to use eyebrow pencils to draw fake seams on the back of their legs to simulate a similar effect. Likewise, since cloth had to be conserved, having less material available made for shifting fashions; men stopped wearing cuffed pants and vests, and women's skirts went shorter and sleeker. In addition, the two-piece bathing suit came into style.

Although full employment wiped out the last vestiges of the Depression, bringing a renewal of prosperity, Americans now faced a different kind of deficiency since every product, every considera-tion went first toward winning the war. Families received ration books that regulated how much gas, sugar, meat, and butter they could buy, and new cars were unavailable because war machinery had to be made at a fast and continual pace.

More people got married since the war brought both a renewal of wealth as well as a sense of urgency for lovers who were about to face uncertain times of separation, and possible death. Family life knew its share of disruptions; for example, many couples ended up living with one set of parents due to a housing shortage. Nor did women stay close to their traditional spheres of influence; during the war, they made up one-third of the work force with five million working in war-related factories.[26] According to one recruiting bill-board, "If you've sewed on buttons, or made buttonholes, on a machine, you can learn to do spot welding on airplane parts. If you've used an electric mixer in your kitchen, you can learn to run a drill press. If you've followed recipes exactly in making cakes, you can learn to load shell."[27]

Women who became known as "Rosie the Riveters" for their factory employment, felt justifiably proud of their contribution to winning the war. One, Lola Weixel, said, "We were happy to be doing it. We felt terrific. Lunch hour would find us spread out on the sidewalk. Women welders with our outfits on, and usually a quart of milk in one hand and a salami sandwich in another. It was an experience that none of us had ever had before."[28]

Prior to the war, most Americans frowned on a married woman working outside the home, unless it was for economic necessity;

that was the husband's duty. Hers was to maintain the home, or else "it would disintegrate."[29] Those convictions still held during World War II, but they had to make way temporarily for an urgent need. In 1943, Margaret Hickey, head of the Women's Advisory Committee to the War Manpower Commission, said, "Employers, like other individuals, are finding it necessary to weigh old values, old institutions, in terms of a world at war."[30] Initially, Rosie the Riveter was single, often just out of high school, sometimes working part-time while still in school. By 1943, however, there weren't enough of them left to fill the urgent requirement for labor.[31] It was to the lady of the house that the nation turned for help. Says William H. Chafe, 75 percent of the women who went to work during 1943 were married.[32] Whereas before the war, the national media had opposed married women working,

> now radio stations and periodicals glamorized war work and pleaded with women to hurry and enlist at their local employment office . . . a national network gave time each week to a broadcast by "Commando Mary" on how women could assist in defeating the enemy. In one radio script, the announcer declared that women possessed "a limitless, ever-flowing source of moral and physical energy, working for victory."[33]

Women may have replaced men in the nation's factories and offices, but they found it more difficult to substitute themselves at home, with their children. In Britain, working women had the support of their government with its "special community centers," "Central Kitchens," and day care, but Americans were loath to depend on the state to prepare their meals or watch their children. The idea of sending a son or daughter to be looked after by strangers "challenged deeply held convictions about the integrity of the family and the importance of a woman's role in the home."[34] As a result, most working mothers arranged for family or friends to watch their children, and if the son or daughter was older, he or she often returned from school to an empty home.

Women might be patriotic enough to leave home to work, but their first priority was family, and many of them changed jobs or just didn't show up for work when their children needed them more than Uncle Sam. Chafe says that "female turnover and absenteeism in one factory alone caused the loss of forty planes a month."[35] In June 1943, for every two women who took war-related jobs, another quit. "Boeing had to employ 250,000 women over a four-year period to maintain a labor force of 39,000."[36] Forty percent of women who left their work in war plants in 1943 did so because of "marital, household, and allied difficulties."[37]

Women entered the working world in such large numbers in the 1940s that their presence helped ensure the victory that the American and Allied forces achieved in the summer of 1945. The impact that they made was, according to the Women's Bureau, "one of the most fundamental social and economic changes in our time."[38] No longer, said Margaret Culkin Banning, would women "be dependent on men for their bread and butter. . . . Able to earn their own keep, they could even support a husband who was wounded or ill."[39] Although a women's march down the path to greater independence seemed inevitable, their time of arrival was still very much in the future. Betty Allie, a State Workmen's Compensation official, summed up the situation in a 1943 newspaper interview: "Women are working only to win the war and will willingly return to their home duties after the war is won. They will look on this period as an interlude. . . . The women are like Cincinnatus, who left his plow to save Rome and then returned to his plow. Women will always be women."[40]

After the ordeals and deprivation, sacrifices, displacement, and uncertainty of two world wars and the Great Depression, it isn't surprising that the majority of women returned to their homes after the industries and offices released them, eager to resume a normal, stable, family life. The new, post-war suburbia with its cars and fully stocked groceries, playgrounds, and schools, its homes to which their alive-and-well husbands came every night, must have seemed like a bit of heaven.

Chapter 12

PLANET HOLLYWOOD

IT WAS A FILM THAT shocked and angered mainstream America, and although its creators claimed to be drawing attention to a societal problem, few people bought that line. The interest it stirred up was not, after all, on the sorry condition of girls whom adults forced to grow up too soon, but on the exploitation of a twelve-year-old actress who bared her body for the camera then romped about naked for a lengthy sequence. Much as this sounds like the hoo-ha surrounding Brooke Shields's appearance as a child prostitute in *Pretty Baby* (1978), the film in question actually came out four decades earlier, in 1938 with Shirley Mills the starlet. Many people remember when innocence pervaded family-minded movies in the early-to-mid twentieth century, but the film industry only went kicking and screaming into that mode.

The origin of moving pictures stretches back to the last years of the nineteenth century when Thomas Edison developed a "kinetoscope" that demonstrated primitive filmmaking. He gave the first public presentation to a New York City audience in 1896, where the first movie studios started. The public paid five cents to watch short films in "nickelodians" where they saw "tiny figures moving against blurred backgrounds," usually depicting "endless variations on the chase."[1] By the 1910s, the movie industry had largely relocated to southern California, to Hollywood where directors could count on fair weather most of the year, and persistent sunshine made for better lighting conditions.[2]

From the dawn of moviemaking, which quickly became one of the country's primary sources of entertainment, objectionable content filled the silver screen, alarming Americans who preferred to maintain a higher moral tone. Film historian Tim Dirks of *American Movie Classics* says that some of the first movies contained "candid depictions of drug use, prostitution, lawlessness, and religious blasphemy."[3] As far back as Eadweard Muybridge's "primitive motion studies" in the 1880s, actors appeared naked with at least two French movies in the late 1890s featuring nude performers; in one, an actress performed a striptease. The 1914 film *Hypocrites* included "full female nudity," while Audrey Munson shed her clothes a year later to portray a sculptor's model, then again in 1916 for a movie titled, paradoxically, *Purity*.[4]

Early motion pictures had a certain proclivity for wayward women with actress Theda Bara holding the title of Hollywood's Baddest Girl. In 1915's *A Fool There Was*, she lured a husband away from his home and family as if she had come straight out of the book of Proverbs, the epitome of a temptress that a man should avoid at all costs. Other movies in which Bara appeared boasted titles such as *Sin* and *The Devil's Daughter* (1915), as well as 1917's *The Tiger Woman* and *Cleopatra*. She reveled in her brand as "the wickedest woman in the world."[5] Other actresses provided their own variety of shock value to the films in which they starred, including swimming sensation Annette Kellerman. Along with advocating the one-piece bathing suit as a replacement for the Victorian era's stuffed seaside costumes, she stripped down to her birthday suit in 1916's *A Daughter of the Gods.* Nakedness in motion pictures even extended into those with religious themes, including *The Penitentes* (1916) that showed frenzied Roman Catholics going about crucifying people on Good Friday, including a young, undressed girl.

From its inception the film industry was out of touch with the values of mainstream America. Once it moved to Hollywood, that name became synonymous with "sin"; some referred to it as "the Sodom of America."[6] Historian John Mack Faragher believes that the people who made up the movie business didn't see the world through the same lens as most Americans. "The physical isolation of (Hollywood), its great distance from eastern cities, the absence of traditional sources of culture and learning all contributed to movie folk looking at life in a self-consciously 'Hollywood' way."[7] Another way in which movies were "out of touch" was how they drew the majority of their talent from cities "at a time when most Americans hailed from rural areas or small towns."[8] Furthermore, studio heads were largely Jewish immigrants from central and eastern Europe, while two-thirds of the actors were under thirty-five—fully three-quarters of the actresses were a full decade younger than that. Ninety percent of the writers had a higher education, and half of those were women at a time when relatively few middle-class females worked outside the home.[9]

For all of their foreignness, however—perhaps even because of it—movies were regarded as exotic and attractive and gained a wide following, achieving "a mythic power in American life" throughout the 1920s when garish theaters were built around themes such as a pharaoh's tomb and the French Renaissance.[10] The public exhibited a mania about its favorite actors, the latest version of the American success story, people who had emerged from modest backgrounds to achieve star status, elevating them beyond the realm of everyday life, as well as conventional morality. Actors, actresses, and directors made the news for such things as drug usage, illicit sex, wild parties, even murder, which made for sensational headlines in papers and sold a steady supply of fan magazines.

In 1921 Universal Studios made some concessions to contemporary values by inserting a morals clause into their contracts so that in the event that its actors "forfeited the respect of the public," they would lose their salaries.[11]

Nevertheless, film makers continued to pour forth movies that shocked and enticed the public, including *Sinners in Silk*, *Ladies of Pleasure*, and *The Joy Girl*, which, according to one press agent, promised audiences "brilliant men, beautiful jazz babies, champagne baths, midnight revels, petting parties in the purple dawn, all ending in a terrific smashing climax that makes you gasp!"[12] In some foreign films, homosexual acts and erotic sadism were portrayed on screen. Even renowned director Cecil B. DeMille included sexual content with his biblical epics, *The Ten Commandments* (1923) and *The King of Kings* (1927). Likewise, the 1925 drama *Ben Hur*, based on Lew Wallace's novel, featured flower girls dancing naked from the waste up.

CRACKING DOWN

Each state had its own decency laws, so there was no uniformity about what was unacceptable content, and little consensus about how to enforce any standards. For example, Tim Dirks says that some states forbade the display of an ankle; others wouldn't allow pregnancy to be mentioned.[13] In 1922, former Postmaster General William H. Hays headed up a new Motion Picture Producers and Distributors of America office that the studios organized as a self-policing instrument "before the public's anger at declining morality depicted in films hurt the movie business."[14] Among the MPPDA's first actions was to expel actor Fatty Arbuckle from the movies for his role in a lurid rape-murder scandal in 1921. He was eventually acquitted after three trials, but Arbuckle had been properly shamed and, some would say, became a scapegoat for the excesses of Hollywood performers.

The morality clauses and the Arbuckle affair did little good in the long run to clean up the film business, nor did a 1927 list of "Don'ts and Be Carefuls" because they were, says Dirk, "open to varying interpretations."[15] The self-regulating list called on movie makers "to establish 'correct standards of life'" as well as to avoid the following: nudity, rape, cruelty to children and animals, men and women in bed, profanity, depictions of capital punishment, perversion, interracial relationships, drug use, excessive violence, "lustful kissing," and the seduction of girls.[16] Dirks maintains that most studios chose to disregard these regulations "because there was no enforcement that was effective" and because, after all, the public kept putting down its money to see objectionable fair.[17] One way that studios side-stepped the restrictions, according to Dirks, was to tack on an ending in which the moral of the story was that fooling around or committing crime did not pay, or in which the bad guy—or gal—repented. "Some of the elicit behaviors could be exhibited," he says, "if later punished within the film."[18] Likewise, if a play could not be adapted for film because it contained offensive subject matter, the producers would disguise it by giving it a new title.

At least two cinematic "bad girls" paraded their way across the screen like preschoolers pushing the limits, trying to find out how much they could get away with. Jean Harlow was a bombshell who flaunted her curves ignominiously as an adulteress and "wise-cracking floozy" while German actress Marlene Dietrich "played seductive, cool females in sexually perverse melodramas."[19] Long before culture was trying to normalize such behavior, she kissed a woman on the mouth in *Morocco* (1930), sang a scorching voodoo song and executed a strip-tease in *Blonde Venus* (1932), and intimated adultery and sadomasochism in a performance as Catherine the Great. It was, however, another actress whose sexy portrayals roused the public's ire to such an extent that for the next few decades, Hollywood was on notice to behave itself or take a major hit in the wallet.

Mae West's "very successful sexual appearances in *She Done Him Wrong* and *I'm No Angel* (1933) threatened a boycott of motion pictures if (censorship guidelines) didn't go into effect."[20] In 1930, a new "Production Code" had been created in which studios faced a $25,000 fine for failure to secure a "seal of approval from the

Production Code Administration" once again led by William Hays; it took four years, however, to go into effect, allowing West's films to slip under the radar. According to what became known as "The Hays Code," filmmakers were to abide by the following guidelines:

1. No picture shall be produced that will lower the moral standards of those who see it. Hence the sympathy of the audience should never be thrown to the side of crime, wrongdoing, evil or sin.
2. Correct standards of life . . . shall be presented.
3. Law, natural or human, shall not be ridiculed, nor shall sympathy be created for its violation.[21]

In addition, studios were to espouse "the sanctity of marriage and the home" and avoid implying "that low forms of sex relationship are the accepted or common thing."[22] Sometimes, the Code recognized that adulterous or forbidden sexual relationships were "necessary to the plot," but they "could not be explicit or justified and were not supposed to be presented as an attractive option."[23] In fact, nothing was to appear on screen that could "stimulate the lower and baser elements," including nudity or "suggestive dances."[24] The problem was that while major studios adhered to these guidelines, lascivious films like *Child Bride* were produced by independents. It is no wonder that the public became increasingly disillusioned with Hollywood's inability to police itself and why the Church stepped in to dispense with the moral riff-raff.

In the 1930s, the Protestant Church still served as the arbiter for American values, a position that, ironically, it would yield in the coming decades to the secular mass media. But not yet. According to a June 1934 *Time* magazine story:

> For many a year the U.S. churches have deplored what they call the brazen indecency of U.S. cinema. Their annual conferences have passed resolutions. Their clergy have lobbied for censorship bills. Their journals have crusades. But for all their zeal the

churches have accomplished very little. Last week, led by members of the Roman Catholic Church, they were embarked on a new crusade, brandishing a new weapon—the boycott.[25]

Organized by the Most Reverend John Timothy McNicholas, Archbishop of Cincinnati, the Catholic Legion of Decency was created to compel the movie industry to clean up its act. Father McNicholas had attended a Catholic Charities Convention in which delegate Amleto Cicognani urged his brothers and sisters in the faith to protect the public from a "massacre of innocence of youth" conducted by film producers.[26] The agency formed by the Church encouraged people to sign a voluntary pledge "to remain away from all motion pictures except those which do not offend decency and Christian morality."[27] Initially, two million people joined the Legion, originally known as the Catholic Legion of Decency but which substituted the word "Catholic" for "National" when the effort drew large numbers of Protestant and Jewish members. It was the first time that the Roman Catholic Church had taken such a leadership role in American life, kicking off the kind of ecumenical effort at moral reform that would occur again after 1973's legalization of abortion.

Archbishop McNicholas's pledge read:

I condemn all indecent and immoral motion pictures, and those which glorify crime or criminals. I promise to do all that I can to strengthen public opinion against the production of indecent and immoral films, and to unite with all who protest against them. I acknowledge my obligation to form a right conscience about pictures that are dangerous to my moral life. I pledge to remain away from them. I promise, further, to stay away altogether from places of amusement which show them as a matter of policy.[28]

The impact of the Legion's boycotts kept the film industry on a short leash for the next thirty years, until the foundations of America's Judeo-Christian culture began to erode. An example of the

Legion's proclamations against particular movies occurred in 1934 when MGM released *Riptide*. It said:

> Unfortunately typical of the pictures that have been built around Nora Shearer, the much publicized wife of Irving Thalberg . . . It seems typical of Hollywood morality that a husband as production manager should constantly cast his charming wife in the role of a loose and immoral woman . . . We advise strong guard over all pictures which feature Nora Shearer. . . .[29]

The Legion uttered similar remarks regarding producer George White, whom it said, found it difficult to create "any type of entertainment he does not soil."[30]

The National Legion of Decency with its millions of members went a long way toward ridding Hollywood of what writer John Dos Passos referred to as its "great bargain sale of five and ten cent lusts and dreams."[31] That it was reviled by filmmakers is a gross understatement.

THE FAMILY IN MOVIES

As early as 1929, a study was made to determine the impact of movies on American children. The Payne Fund Foundation discovered that in the year from 1929–1930, children in over fifty Ohio communities went to the movies weekly, usually unchaperoned and without any rating system to guide their parents.[32] The study concluded that the minds and spirits of American youngsters were at great risk at the hands of this powerful medium, "and that there could be no doubt that what they saw deeply affected them."[33] Furthermore, "attitudes concerning ethnic, racial and social issues were changed by movie viewing . . . (children) retained information they received in the movies. . . . (and) certain movies disturbed healthy sleep."[34] Avid young film watchers also did worse in school than children who went less frequently, and they tended to imitate what they saw on the screen, both good and bad. Furthermore, "these effects were cumulative and persistent over time."[35]

Children had not figured largely in movie plots before the 1930s, but one particular little girl became the highest paid actress during the Depression era. The first child to rise to stardom was actually Jackie Coogan, who appeared as Charlie Chaplin's sidekick in *The Kid* in the 1920s and who became the first film celebrity to have a series of products marketed around him. (In the 1960s he famously portrayed Uncle Fester in the whimsical sitcom *The Addams Family*.) In the 30s, movie studios "began making films that gave a more persistent image of children: they were precious and precocious, eager to fix problems in the small world around them and wise beyond their years.[36] That era's pictures featured children as orphans and kidnap victims who nevertheless prevailed, tykes who exhibited their "plucky nature in dealing with poverty and adversity."[37] The characters they played demonstrated concern for their parents and siblings during tough times and found joy in unadorned pleasures.

Ironically, the biggest child star of the 30s, perhaps of all cinematic history, first appeared in a series known as *Baby Burlesks*, which depicted "young children in adult situations" replete with sexual innuendo.[38] Shirley Temple became the wealthiest star of the 1930s through her adorable roles as "taskmaster and problem solver whenever there was a family crisis."[39] Her first major film was *Stand Up and Cheer* (1934) when she was six and had already been acting in films for half of her life. Like Jackie Coogan, her likeness, replete with a proscribed number of ringlets in her hair, adorned various products, especially three-dimensional and paper dolls. At the pinnacle of Temple's fame, President Franklin D. Roosevelt reportedly said, "As long as our country has Shirley Temple, we will be all right."[40]

She became representative of a characterization of children as resilient and capable, yet "innocents deeply in need of the love and affection of adults around them. While Hollywood preserved the dominant notion of the nuclear family, it gave children the clear message that they could not make it in the world on their own."[41]

Professor Kathy Merlock Jackson, who wrote *Images of Children in American Film: A Sociocultural Analysis*, says this was characteristic of the period. Children "were innocent . . . they were also fix-its, able to solve adults' problems."[42]

She disagrees, however, with the idea that the nuclear family appeared in most scripts, saying, "Families in film were not always nuclear, owing to the death of a spouse due to war, disease, accidents, etc."[43] As a result, children in movies faced obstacles, including "many Shirley Temple films in which the child finds a mate for her single parent."[44] She believes that the frequent portrayal of families that were not intact was "a reflection of the challenges of balancing marital and parental relationships and responsibilities, often amid great odds. Who can't relate to that? Films were a shorthand for people's hopes, dreams, values, and fears, which may have been intensified during the Depression and World War II periods."[45]

While the 1930s saw a spate of a "ludicrous but brief run of films" about precocious infants, most notably those dealing with the adventures of *Baby LeRoy* and *Baby Sandy*, a more persistent trend in the latter part of the decade was to showcase adolescent stars. Among the most celebrated were Mickey Rooney and Judy Garland, who often performed together. Garland starred in the iconic *Wizard of Oz* (1939) in which she played a girl who lived with her aunt and uncle and who, according to Kathy Merlock Jackson, "sought 'home' and belonging."[46]

It might also be argued that movies of this period that dealt with courtship, even marriage, frequently failed to progress beyond a juvenile level either. Formulaic portrayals of romance abounded, replete with runaway heiresses, love at first sight, farce, kissing bandits, mistaken identity, bumbling bachelors, coy women, rich people attracted to those beneath their station, and the proverbial happily-ever-after ending. Barbs proliferated between crusty married couples to the extent that moviegoers might have wondered why anyone should want to tie the knot in the first place, or how there could possibly be fairy tale endings. Another feature of romance in those early days of film was the taken-for-granted conclusion that once a couple kissed, they were destined for the altar. As in real life, reel life conveyed the expectation that marriage followed love.

Screwball comedies and Busby Berkeley musicals fed the public a variety of fluff and fantasy throughout the Depression. Although high levels of unemployment prevailed, to the movies Americans still went, where they were dazzled by the likes of Fred Astaire and Ginger Rogers engaging in cat-and-mouse rendezvous, a prominent theme of the era according to Jackson. In the dancing duos' *Top Hat* (1935) and *The Gay Divorcee* (1934), Astaire's characters pursued an indifferent or downright hostile Rogers, refusing to give up, or respect, her wishes to be left alone. At the height of each screen conflict, the debonair performer led the gorgeous Ginger in a heart-melting dance that left her breathless, and totally his. One recent source comments about *Top Hat*, "Plot-wise things are a little strained . . . But then again, who wants realism? It's supposed to be diversion, right?"[47]

It seemed that "rich heiresses" populated the most successful romantic comedies before World War II, as in *It Happened One Night* (1934) and *The Philadelphia Story* (1940). Of the latter, Matthew Bernstein says it "endorses the man's greater wisdom, teaching his ex-wife where her true desires lie."[48] Women in such films could be endlessly sophisticated and independent, as well as wise-cracking, but in the end, the man subdues them, and in the movies there's a sense that this was how things should be. In *The Philadelphia Story*, director George Cukor "focuses on an independently minded heroine who has to be taught by the man in her life what she truly desires—himself."[49]

Jackson maintains that, in spite of the cat-and-mouse scenarios, Hollywood did put out some movies in which couples "loved deeply but faced obstacles that kept them apart."[50] Dirks believes that "tear-jerkers" like *Four Daughters* (1938) and *The Yearling* (1946) had "moral lessons to be told" in an era that reflected "only conservative family values" and were "extremely typical of the entire period."[51] *How Green Was My Valley* (1941) also was "a repository of the classical virtues"—including "self-sacrifice, romantic love, loyalty to family, hard work."[52]

Although Hollywood values did not always reflect what most Americans believed or the way in which they conducted themselves up until World War II, eventually they came to replace standards set by the Church, those which had been in place throughout American history to that point. Although they had not been consistently followed, they were still the gold standard that society in general agreed upon. Morison and Commager say, "Inevitably the mores and the vocabulary of the movies were imitated by those to whom they represented the fulfillment of every ambition. They set the popular fashion in dress, home furnishing, play, morals, even in marriage and family life, and increasingly human nature came to conform to commercial art."[53]

Chapter 13

HAPPY DAYS: THE 1950S

IN 1950, ACTRESS Ingrid Bergman's sin found her out. On the set of the movie *Stromboli,* the acclaimed Swedish star had an adulterous affair with her also-married director, Roberto Rossellini, and she became pregnant. (She also had a young daughter at home, by her husband.) The public chorus of disapproval reverberated from coast-to-coast with newspaper editorials accusing the couple of glamorizing free love as they engaged in "the dirt and muck of immoral behavior.[1] The *Boston Pilot* commented on how "some people have tried to make 'romance' out of a cheap, sordid, immoral affair."[2] In Washington, D.C., Edwin C. Johnson, a Democratic senator from Colorado, denounced Bergman for being "a horrible example of womanhood and a powerful influence for evil." His fellow members of Congress censured her and declared her *persona non grata.*[3]

Today when commentators assess the actress's life, they usually condemn her detractors for having been narrow-minded, religious fanatics who pilloried a basically decent woman. When Bergman got pregnant by another woman's husband back in 1950, however, the times were very different indeed. During the twentieth century's middle decade, the hub around which everything turned in America was the family in all its clean-living glory. Optimistic and eager about the future, young parents began having children in record numbers; these were fathers and mothers who had grown up during the Great Depression and come of age during World War II. They'd battled first deprivation and fear, then evil on an unprecedented scale in human history, and they'd come out victoriously. It was time for them to reclaim the youth that had eluded them on the battlefield and on the apprehensive home front. They didn't try to act like the kids they no longer were; rather, they had kids of their own, lots of them.

David Halberstam, author of *The Fifties*, notes, "For the young, eager veteran just out of college (which he had attended courtesy of the G.I. Bill), security meant finding a good white-collar job with a large, benevolent company, getting married, having children, and buying a house in the suburbs."[4] They looked to life's wholesome basics, to the home and the family in which to pour out their considerable energies after years of sacrifice. Tom Brokaw says, "They won the war. They saved the world. They came home to joyous and short-lived celebrations and immediately began the task of rebuilding their lives and the world they wanted."[5]

For those men and woman, "the preservation of the family was the collective goal."[6] That generation held the marriage vow in the highest esteem, clinging to it no matter what because, for the most part, divorce simply was not an option. Brokaw recalls growing up in the Midwest where he couldn't "remember any of my parents' friends who was divorced. In the communities where we lived, it was treated as a minor scandal."[7] He believes that more than societal pressure kept husbands and wives together in spite of forces that often put asunder contemporary couples; he thinks that the hard times they had known produced a certain kind of strength. "These relationships were forged when the world was a dangerous place and life was uncertain. If their relationships could withstand the turmoil and strain of the war years, it should only get better after that."[8]

Some of those young husbands endured nightmares of their war experiences, among them a man who sometimes slept on the floor next to his bed because he'd start kicking things over in his sleep, and he didn't want to disturb his wife. He knew that they would get through the ordeal by depending on each other, saying, "With the help of my wife—and the love she has for me—that's how you get over it."[9] In his book about that "greatest generation," Brokaw reflected with deep admiration on "the tensile strength such marriages bring to a society."[10]

SUBURBIA

A grateful nation needed to house war veterans and their multiplying families, but a serious shortage initially confronted the GIs. That's when "the stored-up energy of two decades was unleashed."[11] The year before WWII ended, 1944, saw the construction of just 114,000 single family homes, but by 1950, that figure mushroomed to an annual rate of 1.7 million.[12] Back in the 30s, a Long Island, New York, realtor named Abraham Levitt had begun to build housing subdivisions, and now it was his son Bill's opportunity to make a name for himself. The eponymous Levittowns ushered in a post-war housing expansion by creating affordable dwellings for young, middle-class families. Those new communities symbolized a kind of perfection, according to Herbert Gans, a 1950s-era sociologist, who maintained that "newness is often identified with perfection in American culture."[13] In the period 1950–1980, some 80 million people called the suburbs "home."

Suburban neighborhoods were not without detractors, however, including writer Ron Rosenbaum, who compared them to the fifties film *Invasion of the Body Snatchers* in which menacing pods from outer space took over people's bodies and extracted their souls, one by one. Only compliant lookalikes remained. He said the houses that Levitt built were like evil pods that "housed the aliens and stole the souls of the humans."[14] Although he was not entirely alone in his opinion, Rosenbaum's was the minority view in that era.

People who chose the suburban lifestyle became cheerful trend-setters who raised their families and nurtured the American dream in a way they could scarcely have imagined when they were younger. Doris Kearns Goodwin, writer and historian, recalls her baseball-besotted childhood in the New York suburbs with wistful tenderness in her memoir, *Wait Till Next Year.* She wrote about the idyllic, though modest-by-today's-standards home in which she grew up in the early 50s, the dwelling that was, for her mother and father, "the realization of a dream."[15] It was a place that housed some of her very best memories:

> On summer mornings, my father would come downstairs dressed in his three-piece suit, glance at the gold pocket watch that was attached to his vest with a slender gold chain, kiss my mother and me good-bye, and leave for work. From the window I watched him greet the other men on our block as they walked to the corner to catch the bus for the short ride to the train station, where, every few minutes, an engine whistled, the platform quivered, and one of the seventy-five daily trains swallowed up a new group of commuters for the thirty-eight-minute ride to Penn Station that had made suburban living possible. Now, the fathers departed, our neighborhood, like some newly conquered province, belonged to the women and children.[16]

In her community, Goodwin lived among stay-at-home mothers whose job was to raise a new generation of law-abiding Americans who would be a credit to their parents, as well as their nation. They enjoyed such innocent fare as the Little Golden Books, Nancy Drew mysteries, *Howdy Doody*, and *The Mickey Mouse Club*, as well as simple neighborhood games—hide-and-seek, hopscotch, jumping rope—as each mother watched over, and felt a right to, discipline every child within her watch. These were women and children who also dressed properly and with dignity because that was how one demonstrated respect toward other people. Goodwin recalls how correctly her mother always presented herself: "She never wore shorts or even slacks," she says. "In the grip of the worst heat waves, she wore a girdle, a full slip, and a cotton or linen dress with a bib apron perpetually fixed to her shoulders. Such modesty was the norm in our neighborhood. Indeed, when one of the mothers took to sitting on her front lawn in a halter top and shorts, her behavior startled the block."[17]

WOMEN

Some time ago writer Peggy Noonan asked former first lady Barbara Bush, who raised her children in those post-war years, "Why did you have children?" In response, "Her eyes widened. 'Why, Peggy!' she said, and laughed me off. She meant, 'Listen, kid, you got married and had kids in those days, one followed the other, you didn't get all scientific.'"[18] The 1950s were about the family; "marriage and children were part of the national agenda."[19] Most men and women believed that men should go to work and women "take care of the home."[20] Only under duress were middle-class women supposed to work, that is, if the man couldn't support his wife and family. Most men considered it a point of great pride to be able to provide for their wives and children; they would have been ashamed otherwise. Those women who did find it necessary to have jobs after the war leaned toward "clerical and service positions."[21]

There was a consensus that "women who chose to work when they didn't need the paycheck were often considered selfish, putting themselves before the needs of their family."[22] Even when it became necessary for a woman to make a living, she could feel conflicted about the breadwinning role, including the highly successful Christian writer Catherine Marshall. Following the death of her husband, Senate Chaplain Peter Marshall, she wrote two books based on his sermons and his life—the latter was made into a major motion picture—which brought her considerable acclamation. Although she was grateful for the financial stability that came with her accomplishments, Marshall "experienced great conflict over her new role. She felt less feminine when negotiating book contracts, train schedules, and public appearances."[23] Her husband had preached long and fervently over the necessity of women to be metaphorical "keeps of the springs," those who guarded the public "waterways" by taking care of their families, including nurturing sound spiritual and civic values. Unless they did so, he maintained, the society would become hopelessly polluted.

In the 1950s the media portrayed American women as positive, wise, and fulfilled in their suburban homes. Conversely, their Cold War rivals, institutionally oriented Russian women, wore "gunnysacks as they toiled in drab factories while their children were placed in cold, anonymous day care centers."[24] Most American girls aspired to grow up to be "Susie Homemakers" like their moms, to maintain spotless domiciles, make great meat loaf, pot roast, and Jell-O molds for the enjoyment of their appreciative families. In fact, the new norm was to get married early, even right out of high school or during college; in the fifties, the average age for a girl to marry dropped to nineteen.[25] Gail Collins notes that "the stampede to the altar was so intense that junior high school students had already chosen their silverware pattern" and were filling their cedar-lined "hope chests."[26]

For white, middle-class women, even more important than securing an education was to get an "M.R.S.," "and if the time was right, a girl would quit (school) to marry. Conversely, black women didn't go to college in large numbers, but those who did managed to graduate because they felt their income would be needed someday due to the inequalities that their men faced in the job market."[27]

"If a woman wasn't engaged or married by her early twenties," according to a PBS documentary, "she was in danger of becoming an 'old maid,'" which carried the dishonor of having been passed over and, therefore, undesirable.[28]A popular 1950s movie *Guys and Dolls*, featured a thirtysomething nightclub dancer who'd been engaged for fourteen years to a marriage-phobic gambler. In her mortifying state of betwixt and between, she learned that her perpetual cold was caused by her relational (and sexual) frustration. Over the years, she had told her mother that she'd actually gotten married, then she began inventing children. Far more to be avoided than singleness, however, was the loss of one's virtue; "being single and pregnant was totally unacceptable."[29] If a young woman "got in trouble," she was most often secretly trundled off to an unnamed location to conceal her moral failure. After putting the child up for adoption, she would return home as people narrowed their eyes and rendered their calculations. There was great pressure on girls not to "go all the way," that boys wouldn't marry them because "why buy the cow when you can get the milk for free?" It was, according to popular thought, up to the female to keep her boyfriend from losing his head.

For those who did things by the book (got married, then had children), the latter usually arrived in rapid succession so that a woman often completed her pregnancies by the age of thirty. Families often consisted of three or four children with the initial baby making an appearance around first wedding anniversary. In case there was an "oops" before the taking of vows, the wedding date would be pushed up so that no one would guess. In spite of the *Guys and Dolls* scenario, engagements were not of a lengthy duration. For those waiting to consummate marriage, the sooner the better.

Helping mothers raise the Baby Boomers was a placid pediatrician named Benjamin Spock, whose iconic book, *The Common Sense Book of Baby and Child Care*, premiered in 1946. Trained as a psychoanalyst, Dr. Spock believed that "much of the prevailing wisdom of that day was flawed" when it came to child rearing.[30] For example, he promoted picking up fussy babies at a time when most "experts" advocated making them cry so they wouldn't be "spoiled." He believed that attending to a wailing infant would make the child more secure. Ironically, rather than follow set rules of discipline issued by specialists, Spock encouraged parents to see themselves as the experts on their own children.[31] He was "completely at odds with the cold authoritarianism favored by most other parenting books of the time," especially when it came to spanking.[32] He wrote, "I don't think physical punishment is necessary or particularly effective."[33]

He believed that corporal punishment could create bullies, teach that "might makes right," and that fear of pain was not a good inducement to good behavior.[34]

Spock became a household name in the 50s when at-home mothers did most of the early child-rearing. At that time, fathers weren't even allowed in delivery rooms, nor did they eagerly volunteer for, or accept, feeding babies or diaper duty. That was a woman's work; only she could do it right. Second only to the Bible in sales, Spock's groundbreaking book sold over fifty million copies in thirty-nine languages.

In the early decades of American history, small children often dressed like little grown-ups and took on adult tasks before they reached school age. With the Victorian period's romanticism about childhood that slowly began to change, but until the 1950s, there was still a pattern of first came childhood, then came the responsibilities and benefits of adulthood. Coming of age occurred early, and it meant preparing for having one's own family. In the 1950s a new category of youth surfaced, the teenage years in which the brief season of childhood was prolonged before taking on an adult role in life. Of course, many girls married before they reached twenty, but this was the beginning in the American family of an expanded state of youth, as well as the infancy of a preference for youth over wisdom.

Those "first" teenagers had as much income per week in the mid-50s—$10.55—as the average family had "after all the essential bills were paid," fifteen years before.[35] This economic boom lent them greater buying power in an age of brassy advertising and merchandizing, and one of the most noted ways in which this new demographic expressed itself was through the new musical style of rock and roll. Many parents and other authority figures denounced the coarseness of Elvis Presley, Bill Haley, Chuck Berry, and Little Richard, but they found it difficult to curb their teenagers. David Halberstam writes,

> A new generation of Americans was breaking away from the habits of its parents and defining itself by its music. . . . This new

generation was armed with both money and the new expensive appliances with which to listen to it. . . . In the past when American teenagers had made money, their earnings, more often than not, had gone to help support their parents or had been saved for one treasured and long-desired purchase. . . . or it had been set aside for college. But now, as the new middle class emerged in the country, it was creating as a byproduct a brand-new consuming class: the young.[36]

Prior to that prosperous decade, parents and children gathered around a household radio or phonograph. In fact, they still got together to watch the one family television set with its three channel choices, but with teens in possession of a significant amount of money, they were able to buy their own transistor radios and portable record players on which to listen to *their* music. According to Halberstam, a "new subculture of rock and roll" emerged in which traditional sources of authority began to recede in favor of the disc jockey.[37] That AM radio Pied Piper "reaffirmed the right to youthful independence and guided teenagers to their new rock heroes," further cementing the status of the newly minted American teenager.[38]

A significant occurrence in the development of this faction came in the mid-50s when Elvis Presley's popularity among the young reached a feverish dimension. At that time, all the major American entertainers appeared on *The Ed Sullivan Show*, hosted by the man who became in those years "the unofficial minister of culture in America."[39] Sullivan was careful to choose only the most wholesome acts so that the entire family could enjoy his programs and was, says Halberstam, "at the exact center of American mass culture."[40] There was no way, he let it be known, that the sexually charged Elvis was going to appear on his show, this young man who "was working the American home," making it "a house divided."[41] Market forces eventually drove Sullivan to reconsider, and he ended up booking Presley for three appearances. Halberstam regards this as a turning point, the beginning of what would be called a decade later "The Generation Gap." He says, "It was . . . a critical moment for the whole society: the old order had been challenged and had not held. New forces were at work, driven by technology. The young did not have to listen to their parents anymore."[42]

THE PERFECT FAMILY

The energy and optimism of the 1950s carried over into the latest technological craze, television. Like humans throughout the ages, the young men and women who were raising their families yearned for a perfected state to replace human fallenness. Why not, then, portray such a desired condition of relative sinlessness on television programs? Sure, there would be some problems to make scripts interesting, but the point was that within the framework of a half-hour show, including commercials, all conflicts would be speedily resolved. It is not surprising, then, that the dominant theme of TV's golden age was the family-oriented situation comedy, and the best-loved of them all was about a kooky, redheaded housewife named Lucy Ricardo, played by Lucille Ball.

When the show was in the planning stages, producers desired a TV husband who would play it straight to Ball's zany character, but she insisted that having her real-life husband in that role would lend authenticity to the program. (Perhaps *I Love Lucy* was television's first "reality TV.") Then the creators zeroed in on the theme of "an ordinary housewife who wants to be a star."[43] Bingo. Americans thronged to their TVs each week to watch the slapstick-style comedy in which Lucy schemed to be famous while her bandleader, Cuban-born-husband, Ricky Ricardo (played by Desi Arnaz), mangled English as he demanded that she "'splane" her actions. Television writer Jack Sher and wife, Marilyn, assessed the show's stunning popularity during the "family decade," saying that *I Love Lucy* held a mirror

> up to every married couple in America: Not a regular mirror that reflects the truth, nor a magic mirror that portrays fantasy.

But a Coney Island kind of mirror that distorts, exaggerates and makes vastly amusing every little incident, foible, and idiosyncrasy of married life.[44]

As for children, they loved Lucy, too, in part because she was a childlike grown-up.[45] By 1954, fifty million viewers tuned in weekly.

Two years into its run, the show faced a considerable challenge when Lucille Ball became pregnant, and the producers decided to incorporate her condition into the story line. It was not an easy choice. "Previously," David Halberstam observed, "pregnant women had just not been seen in films or on television," the latter medium having an even stricter decency code than Hollywood.[46] The powers-that-be concluded that Lucy Ricardo could be pregnant, but that the word must never be used; instead, the program used "expecting" or "expectant mother." Furthermore, to ensure discretion and secure public sanction, CBS lined up a minister, a priest, and a rabbi to review all of the scripts.[47] The actual birth episode aired the night before President Eisenhower's first inauguration, and it drew an audience of 44 million, twice the number for the new chief executive's swearing in.[48]

Like the Ricardos on *I Love Lucy*, the Nelson family on *The Adventures of Ozzie and Harriet* "seemed to embody every virtue of the all-American family."[49] Halberstam says, "By the midfifties television portrayed a wonderfully antiseptic world of idealized homes in an idealized, unflawed America."[50] It was also an essentially white, middle-class America. There were no minorities in onscreen families, except for Desi Arnaz, no divorce, no serious misbehavior or illness, a place where dads were steady and though sometimes awkward, they were always good.[51] TV moms were the comforters, the "perfect mistresses of their household premises," but as they "ventured from their houses," they appeared "less competent."[52] In one episode of *Father Knows Best*, the mother was seen as feeling inferior next to her successful friend from college, who came to visit, but then she realized that her single pal was basically lonely and in terms of relationships, unfulfilled, and that was what really mattered.

TV children got along well with their brothers and sisters, and even when there was rivalry between them, their love was greater.[53] They lived in white-collar suburbs where people always dressed up to go out, mothers wore dresses and high heels at home and donned a hat and gloves to do the grocery shopping or go to the dentist. Family life on television was idyllic; "these television families were to be not merely a reflection of their viewers but role models for them as well."[54] On *Leave It to Beaver*, "the family always seemed to eat together and the pies were homemade."[55] In one episode, however, when Ward sniffed approvingly at June's pot roast, saying how wonderful it was to have old-fashioned food, June responded, "At least that's what the package says." Thus, American housewives had permission to use prepared meals because even June Cleaver resorted to them on occasion.

Of course, that isn't what life in America really looked like. Not all of its families enjoyed the comforts and blessings of middle-class, suburban life; some preferred to reside in cities or on farms, while others worked long and arduously to earn their livings. Black families were beginning to struggle openly for basic civil rights under the law, and immigrants strained to fit in. As in all ages, couples faced marital difficulties, problems with in-laws and other family members, including wayward children, while others dealt with mental and physical issues, as well as substance and relational abuse.

Even sitcom families didn't live in a perfected state offscreen. Desi Arnaz was a notorious womanizer, who freely imbibed drugs and alcohol to cope with the pressures of life. Desi Jr. once spoke about how strange it was to have parents be so loving and funny on their show, then be entirely different in reality. "Those were difficult years," he said, "all those funny things happening on television each week to people who looked like my parents, then the same people agonizing through some terrible, unhappy times at home."[56] Similarly, onscreen Ozzie Nelson was a docile, amiable, and ever-present father, but in reality he was a driven, insensitive workaholic.

The picture of family life that American television portrayed in the 1950s might not have measured reality exactly, but it did represent a vision of that era's "good life." Those delightful old shows also reflected the optimistic spirit of that age when America stood tall in the world, and for many, anything seemed possible.

Chapter 14

MUTINY IN THE BOUNTY

IN THE 1950S, as in every generation, America had its misfits, unconventional people who had difficulty fitting in with the mainstream. Often they felt rejected because of some perceived or real deficiency in themselves or their backgrounds. Prior to the 50s, such people usually tucked themselves away quietly in society's back roads and hollows, aberrations that others glanced at as they went about their normal routines. In that transitional era, however, a certain culture of nonconformists emerged that eventually became a hip subset of society. Known as "Beatniks," they came though New York's Columbia University where the administration initially shook its collective head at the group and labeled them kooks. They included Jack Kerouac, Allen Ginsburg, John Clellon Holmes, and Lucien Carr. Playing Pied Piper to those young men, 1936 Harvard graduate William Burroughs lived in freewheeling Greenwich Village, where he introduced his followers to a countercultural lifestyle.

According to one source, Kerouac came up with the moniker "Beat Generation" in 1948 to describe his "anti-conformist" pals. "Beat" itself was jargon to describe "the world of hustlers, drug addicts and petty thieves, where Ginsburg and Kerouac sought inspiration. It was also slang for 'beaten down' or downtrodden, but to Kerouac, it also had a spiritual connotation as in 'beatific.'"[1]

David Halberstam had much to say about the Beatniks, noting for example, that although they were primarily writers, "their lives tended to be more important than their books."[2] Their favorite theme was themselves; rather than recede into the shadows as those who could not, or would not, keep to the middle-of-the-road, they proclaimed themselves as superior to all the unsuspecting dopes who inhabited the nether regions of conformity. They were "exceptionally self-absorbed: They recorded their thoughts, dreams, and emotions meticulously," says Halberstam, "as if they were the first who had ever had them."[3] They imagined a new social order consisting of "artist-citizens" who would triumph over the banal and mundane.[4]

In *Go*, John Clellon Holmes created a scene in which his "anti-hero" sees a group of chirpy Girl Scouts on a subway—they're going on a field trip, and he's on his way home after a dissipated all-nighter in the Village. He surveys their happy faces, these "upbeat, optimistic emissaries of traditional wholesome American values and wonders: 'To be like them or like us, is there any other position?'"[5] Halberstam says, "The Beats . . . revered those who were different, those who lived outside the system, and particularly those who lived outside the law."[6] They unleashed a snarling rebellion that initially encircled American thought, then howled until the doors were opened to it. In the movies new champions appeared who bucked the system, including the iconic Marlon Brando in *The Wild One* and his adoring protégé James Dean in *Rebel Without a Cause*. They played characters who, in an earlier generation would have simply been portrayed as bad seeds, but who now were described as misunderstood by their parents and a mean-spirited society, authorities who were far less enlightened than they.[7] The more muttered verbiage that flowed from their mouths and pens, the more profound they seemed, or tried to seem.

The Beatniks, as well as other assorted dissenters, "were the first to protest what they considered to be the blandness, conformity, and lack of serious social and cultural purpose in middle-class life in America."[8] They experimented with drugs, including Benzedrine and marijuana to reach heightened states of consciousness that the conventional middle class couldn't achieve by paying the bills, voting, and mowing their lawns. Halberstam points out, however, that it was only the affluent culture that gave them the ability to live in disharmony with the times. "It was no small irony," he says, "that the magic ingredient that allowed them to forgo regular jobs and still manage reasonably comfortable lives was the sheer affluence of the mainstream culture that they so disdained; the country was so rich that even those who chose not to play by its rules were protected."[9]

Furthermore, in America, the Beatniks were not only tolerated, they achieved a degree of celebrity. Memoirist Joyce Johnson says, "'Beat Generation' sold books, black turtleneck sweaters and bongos, berets and dark glasses, sold a way of life that seemed like dangerous fun—thus to be condemned or imitated. Suburban couples could have beatnik parties on Saturday nights."[10] Madison Avenue advertisers turned the concept into a marketing device, and "'hip' record companies in New York used the idea of the Beat Generation to sell their new long-playing vinyl records."[11] In the 1957 film *Funny Face*, Audrey Hepburn played a Beatnik bookstore clerk who wore utilitarian outfits and studied "empathicalism." Even television incorporated the Beatniks into the popular sitcom *The Many Loves of Dobie Gillis* in which Maynard G. Krebs became instantly recognizable as a lovable, goatee-wearing hipster who was allergic to work.

Some of the original Beatniks struggled with the success that a culture they were at odds with afforded them—"publishing contracts, requests to write for magazines, lecture offers for the unheard-of sum of five hundred dollars a night."[12] In fact, Kerouac, according to

Halberstam, "ultimately found fame hard and destructive, ending his life in a cloud of alcoholic rage and bitterness," but those like Allen Ginsberg, "who had felt so ugly and unattractive as a boy, loved flirting with success."[13] In the late 50s, on the eve of a defining decade in American history, Halberstam rightly observes that "their success, above all, was a sure sign that the old order was changing. The walls were tumbling down."[14]

THE MYSTIQUE OF FEMINISM

In the post-World War II era, magazines portrayed women as mainly housewives and mothers whose interests were focused on domestic affairs.[15] There was, according to an academic study of that period, "no culturally approved alternative to homemaking."[16] Nevertheless, most suburban housewives expressed contentment with their lives, including one Philadelphia area woman who recalls those days with great fondness as a time when she was involved with her children on a daily basis, engaging them in many fun activities. According to a 1962 Gallup Poll, three out of five women said that they were happy with their lives.[17] William Chafe says that women weren't being treated worse than at any other time in American history, but as with the Beatniks, a restless few drew considerable attention to themselves.[18] At the heart of their grievances was "the assertion that women had been deprived of the chance to develop an identity of their own."[19]

In 1962, Helen Gurley Brown expressed thoughts considered improper even a few years earlier in her bestselling book *Sex and the Single Girl*, a work that not only broke ground, but created a cultural avalanche. Going in an extreme opposite direction from American culture, she advised young women, who had emphasized getting married young so they wouldn't turn into "old maids," to instead enjoy their early adulthood, to make it carefree and self-indulgent. She believed that single girls should live like worldly bachelors, to have sexual adventures with multiple partners, including married men, to create a good career and acquire plenty of money.[20]

As if engaging in adultery wasn't shocking enough, Brown told her readers that marriage was not, after all, the pinnacle of human happiness, but instead "insurance for the *worst* years of your life. During your best years you don't need a husband."[21] Although most women rejected Brown's over-the-top views, she intrigued and entertained, and her outlook lent itself to a gradual diminution of the persistent fear "of sterile and possibly unnatural singlehood."[22]

If American society regarded marriage in those days as the epitome of contentment for a woman, it made few allowances for those who became disgruntled with the day-to-day running of a household. The culture gave widespread support for the family, but it tended to define the roles and expectations of men and women along narrow, sometimes confining lines. For example, even if women married and had children early, how were they to express their other talents and interests once they had fulfilled the requirements of the intense child-rearing season of their lives? Most of the professions, except for teaching and nursing, still closed their doors to women, or begrudgingly allowed them entrance. Chafe notes that in the years after World War II, "millions of women had joined the labor force . . . without fanfare . . . (unaccompanied) either by progress toward equality or an organized effort to protest traditional definitions of 'woman's place.'"[23] One woman's effort led not only to the flourish that was initially missed, but turned into a cacophony of voices inciting radical change in the 1960s and early 1970s.

Betty Friedan was born in 1921 to Jewish parents who owned a jewelry business in Peoria, Illinois. A child of affluence, she became a self-avowed Marxist and went to prestigious Smith College. She married and had children, which slowed down her career as a leftist journalist, but a piece she wrote about her fifteenth college reunion gained national attention. She discovered that many of her classmates felt restive about their lives, something she referred to as the "Problem That Has No Name." Her subsequent book that she built along that premise, *The Feminine Mystique*, sold one million copies after its 1963 publication. In it, Friedan argued that "women could find their true identities only outside of the home, that they were of little worth to themselves or society if they only existed as housewives."[24] Chafe says that she "generated the kind of attention that made feminism a popular topic of conversation once again."[25]

As she made her way around the country, Friedan said that the way in which the culture demanded a woman's "total involvement in the roles of wife and mother" held her "captive," that the home had become a "comfortable concentration camp" that "infantilized" women and "forces them to 'give up their adult frame of reference.'"[26] In fact, she argued that the entire family unit had become an unhealthy "breeding ground for discontent and unhappiness," in which "children were treated like 'hothouse plants,' women over identified with their offspring, and a vicious cycle of repression and frustration ensured."[27]

Chafe believes that the convergence of Friedan and other feminists with the civil rights movement in the South caused "women to develop a heightened consciousness of their own oppression" that otherwise wouldn't have become an issue.[28] He argues that in the 50s, any challenge to the traditional family was seen by society as "part of a larger 'plot' to destroy America."[29] Since civil rights was a respectable battle against systemic evils, however, it became possible to question other societal problems.[30] In addition, there had been some changes for women after the war, along with "the continuation of structural barriers to real equity," a combination that "made both possible and necessary the ideological challenge to develop new norms of relations between the sexes."[31] Furthermore, even if feminism appealed to relatively few numbers, especially at first, eventually it touched all Americans.

By the end of the 1960s, nearly half of the mothers who had adolescent girls were working outside the home, and surveys showed that those girls tended to regard their parent more highly than those whose mothers stayed at home.[32] Most Americans didn't have a problem with the concept of a woman working for a paycheck, if she wasn't neglecting her home life, so in that sense feminism went mainstream. Its dark side caused far more divisiveness, the lobbying for legalized abortion, as well as the shrill diatribes against marriage, the traditional family, religion, and heterosexuality because feminists regarded them as tyrannical institutions that kept women down.[33] Some of the more radical among them advocated lesbianism because they believed it would empower women to live more in tune with their femaleness, as well as alleviate the need to become dependent on a man for her sexual completion. In the early days of the movement, the leadership kept those voices as muffled as possible so as not to alarm middle America.

THE RADICAL FRINGE

In the 1960s, many discontented people began to air their grievances publicly, some of them peacefully, such as the early civil rights activists, while others belligerently demanded an end to the draft and the Vietnam War. American public opinion, even among college students, supported the war until President Lyndon Johnson ended the automatic draft deferment that opened the way for college men to be conscripted. Massive, campus-wide protests ensued, often spiraling into viciousness and mayhem. Students "sat in" the administrative offices of their colleges and universities, burned draft cards, and marched in the streets. All of these protests represented a rebellious attitude toward established authority in a way that America had never before experienced. Gail Collins attributes much of the upheaval to the war:

> The growing disillusionment with the conflict, even among people with fairly traditional political outlooks, did more than create bad feeling toward the politicians in Washington. It cast a cloud of illegitimacy over authority in general. If the people in charge could be so wrong about something as important as a war, why should anyone assume that they were right about the necessity of maintaining one's virginity, avoiding drugs, or obeying a school dress code?[34]

A spirit of revolt, fueled by drugs, "free sex," and the music of Janis Joplin, the Beatles, the Doors, Eric Burden, and Jimi Hendrix spread over the country, causing some adults to wonder what in the world had gone wrong. When he acquiesced to allow the Rolling Stones to perform on his family-oriented show, Ed Sullivan insisted that their lyric "Let's spend the night together" be changed to "Let's spend some time together." As Mick Jagger got to that part of the song, he rolled his eyes as if to say, "Let's humor the old man. We know what's really going down." Morris believes that the student uprisings of that era "seemed to flip values upside down . . . Instead of being credited with building a peaceful prosperity, (parents) found themselves accused of creating a corrupted system of institutionalized racism and soulless technocracy, of immorality in the Third World and Vietnam, of exploitation of the world's poor."[35]

The rebellion that occurred could be traced back to the initial discontentment of the Beatniks that eventually caught hold in mainstream society. "There was a spirit of liberation in the air," Morris says, "not only of blacks, but of homosexuals, of women, of students themselves, the whole group whom the psychiatrist and historian Erik Erikson called 'the other.'"[36] There was among those radicals an "elitist exclusivity" that found the whole middle-class experience banal.[37] Betty Friedan, for example, had barely a nodding acquaintance with the average American woman. Many leaders of the early feminist movement were, in fact, part of a privileged upper class, white women who had college and sometimes graduate degrees, people who often had a certain "disdain . . . for the 'sterile suburbs.'"[38] The majority of the reformers tended to deride, for example, the lower-middle class "Levittowners," who were, in fact, often quite happy with their new and improved lives, those who were "delighted to have escaped the cramped housing, the dirt and noise, and the raw edge of city life."[39]

Although the militants were in the minority, their influence shook the very foundations of American culture in large measure because of media coverage.

Those who dissented took for their heroes men like Che Guevara and Jean Paul Sartre, who believed that "man invents his own law," and "humanity 'begins with rebellion.'"[40] They commended writer Norman Mailer, whose character Stephen Rojack in *The American Dream* tries to become liberated from "the mildew of discipline."[41] They worshiped youth and disparaged old age. Prior to that time, childhood was an innocent season of preparation for adulthood. The young imitated grown-up dress and manners in an effort to reach their fullest human potential as a mature man or woman, to be good, law-abiding citizens who helped one another and lived peacefully with their fellow human beings. After the 1960s, the aspiration was to be forever young. Abbie Hoffman, cofounder of the Youth International Party—the Yippies—once proclaimed, "We ain't never, never, never gonna grow up!"[42]

WOMEN'S LIB

The young women who got caught up in the search for personal liberation frequently found themselves on unreceptive ground. Men who were involved in radical politics, including opposition to the Vietnam War, tended to be condescending toward the women who stood with them, expecting them to do all the progressive things, then fall into a traditional, domesticated role when they got home. Those women burned their bras, attended sit-ins and demonstrations, then cleaned and cooked for their men, who often failed to take their views seriously. At one meeting, a leader patted a feminist on the head when she tried to make a point telling her, "Move on, little girl; we have more important issues to talk about here than women's liberation."[43] The high-minded, antiestablishment "hippies" advocated "free grass, free food, free shelter" and "free chicks."[44] When someone asked the black militant Stokely Carmichael what he thought the proper position was for women he answered, "Prone."[45]

The modern civil rights movement had been given momentum by a woman, Rosa Parks, who, in 1955, inaugurated a citywide bus boycott when she refused to give up her seat to a white man in Montgomery, Alabama. Since then, many women have taken up the cause, often risking their safety to achieve racial equality. At the massive 1963 March on Washington, however, not one woman appeared on the program to speak, not even Parks. Gail Collins believes that "many black women were willing to defer to the men simply because they felt there was a need for strong male role models in their community."[46] She also argues that the sexual revolution of the 1960s often put women, whose "liberation" took place later in the 1960s and 1970s, at a disadvantage in their relationships. She says that "many girls felt free to say yes before they figured out that they had the right to say no. Refusing a date's demand for sex had been difficult enough when both parties grudgingly accepted the idea that women should remain virgins until they married."[47]

In 1969, 68 percent of Americans expressed a traditional opposition to fornication, but by 1973, the majority had swung dramatically in the other direction. That same year, a survey of eight colleges revealed that by their junior year, 76 percent of the coeds had engaged in sex.[48] It truly was a sign of the changing times and mores when First Lady Betty Ford answered a TV interviewer's forthright question with an even more candid answer. He asked how Mrs. Ford would react if her teenage daughter Susan told her she was "having an affair." Ford replied, "Well, I wouldn't be surprised. I think she's a normal human being like all young girls."[49] The First Lady of the United States had given her implicit approval to the rightness, the *normality*, of teenage sex. Needless to say, it marked a turning point.

As in every generation, people have faced challenges, and in that respect, the era of protest was no exception. In the nineteenth century, activists had addressed the evils of slavery, poor treatment for the mentally ill and prisoners, and the depersonalization of an industrial society. Civil rights marchers had legitimate complaints against a culture that routinely denied them basic human rights, many believed that the war in Vietnam was not executed in a proper way, and women were expected to walk a very narrow road that seldom veered away from family, teaching, or nursing. However, some of those who found fault with America in a public manner demonstrated high levels of selfishness. Although she was just a fictional little girl, Charlie Brown's kid sister, Sally, summed up the position of those protestors in *A Charlie Brown Christmas* when she asked her brother to write a letter for her to Santa Claus. After telling the right jolly old elf that she'd been extra good, she explained that she had a right to the long lists of presents she was expecting, but if they were too much trouble, she'd be just as happy with money, especially "tens and twenties." When Charlie Brown rebuked her attitude, she responded, "All I want is what I have coming to me. All I want is my fair share."[50]

In the nineteenth century, activists sought not to destroy society but to right what they deemed to be wrong; they set out to heal, love, and build up. They protested to make conditions better for themselves and for other people who were struggling. On the other hand, many mid-twentieth century militants (peaceful civil rights marchers excluded) had a "what's-in-it-for-me?" attitude. After all, were hippies mainly into peace and love, or sex and drugs? The Rolling Stones and the Doors weren't advocating true women's liberation when they cajoled, "Let's spend the night together" and "Come on, baby, light my fire."

Chapter 15

WHAT'S LOVE
GOT TO
DO WITH IT?

IN THE 50s, television led the mushrooming mass media into a new age of American culture and left an ineffaceable mark. With the growth of suburban communities, residents tended to spend less time with their extended families, and once they got to know them, often got together with neighbors far more frequently than with grandparents, uncles, aunts, and cousins. The people they saw regularly on television also seemed nearer than their dearest because they came into their homes on a regular basis and so were more immediate and accessible. In 1965, a "demonstration" for Chicago advertising firms by Gardner Murphy of the Menninger Foundation focused on the effects of this new medium on its audience and, according to David Halberstam, Murphy "directed a team of social scientists to study advertisers and the programs they sponsored."[1] That team made interesting discoveries, including the way in which many American women thought about the popular morning TV host Arthur Godfrey:

> Psychologically, Mr. Godfrey's morning program creates the illusion of the family structure. All the conflicts and complex situations of family life are taken out and what is left is an amiable, comfortable family scene—with one important omission: there is no mother in the Godfrey family. That gives the housewife-viewer the opportunity to fill that role. In her fantasy Godfrey comes into her home as an extra member of her family; and she fancies herself as a specially invited member of his family . . .[2]

Undoubtedly, television wielded tremendous influence, including an ability Halberstam says "to soften the edge between real life and fantasy."[3] For many Americans, it became a constant presence, initially in their living rooms and eventually throughout their homes as portable sets made the ownership of several TVs financially feasible. Some people had them installed under kitchen cabinets and in bathrooms so they could always stayed tuned in. Today they are ubiquitous in public places as well, from drug stores to mall walkways to fast food restaurants and waiting rooms. One female nursing home resident told a newspaper reporter that from the time she gets up in the morning until she retires at night, her TV is on. She "moves" from one channel to another, knowing just what programs are on during each part of the day, the news people, talk show hosts, and fictional characters being more immediate and real to her than her family, who cannot be with her with that kind of constancy. She concluded that if her TV were ever taken away, "I'd be lost without it." She is far from alone.

In many American homes the television is also on throughout the day, even during meals. So-called TV dinners first appeared in 1954 to facilitate the serving of food so that families could eat on trays in front of the television. One might argue that at least in those early days of the medium families still ate together at all. They also might point out that there were only three channels from which to choose so it wasn't difficult to reach a consensus, or be afraid that something inappropriate for the children might pop up on the program or the commercials surrounding it.

Initially, television portrayed a church-going society that followed mostly Christian values, was mostly white, and mostly middle class/suburban. The content of programs was safe for family viewing, and it provided people with an ideal image of what it meant to have loving, take-charge parents, obedient children, and communities in which people were caring and well-connected. Into the 1960s, the medium continued to retain a basic wholesomeness, even in the daytime soap operas, but cracks began to show as that uneasy decade neared its end. For the most part, however, TV families were intact, and when single parents did appear, as in *The Andy Griffith Show, My Three Sons,* or *The Courtship of Eddie's Father,* it was because the wife of the main character had died. There was virtually no divorce, and blended families had to wait for their debut until *The Brady Bunch*—the father was widowed, and it was assumed that the mother was as well, although the show's creators initially made her divorced. They decided not to be explicit about it, however, because advertisers and viewers might object.

On productions about single people, such as *That Girl, The Patty Duke Show, Petticoat Junction,* and *Gidget,* innocence remained a hallmark. The boy-girl encounters in those series amounted to simple disagreements and misunderstandings, sweet activities, and light smooching, and as far as the public knew, the stars of those shows, with a few exceptions, lived as chastely as the characters they played.

CHALLENGES

The musical British invasion of the mid-1960s introduced America first to a group of long-haired (for that era) lads from industrial Liverpool who had a rather strange effect on female fans.

When the Beatles sang "I Want to Hold Your Hand," girls shrieked, clutched at their hair, cried, reached out to touch the musicians, and some even fainted. The Beach Boys and Frankie Avalon might have sent them into a swoon, but this was something feral, and it frightened many parents. Within a year or two, new acts appeared from Britain including ones with blatantly sexual, morally edgy messages, including the guttural sounds of Eric Burden and the Animals and the Rolling Stones. The Beatles also moved out of the mainstream and into a different mode with far earthier songs about revolutions and lost souls in a place where Christianity was irrelevant ("Eleanor Rigby").

Rock's influence on young people helped to create a new "mainstream" that allowed for looser attitudes toward sexual relationships, experimental drug use, and experimentation with Eastern religions. Protestant Christianity may have been the cultural authority and trendsetter earlier in American history, but that era was ending. A new generation set the stage for two key changes. First, youth gained in status and importance over maturity; it was no longer preferable to be older and wiser, to aspire to be all grown up. Now it was almost a crime to be anything but young and without "preconceptions" or "withered" standards. One 60s slogan put it this way: "Don't trust anyone over thirty." Second, the worldview of postmodernism arose, its basic premise that there is no source of absolute truth or authority. Instead, each individual must define his or her own truth and standards. The shift came quickly, aided by mass media.

While television remained mostly family oriented during the 1960s, there could be little doubt that the counterculture was making headway. Those calling for sexual "freedom," women's liberation, and a movement away from traditional values attracted a great deal of airplay. The people behind those messages still frightened advertising executives, who knew that middle-class Americans would write angry letters and stop buying their products if they put shows on the air that deviated from certain values. There were, however, a few programs that veered sharply away from the

Christian ideal. (As in the 50s, movies had begun to break away from that standard far more quickly than television, which, after all, occupied people's living rooms. That was family territory. Conversely, people could choose to see or not to see a certain film.)

Some films were more discreet than others. For example, *The Children's Hour* (1961) dealt with the ruination of a private girl's school after rumors about their sexual orientation surrounded the two women who ran it, but the film did so in a tactful manner. Less discreet was 1967's sensation *The Graduate*, in which a recent college graduate had an affair with a significantly older, married woman, then decided he was actually in love with her daughter.

In 1964, ABC introduced a prime-time drama about the lives of several characters in a fictional New England town. *Peyton Place* ran for five seasons, during which the players conducted far-from-ideal relationships involving murder, divorce, infidelity, and family discord. It stood mostly alone as something apart from the norm until 1967 when CBS aired *The Smothers Brothers Comedy Hour*, a variety show that bore little resemblance to the family-oriented formats of comparable programs. According to Wikipedia, the show was cancelled after a year-and-a-half, not because it wasn't popular, but because of "the brothers' penchant for material that was critical of the political mainstream (and sympathetic to the emerging counterculture)."[4]

Pushing social boundaries to an even greater extent was *Rowan and Martin's Laugh-In*, a comedy program that borrowed heavily from the hippie subculture. Premiering in January 1968 on NBC, *Laugh-In* (a word play on campus "sit-ins" and "love-ins") featured "a rapid-fire series of gags and sketches, many of which conveyed sexual innuendo"—"sock it to me"—"or were politically charged."[5] Go-go dancers strutted in bikinis, their bodies covered with slogans. Although this was no family-oriented show, it gained such a strong following, including among children, that when presidential candidate Richard Nixon made a brief appearance in September 1968 asking, "Sock it to me?" Vice President Hubert Humphrey decided not to accept his own invitation to appear on the show and, according to one source, "later said that not doing it may have cost him the election."[6]

THE CUTTING EDGE

Perhaps fictional Archie and Edith Bunker would have longed for the wholesome good old days of Donna Reed, the Cleavers, and the Nelsons, but ironically, the show that made their names household words signaled the beginning of the end for idyllic TV relationships. Once that frank family from Queens, New York, debuted in 1971, television's interpretation of the American home began to change. Although *All in the Family* presented its own kind of fantasy, producer Norman Lear held up a mirror to society and showed America what he believed one working-class family looked like. Unlike earlier TV fathers, Archie Bunker wasn't so much all-knowing as know-it-all. His wife, Edith, was no well-coifed, pearl-wearing college graduate who ran a pristine home; rather, she always appeared slightly rumpled wearing a simple housedress and a vacant expression as she dusted her souvenir knickknacks. Archie frequently disparaged her efforts and called her "Dingbat." Their only daughter had married a left-wing college student, hippie type who espoused far different political and social views than his father-in-law, whose house he occupied. Archie dubbed him "Meathead" and regularly made cutting remarks about his Polish ancestry.

The show pushed the envelope of contemporary taste and censorship as it attempted to display a more realistic view of blue-collar family life on Main Street, USA. For the first time, a toilet was flushed on TV, which garnered huge laughs, at first because it was so unexpected, later because the producers had gotten away with it. Potty humor was here to stay. Bubbly Edith went through an unusual grouchy phase on an episode that mentioned her entrance into menopause. (Archie was going to give her thirty seconds to get over it.) *All in the Family* touched on racism and ethnicity, miscarriage, rape, and breast cancer. It regularly addressed political issues, the feminist movement, even impotence, "issues previously considered unsuitable for U.S. network television."[7] It became wildly popular, perhaps because it pushed boundaries, possibly because many people could at last relate to a less-than-perfect, yet still loving family.

Increasingly, television began to abandon the concept of a model family that oriented itself around mainstream Protestant mores. *Maude*, a spin-off from *All in the Family*, was no Donna Reed. Married four times, she wore the pants in the house, regularly sounding the battle cry for women's lib. In one episode, she decided to end a midlife pregnancy, a shocking development for most 1970s American families. Other shows centered around divorced people for the first time, including *Alice* and *One Day at a Time*. The series *Family* purported to be about average middle-class people who dealt with the things that many families face, such as disease, adultery, senility, divorce, and a teen's struggles over whether or not to have sex. (She decided not to.)

Although television still maintained a certain overall wholesomeness (think *Little House on the Prairie*, *The Waltons*, and *Happy Days*—even *Charlie's Angels* tended to behave themselves), the decade's music had moved into a looser realm. Many chart-toppers that provided the backdrop for dating teenagers featured sexually charged lyrics. In fact, the three-fold message of disco music was party hearty, have sex, and do drugs. Donna Summers, Rod Stewart, the Starland Vocal Band, Sylvia, and K.C. and the Sunshine Band never would have made it on *The Ed Sullivan Show* with their moaning, morally questionable ballads. Although the magazines that youngsters read maintained a traditional concept of dating and sexuality, they were fighting a rising tide.

With the decline of the church as the keeper of the keys to the cultural kingdom, 70s media began to promote individual and family relationships based entirely upon emotion, societal trends, and one's own opinions. The media, now loosened from a religiously based view of life, went in a decidedly more secular direction.

MATERIAL GIRLS

Many American parents of young children look back with fondness to the family shows of their youth, to *Growing Pains*, *The Facts of Life*, *The Cosby Show*, and *Family Ties.* They differed from earlier counterparts by portraying an upper-middle-class black family, for example, in which the mother, who was a lawyer, always had time for her children and her husband. In fact, on most 80s shows, mothers worked outside the home; that was the new model of married womanhood. Not only was that considered to be the principal way to female fulfillment, it was expected. TV and movies also took for granted the dissolution of marriages and experimented with story lines involving divorced parents, dating, and blended families, including *Kate and Allie* in which two college friends decided to move in together to help each other raise their kids as they recovered from broken marriages. In addition, there was a stronger representation of sexual activity among the young as their "old-fashioned" parents tried to cope with a new reality, including *Too Close for Comfort.* While TV families still had a certain glow—who didn't love Cosby?—many nontraditional ones filled the screen including *Mama's Family*, *Married with Children*, *Dallas*, *Dynasty*, and *Roseanne.* Television not only gave Americans permission to be less than perfect, it had begun to glamorize nontraditional families, as well as kids who seemed wiser than their parents, who were seen as mostly clueless, especially the fathers. No longer under control of the big three networks and with a surfeit of cable channels from which to choose, television offered many times over images of broken relationships and reordered families.

On-screen children caught up in their family's dramas often came across as world-weary at a tender age, a story line that crossed into reality for child star Drew Barrymore, who by the age of ten had started drinking and smoking marijuana. In her autobiography, *Little Girl Lost*, she wrote about her partying lifestyle, including one heartbreaking photo of her at an adult function, leaning her head on her hand as if she were sinking under the weight of growing up too soon.

What's Love Got to Do with It?   187

She was a star in one of the most successful family movies of the 80s, *E.T.*, in which a recently divorced mother tried to hold herself and her three unhappy children together. The movie spoke for a generation rocked by divorce.

If television moved with a certain cautiousness toward a more realistic, yet in some cases still romanticized portrayal of the family, popular music spit any sense of discretion into the prevailing winds. In the early 80s, two singers in particular thrust music into greater permissiveness, promoted heavily by the new MTV music video channel. Michael Jackson had grown up in the spotlight of his famous singing family, and emerging as the dominant personality, went solo by the late 70s, his allure breaking ground by appealing to a cross-racial, international, and largely female, audience. In 1984, he had a colossal bestseller with his *Thriller* album, and in its aftermath became as influential to pop culture as the Beatles had been in their day. His manic, sexually charged dances and lyrics frequently included raw violence, but instead of facing censorship, he was widely embraced as a master performer.

Along with the "King of Pop" came Madonna, a Catholic girl from Michigan whose blend of crude sexuality and religion initially stunned parents and delighted their little girls, who set out to imitate the new star with her bustiers and in-your-face attitude. She enjoyed monster successes with "Like a Virgin," "Papa Don't Preach," and "Borderline," and when the public started taking her act for granted, Madonna ramped it up, a master marketer of her own product as she continually reinvented herself. Over the 80s and 90s she repeatedly drew attention to herself with vulgar on-stage performances that featured sex acts, sadomasochism, nudity, and lesbianism. She famously kissed two other female pop stars at 2003's MTV Music Video Awards show, and her book, *Sex*, showed her having relations with both men and women. She once dedicated "Papa Don't Preach" to the pope—Italians call him "Papa." One commentator remarked, "From the moment Madonna burst onto the nation's radar screen in the mid-1980s, she did everything in her power to shock the public, and her efforts paid off . . . (she) thrived on the criticism, and continued, throughout the decade, to reiterate the most fundamental of her issues by consistently celebrating women's sexual power."[8]

After the material girl had her first child, out of wedlock, she told an interviewer that she was going to raise the little girl carefully, that she wouldn't be exposed to a lot of media because of its bad influences.

The effect of Michael Jackson, Madonna, and other 80s and 90s musical stars on young Americans is hard to overestimate. Coarse songs and dances that would have been considered pornographic by earlier generations are now mainstream; hip-hop and rap music have continued this trend. At least since the 80s, the mainstream media has been freed from adherence to traditional standards, creating a very different image of family and relationships than the one that had existed for centuries. Even television commercials have become eyebrow raising with their soft-porn promotion of everything from feminine products, birth control, perfumes, underwear, clothes, cosmetics, and drugs for erectile dysfunction. When advertisements aren't selling sex, they're stimulating people's minds with fast-paced images of violence, gore, and its aftermath. Television is not a family-friendly place anymore, nor is the image of mainstream American culture that it presents.

Parents who were raised on Madonna may not be as sensitive as their folks were regarding how such programs and images affect little minds. It isn't unheard of today for elementary-aged girls not only to imitate *Hannah Montana*, but also Carrie, the lead character in *Sex in the City*, or to be able to name each of the *Desperate Housewives*. Adolescent girls even have their own version of *Cosmopolitan* magazine to teach them how to be sexually liberated, take-charge females.

THE CLEAVERS DON'T LIVE HERE ANYMORE

The media no longer portrays boy-meets-girl in a straight line from first kiss to the altar; rather a circuitous route now leads young people, and not always to matrimony. Instead it may involve a meandering path that begins in the aftermath of their parents' divorce and reentry into the world of dating, several failed relationships of their own, sometimes including a same-sex fling, followed by a heterosexual season of living together. The wildly popular show *Friends* demonstrated that while people can get married, it is only one of many options. So-called reality shows involving romance that are not aired during prime time are nevertheless advertised while younger viewers may be watching. Daytime TV features a veritable sideshow of the wreckage of human relationships in their most outlandish facets.

The media generally presupposes that people will engage in sex before (or in place of) marriage. To do otherwise is considered unusual, even unhealthy. A case in point is a scene in the 1995 movie *While You Were Sleeping* in which Lucy, a single woman, told her coworker and friend Celeste that she was about to be married, a sudden development. Celeste asked if Lucy was pregnant, but Lucy told her that you have to have sex to have a baby. At that, Celeste got a totally confused look on her face as she said, "But I thought you were engaged." Lucy hesitated, then remarked, "Well, we're . . . waiting." To which Celeste sputtered, "Waiting?" as if it were the strangest thing in the world. Two of the most popular shows of the late 1990s and beyond revolved around the lives of single friends making their way in New York City, and their behavior not only reflected but helped set the tone for millions of young Americans when it came to romantic relationships. Sex outside of marriage was assumed in both shows, and while matrimony was embraced, so was living together apart from it, as well as homosexual and bisexual affairs and having a baby outside of wedlock. This, proclaimed the writers and actors, was the new American reality.

In the 1950s and early 1960s, television provided the nation with shows that conveyed ideal marriages and families. In the last few years, the media has instead given Americans many alternatives. Perhaps one of the saddest recent depictions of family was the "reality" program about a young couple who allowed the cameras to film their everyday lives with their many children. During the course of the highly rated show, Jon and Kate Gosselin went from a modest, church-going couple to celebrities with a book tour, twenty dollars a pop for an autographed picture, a gorgeous new house on many acres, magazine covers, and associations with other celebrities; Emeril even came and cooked for them in one episode. It was more than their marriage could stand; Jon resented the loss of privacy, but Kate reveled in the attention and the money. Their relationship ended, not happily ever after, but in divorce.

As the media permeates contemporary American life and thought, its influence is enormous on families, children, and those who are dating. In the past thirty years, TV, movies, the print media, and Internet have steered people away from the values that guided national life previously, into a murky sea without any strong Christian presence or firm set of relational boundaries.

Chapter 16

WE ARE FAMILY

THEIR WEDDING DAY promised to be perfect, an ornate church providing a storybook backdrop: a beautifully attired bride, groom, and attendants; a limousine; a reception at a tony hotel; a Caribbean honeymoon. Not that there hadn't been challenges, like the way in which the young woman's mother kept referring to the groom as her daughter's "first husband." (Comedienne Roseanne Barr told her about-to-be-wed daughter, "Take this marriage thing seriously—it has to last all the way to the divorce."[1]) She herself had been married for fifteen years before she got divorced, followed by a season of living with a man who eventually became number two. The bride's father had also remarried. One set of her grandparents had divorced; her grandfather was remarried, but they lived in separate homes, and her grandmother couldn't stand being with either her ex-husband or his wife. The groom also came from a broken home, and both of his parents had remarried and taken on stepchildren.

Before the wedding, the bride and groom had spent considerable time on diplomatically seating their families at the ceremony and reception and with considerable sensitivity and flair, they pulled off this difficult assignment. After their children were born, they began an annual choreography around holidays and birthdays, trying to spend equal amounts of time with each set of parents and grandparents so as not to cause conflict or hurt feelings.

The once dominant "traditional family" still exists, but to a much lesser degree than before the 1970s. According to a 1972 study by the National Opinion Research Center, nearly three-quarters of American children lived with their biological mother and father, but by the end of the twentieth century, that number had dwindled to just over half. "Marriages decline, divorces climb as families evolve into 21st century."[2] In 2007, 2.2 million children under eighteen lived with "two unmarried parents," while 25.8 percent resided with a single parent, and 2.5 million cohabitating couples had at least one child belonging to either partner living with them.[3]

Researcher Tom Smith says, "Marriage has declined as the central institution under which households are organized and children are raised. People marry later and divorce and cohabitate more. A growing proportion of children have been born outside of marriage."[4] In fact, he has discovered that "the most common living arrangement" today consists of two unmarried people without children.[5] In the United States, nearly 1.5 million children annually are born to unwed parents; in Cook County, Illinois, which includes Chicago, the figure was 34.5 percent. The same source concluded, "The marriage rate in the United States flirts with an all-time low."[6] Moreover, Smith's survey revealed that the majority of Americans believe that marriage is mainly "an institution for romantic love and companionship," rather than the place in which children are born and raised, a sharp deviation from past generations.[7]

One Iowa woman says that her generation

doesn't know how to make marriage work. We don't have any examples of what marriage should be. If you look at our families, there's generally not a lot of good modeling there. If you look to Hollywood, you're not going to find any positive examples of good marriages . . . Instead we have reality dating shows like *The Bachelor*, in which someone proposes after six weeks of dating twenty-five women at once![8]

Author Tricia Goyer says she wasn't thinking about marriage when she started getting intimate with guys in high school. She did, however, want to make her marriage work when, at the age of eighteen, she found Mr. Right, a man who loved God and wanted to be a good husband to her, as well as a good father to the child she'd had from a previous relationship. She says in her book *Generation NeXt Marriage*,

> As someone who was raised by a mom and stepdad who were already contemplating divorce on my wedding day, I couldn't think ahead to what the next year held for John and me, let alone the next fifty years. I wanted the best marriage possible, but I had no idea how to make that happen. That . . . is an anxiety-filled, confusing place to live.[9]

Apart from exceptional cases, couples from the World War II generation stayed together once they were married, a pattern that their offspring did not imitate. By 2004, men who were born during the early part of the Baby Boom, from 1945 to 1954, had a divorce rate of 38 percent, and 41 percent of Boomer women had severed their marital ties.[10] One organization devoted to stepfamilies claims that today, 60 percent of marriages end, and about 75 percent of divorced people remarry; about 65 percent of those remarriages involve children from previous unions. It concludes, "More than half of Americans today have been, are now or will eventually be in one or more step situations during their lives."[11]

THE DATING GAME

In the 1950s and even throughout most of the 1960s when single people dated, most accepted, however grudgingly, that sex wasn't something nice girls did. Maybe, just maybe, if you were engaged, you might have sex outside of marriage, but that wasn't the norm. Presently, however, some 46 percent of senior high school students have had intercourse, and there is a phenomenon that many engage in called "hooking up," which amounts to having casual sex devoid of any commitment or expectations. It isn't just the boys who are after that kind of sex, but girls also aggressively pursue it.[12] There are, however, emotional consequences with many teenage girls experiencing depression in its aftermath; 60 percent of all sexually active teens say they regret their behavior.[13] Perhaps surprisingly, most teenagers want to discuss sex with their parents, but the latter are not always available or just don't know how to talk to their children. Sarah Brown of the National Campaign to Prevent Teen and Unplanned Pregnancy says, "Teens consistently say that their parents have the most influence over their decisions about sex—not the media, not their boyfriend or girlfriend and not their best buds in school."[14] Another expert says that families are so busy with a myriad of activities that "there are fewer opportunities to sit down and talk about what they're experiencing."[15] Those who do, however, demonstrate a difference; "the research shows that teens who talk with their parents are more likely to wait."[16]

In most media presentations, singles take sex outside of marriage very much for granted; it is simply part of life and not to be questioned, much like the assumption that most non-married couples will live together. And yet some voices are pushing back, saying that living together isn't the best way to go because it adds up to a lack of commitment. Instead, singles should wait—at least until the fourth date anyway—to have sex. In 1995, Sherrie Schneider and Ellen Fein wrote a bestseller, *The Rules*, in which they outlined a system for women to find "Mr. Right." The "dating coaches," for example, encouraged women to avoid having a "fantasy relationship." In other words, if the guy doesn't ask you out, they said, "He's just not that into you."[17] Furthermore, they maintain that a woman shouldn't date a man for more than two years, that one is sufficient to find out if he's going to marry you. Nor should a woman ever call a man because males need a challenge, it's the "natural way."[18]

Schneider and Fein believe that while their rules may seem out-of-step with contemporary society, they work because a guy is a guy is a guy no matter what era he lives in, and a man naturally needs to be challenged. He is turned off by women who are easy to get. They say, "With all due respect, feminism has not changed men or the nature of romantic relationships. Like it or not, men are emotionally and romantically different from women. Men are biologically the aggressor. They thrive on challenge . . . while women crave security and bonding. This has been true since civilization began!"[19]

CAT'S IN THE CRADLE

In 1974, singer Harry Chapin came out with a heartbreaking song about a little boy who craves his father's attention, but his every effort is thwarted by the unresponsive parent who always has something seemingly more important to do. When the dad retires, he calls his son and asks if they can get together, to which the boy says his kids are sick, and his job isn't going well, so he cannot. When the father hangs up, he realizes that his son has grown up to be just like himself. Listeners wondered how a dad could be so pre-occupied. If, however, a contemporary singer were to do a cover of that song, he or she could just as easily sing about an indifferent mother. In the 70s, feminists convinced vast numbers of American women that unless they worked outside the home, they would never be fulfilled, they would never be respected, and that they would never find happiness through marriage and child rearing. They promised that work would liberate them. Thirty-five years later, propelled by that lingering message, economic necessity, divorce and the fear of it, as well as consumerism, motherhood looks very different from the way it was when today's grandparents grew up. First-wave feminists diminished homemaking and now many contemporary mothers are allowing others to raise their children. *Parade* magazine states that "two-thirds of all American women are working by the time their first child is a year old, compared with only 17 percent four decades ago. Single-parent households, most of them headed by women, constitute a quarter of all U.S. families."[20]

Suzanne Venker has addressed this issue thoroughly and with clear-eyed passion in her book, *7 Myths of Working Mothers*, in which her main premise is that motherhood is a worthwhile, full-time job and that the feminist creed that says women can simultaneously excel at work and motherhood while entrusting their children to others is "bogus."[21] Author Ann Crittenden agrees, saying that doing both is "like running in a marathon with a ten-pound weight strapped to each leg."[22]

Working outside the home has left mothers frazzled and unable to connect with their children with the remains of their days, after work when it's time to throw something together for dinner, do laundry, pay bills, grocery shop, and clean—maybe. In an article for *Parents* magazine, one mother confessed, "My kids, ages three and five, jump on me as soon as I walk in the door, but the transition sometimes overwhelms me—and there are just so many things I need to get done." Another wonders what to do when her child calls her at work, and she's busy.[23] As Venker notes, it has been difficult for American mothers to raise their children "with leftover time." In her candid assessment of contemporary motherhood she writes:

> So we've come up with a new way to raise children. We begin by removing babies from their cribs every morning while they are still asleep so we can get them to day care in time for work. We shuffle older children around from home to school to activity as though they are in our way and we need a place to put them. We no longer feed children three healthy meals a day because it takes us too much time to prepare them and children too long to eat them. Finally, we no longer talk to our children—really

talk—because we're just too tired to give them our full attention. And still we wrinkle our eyebrows and wonder what's wrong with children today: Why are they not doing well in school? Why are they overweight? Why are they getting into so much trouble? Why are they sleep deprived? Why are they on Ritalin? Why are they so disrespectful? Why are they having so much sex? Why are they spoiled? We simply refuse to see the connection between the problems that exist among today's children and the fact that mothers aren't at home. Just what did we think mothers were for?[24]

She concludes that women who have left the workplace for home have discovered how stimulating it is to "be your own boss," and that women can never replace what they miss at home with what they find at work; "the workplace is about money and success; family is about human connection, love, and personal growth."[25] She rejoices that contemporary women live at a time when today's technological innovations and conveniences have rendered much of housekeeping drudgery obsolete, that "women can now spend the bulk of their time enjoying their children."[26]

Betty Friedan told women that "raising children is a life of 'empty, purposeless days.'" Venker counters, "Motherhood is a gift, a chance to become a better person. What could be more liberating than that?"[27] In fact, the U.S. Census Bureau discovered that the percentage of working women with infants has been dropping over the last ten years.[28] Perhaps they are discovering, as one successful career woman did to her dismay, that she was missing too much. She asked her teenage son to spend a week's vacation with her, but he said, "It's too late. I'm all grown up. You missed my childhood."[29] Historian Benjamin Hunnicutt says, "I think women are beginning to feel betrayed by work. What they seek at work, this identity, community, meaning, is not being found."[30] "We want," says Danielle Crittenden, "at the end of our lives, to look back and see that what we have done amounts to more than a pile of pay stubs, that we have loved and been loved."[31]

AN AMERICAN CHILD

Molly Gordy is the mother of two girls, and she told *Parents* magazine that her three-year-old likes to stand before a mirror singing to a Britney Spears song, "Oops! I Did It Again."[32] In one Chicago preschool, the teachers are keeping a closer eye on the kids after they found a four-year-old boy inside a big cardboard box lying on top of a girl, trying to kiss her. The adults concluded that he had been acting out something he had seen on television.[33] Writer Dianne Hales remarks, "What's coming out of the mouths of babes hardly sounds innocent—even though it usually is."[34] She says most parents "wonder where their youngsters are picking up such words and ideas. But the answer is simple: everywhere. Long before they can read, today's kids are bombarded with sexual imagery."[35] Gone are the days when parents can feel safe allowing their children to watch children's movies; even many of those contain sexual innuendo and images, as well as uncouthness. Hales reports that the mother of a four-year-old had a game show on, and she thought her son wasn't paying attention until he asked her what erectile dysfunction was. The mother was able to satisfy him with a brief explanation that it was a medical problem, but she said, "I'm glad he wasn't watching television with his twelve-year-old cousin. Who knows how he would have explained it."[36] Perhaps it is no surprise, in light of our culture's emphasis on the physical aspect of relationships that sexual experimentation is happening at increasingly earlier ages.

According to Common Sense Media, 70 percent of TV shows depicted sexual material, but less than one in four teen-oriented programs "featured any discussion of risk and responsibility." Likewise, "60 percent of female video game characters are presented in a sexualized fashion."[37] Moreover the report stated, "Many of these images are played for shock value, so they often contain graphic or violent sex. Even mild shows use sexual situations for humor. Sexual humor is a mainstay of adolescent entertainment."[38] Not so long ago, young people with raging hormones were expected to discipline themselves and wait until marriage before having sex with a lifelong spouse.

During the course of American history, there have been several periods when being young presented great challenges. This is one of those eras. Most children are connected to the TV, Internet, iPods, games, and text messaging an average of five-and-half hours a day. While those ages eight and older log up to seven hours a day of such activities, many are without real guidelines.[39] This has contributed to childhood obesity and related medical problems, including early onsets of diabetes and heart issues. Kids are growing up not only on unrestricted television, but on day care, after-school care, fast food—who has time to cook?—over-scheduling, little leisure time, and lack of sufficient sleep.[40] Add to that mixture a lack of discipline; Venker maintains that working moms don't want to come home to the few hours they have with their children and discipline them.[41] Nor do separated or divorced parents with visiting privileges.

Author Inda Schaenen has written of the way in which contemporary American children are so rushed and scheduled, concluding, "Children flourish (only) when they are unhurried . . . by their very nature, (children) move like snails."[42] Venker concurs. "Previous generations understood this and adapted their lives to accommodate the needs of children . . . But today we expect children to adapt to their parents' needs."[43] Family therapist Dr. Ron Taffel says, "In my conversations with them, children from kindergarten to age twelve overwhelmingly indicate that what they want most is more time, as in undivided attention. The quality of family life has changed dramatically."[44] Not only do children not have enough time with their parents, many live far from grandparents, who often reside at adults-only venues in other states. Venker believes that "today's children are growing up without a childhood, an honest to goodness childhood—complete with mothers who would rather be with them than anywhere else in the world."[45]

Some children, however, never experience life at all. Since the Supreme Court legalized the procedure in 1973, estimates are that nearly 40 million children have been aborted.[46] The results have been devastating to two generations; a high percentage of women who have abortions have more than one, and women who have them are at increased risk for damage to their reproductive systems, depression, suicide, and substance abuse.[47] Women who get pregnant after age thirty-five are routinely encouraged to undergo genetic testing (that poses a risk to the fetus) in order to determine whether their unborn children have abnormalities. Of those who learn that their babies *may* have Down syndrome, 84–91 percent terminate their pregnancies.[48]

There are, however, people who do everything in their power to have children because they struggle with infertility; the Mayo Clinic has determined that about 15 percent of American couples have difficulty conceiving a child.[49] There are many causes, but a prevailing one for today's men and women is that they are marrying later and/or putting off having children, sometimes to build up their careers. Just a few decades ago, little could be done to help people yearning for children fulfill their dream, leaving them few options, including adoption or remaining childless. There are, however, a variety of assisted reproductive technologies that provide hope for infertile couples, among them in vitro fertilization, assisted hatching, various kinds of drugs, and male-oriented procedures to address their specific infertility problems, in addition to receiving outside help from sperm and egg donors and surrogates. While these pose certain ethical challenges, they also offer hope to those who, using them responsibly, can have the children they yearn for.

Author Marlo Schalesky chronicled the difficulties she and her husband experienced getting pregnant in her book *Empty Womb, Aching Heart*. They consider themselves greatly blessed that in spite of several miscarriages, among other setbacks, they now have five children. She said,

> One thing I love about having my family today is that God has opened up so many more avenues of blessing through medical advancements. For my family, those blessings have come in the area of advanced reproductive technologies. I'm very grateful

for the advancements that have allowed my husband and me to have four of our five children, and have also taught me so much about trusting God and seeing Him act through a medical journey. Plus, going through IVF has taught me a greater respect and awe for life in seeing how many aspects of reproduction have to be perfectly aligned in order to conceive and have a baby. Without these advancements, my family wouldn't be the wondrous thing it is today, and I wouldn't have realized just what an incredible miracle each child is. ART not only gives us better chances for the much-hoped-for baby, but it also makes us more aware of the wonder of reproduction. If you've gone through ART, you never take a baby's life for granted. You know what a miracle it is![50]

A NEW KIND OF FAMILY

By traditional definition, a family is made up of a husband, wife, and their children. Today, however, Americans have come to embrace a wider concept of family such as children living with one parent or who move between divorced parents, kids who live with one parent and a live-in partner, and those in stepfamily situations. (Some people even treat their pets like children.) The most common new-style "family" includes two unmarried adults, which was rare in 1960 when just 430,000 Americans lived together outside of marriage. Forty-five years later that figured had skyrocketed to 5.4 million.[51] Today, 50–60 percent of marriages begin with the couple living together first.[52] It is routine to hear those celebrating anniversaries say something like, "We've been married for ten years, but we've been together for fifteen." On TV shows dedicated to house hunting, the pair frequently isn't married or engaged. Author Mike McManus says, "Women see [cohabitation] as a step toward marriage . . . Men don't because they like to have the ready availability of sex and having someone share their living expenses."[53] Some say that it's a good way to determine future compatibility. However, cohabitating is fundamentally different from matrimony since it lacks the abiding commitment of marriage.

The statistics reveal the downside. Sixty-seven percent of couples who do so and then marry, eventually divorce.[54] Forty percent of those who live together never even make it to the altar or justice of the peace.[55] A Columbia University survey found that "the average cohabitant has several partners in a lifetime."[56] Yale sociologist Neil Bennett discovered that 80 percent of women who live with a man are more likely to separate or divorce than other women who didn't live with spouses before they married.[57] Those wives also tend to be unhappier in marriage, more likely to commit adultery, experience more trouble with conflict and communication, and they often lack emotional and relational maturity.[58]

OUT OF THE CLOSET

Much media fanfare accompanied the union of Ellen DeGeneres and Portia de Rossi after California courts overturned a ban on same-sex marriage. An article in *Real Simple* magazine featured "a beautifully unconventional family," of two women in a lesbian relationship who got pregnant at the same time, with outside help. One of the partners said, "On the street, people probably thought we were friends who had just come from pregnancy class. When I was registering us . . . the woman who worked there was freaking out because she had never seen this before."[59] Model and talk show host Tyra Banks featured a couple on her program who were lamenting the refusal of one of their mothers to attend the ceremony because it was between two lesbians. Banks, with audience support, browbeat the mom, chiding her for ruining the biggest day of her daughter's life. She mentioned that mothers of murderers still visit their children in jail so why couldn't this women support her daughter, who wasn't guilty of any bad thing.[60]

Media programming and public school curriculum often uphold homosexuality as an alternative lifestyle that reasonable people accept. Those who object are often viewed with disdain, sometimes with pity, as suffering from homophobia, even though until a few decades ago most Americans considered same-sex relationships an oddity. A recent case in point was the media hoopla over Carrie Prejean, Miss California in the 2009 Miss USA Pageant, who answered a judge's question about gay marriage. She said that although she thought it was great that Americans could choose one way or another, she believed that marriage was between a man and a woman. She ultimately lost her crown.

Not all homosexuals consider marriage to be the epitome of a relationship. One lesbian feminist wrote in *The Philadelphia Inquirer* that she believes same-sex individuals are mistaken in pushing so hard for legally recognized matrimony. She says of those who, like herself, "came out" thirty years ago, "We were going to live our own lives, do what we wanted, and be independent. We certainly weren't going to get married—to anyone. Marriage was all about being in that limiting little box. Wedding bells sound too much like chains clanking."[61] She advocates for something very different from a standard marriage model, something radical. "I'm going for a model that is conceptually broader. I want love and intimacy, and I want freedom, which means not being tied down. . . . Those of us who are choosing these kinds of options are on the cutting edge of something absolutely new in Western culture." Regarding children produced by these new unions, she believes that "in a village type of community, children have half a dozen people, or more, to parent them, and, in my opinion, that's much healthier than having only two."[62]

REFLECTIONS

Suzanne Venker writes that although contemporary American couples may differ from those in previous eras in their views on marriage and family, people don't really change in the way they are wired from one generation to the next. We might have thought we could change the relationship between the sexes, especially the old-fashioned notion that men and women are fundamentally different, but, Venker concludes, they are not. She lists current myths: Men can be just as nurturing with children as women. Children will do fine in day care. Men and women should have sex before marriage and frequent, extraordinary sex thereafter. Venker asserts that years ago, there wasn't that kind of pressure on people; sex had its place within marriage, but it wasn't the be-all and end-all of the union. She says, "If (the couple) weren't having a lot of sex when they were married, or if it wasn't the most fulfilling sex in the world, they had nothing with which to compare it. This is no longer the case."[63]

Our culture's marriage myths also overlook the joys and meaningfulness of traditional family life.[64] Venker concludes,

> Candlelight dinners are nice, yes. But they can't compare to the glance between a man and a woman over the head of a sleeping child. They can't compare to the rush of emotion a woman feels as she watches her husband make her child laugh . . . we overlook the romance of family. Indeed, moments of passion are often fleeting, but real love lasts forever.[65]

Chapter 17

FOLLOW
THE LEADER

SHE WAS AMERICA'S sweetheart, a celebrity from the age of six who sang at fairgrounds, on the radio and television and who at eighteen captured the Miss Oklahoma title. She came in second at the Miss America pageant the following year and went on to have a successful recording career with hits like "Paper Roses" and "Till There Was You," as well as becoming famous for her orange juice commercials on TV; many people still recall her memorable pitch, "A day without orange juice is like a day without sunshine." In much demand and greatly admired, Anita Bryant performed at a Super Bowl and sang at President Lyndon Johnson's graveside service.

An evangelical Christian, she became alarmed when homosexual advocates began championing "antidiscrimination" ordinances and laws, believing that they would eventually unravel the American family. Bryant used her influence to begin a "Save Our Children" campaign that helped repeal a 1977 Dade County, Florida, pro-homosexual law, and her effort quickly extended to other states. Although it met with various successes, including a prohibition against homosexuals being able to adopt children in Florida, Bryant paid highly for her activism. Her opponents organized a boycott of orange juice; at gay bars, a new drink known as the Anita Bryant (containing vodka and apple juice) replaced the standard screwdriver, which used orange juice as a key ingredient. At a televised Iowa press conference, an irate man threw a pie at her, hitting Bryant in the face, and there were regular kidnapping and death threats against her and her family, in addition to attacks on her home. According to Janet Porter, "Like a scene out of Sodom, homosexual activists surrounded her home screaming at the top of their lungs. Her mother was afraid to open the door."[1] As her popularity nose-dived, she eventually lost her livelihood and her marriage ended in divorce. Porter calls Bryant "a sacrificial lamb to wake a sleeping nation."[2] More than thirty years later, the homosexual community still reviles her, and many Americans associate her name with bigotry.

In past years the church acted as a bulwark to uphold traditional values. As often as not, it follows the broader culture's lead today. As a believer in Christ, Bryant saw radical changes and threats to the family in the late 1970s, and she decided to challenge them head-on. Many evangelicals agreed with and supported her, but far from all Christendom concurred. Leaders in mainline churches often welcomed the cultural shifts. They regarded those changes as a refreshing breeze, maintaining that women and children had been under the thumbs of men far too long and the church, as a purveyor of such attitudes, needed to repent and embrace the new day. Within those denominations a fracture took place between those who fought for traditional values and others who sought to reinterpret Scripture according to the new cultural trends, which included overcoming what they deemed patriarchalism, sexism, and homophobia. The Roman Catholic Church officially held its ground on a traditional concept of family, but countless Catholics chose to ignore its teachings about birth control and divorce.

The implications were deep for relationships between the sexes, as well as the way in which people related to God. Within the older Protestant churches, women were often permitted to serve as pastors and church officials. Many mainline leaders also demanded that inclusive language replace the "sexist" language contained in hymnbooks, books of worship and confessions, even in the Bible itself. No longer was it acceptable to call God "Father" or refer to the Almighty as "Him" or "He"; the Holy Spirit became for many a female expression of the Trinity. Beloved songs like "God Rest Ye Merry, Gentlemen" became "God Rest Ye Merry, Gentlefolk," and Jesus, likewise, fished for persons, not men. Eventually that movement led some within mainline Protestant churches to promote "reimagining." Sylvia Dooling, leader of the Voices of Orthodox Women group in the Presbyterian Church (USA), explains that it "was about breaking down the walls of the existing church that (a) group of radical feminists believed had been imagined by men, then they set out to re-imagine God according to their own experience."[3]

At mainline seminaries, many students and faculty began advocating for a mainstreaming of homosexuals within society, claiming that their sin wasn't any greater than gluttony or gossip. Others took that argument a step further by saying homosexuality wasn't a sin at all, but rather an alternative lifestyle, and the problem wasn't homosexuality but homophobia. Pressure occurred to allow openly homosexual men and women to become pastors, as well as to bless their unions along the same lines as heterosexual marriages. These views among the church's seminaries and hierarchies eventually filtered down to the pews, and even Sunday schools began teaching small children to embrace the new tolerance. One young man who graduated from a Bible college and entered Princeton Theological Seminary in the early 80s, says it was like going right into the culture at large. Dominating the scene were women who were feminists first, "Christians" second.

As a result of liberal theology and a left-leaning political orientation, the Presbyterian Church (USA), for example, along with most other mainline churches, have experienced polarization with activists on both sides of issues pertaining to marriage and the

family. Dooling has witnessed droves of members leave her denomination, either "dropping out entirely" or switching to more conservative Presbyterian groups. She believes that her church is "living
through a crisis," but she also sees that "healthy, biblical changes
(are) taking place because of the reality that unless changes are
made, the denomination will go down in flames."[4] Her group, VOW,
provides an alternate voice for PCUSA women, whose denomina-
tionally based Presbyterian Women has grown increasingly radical
over the years. "There were those on staff in our denomination,"
she says, "who were attempting to break down the biblical and traditional heritage of our church." She and others like her felt led by
God "to speak out and encourage others to do the same."[5]

A fundamental issue that separates the liberal and conservative
factions within mainline churches is how they approach and interpret
Scripture. For the latter, the Bible is God's infallible, inspired Word
that guides people in all cultures and generations universally. For the
former, however, it *contains* God's word, but because it was written
by fallible men who came out of various times and cultural practices,
it does not apply to everyone across the board. On that side is Victor
Paul Furnish, Distinguished Professor Emeritus of Southern
Methodist University's Perkins School of Theology. He says:

> Some people believe . . . that scripture is the written deposit of
> God's truth, mediated through inspired writers in centuries
> past, but valid in both general and specific ways for all times
> and places. This may be called the sacred cow view of the Bible.
> It leads to the conclusion, when applied to the concrete ethical
> teachings of Paul, that they are in fact God's commandments
> and thus eternally and universally binding.[6]

By asserting that the apostle's directives regarding the roles of
women and men in the family were intended for a first century
audience, Furnish is able to dismiss Paul's teachings.[7]

According to the Presbyterian Church in America and many
other evangelical denominations, men and women are equal in

importance before God but are also fundamentally distinct. As such, they have God-ordained roles that correspond with His created order, including man's "headship" over women. Therefore, men are to function as the authorities in both the home and the church while women are to remain submissive to them. If men usurp that role, and women refuse to accept that male leadership, those proponents believe there will be increasingly destructive consequences in families, churches, and the culture at large.

The matter does not stop there in contemporary American churches because the lines cannot be drawn simply between liberal and evangelical groups. There are many evangelical egalitarians who believe that "the Bible teaches the full equality of men and women in Creation and in Redemption," and who find support for their position in scriptural passages such as Genesis 1:26–28; 2:23; 5:1–12; 1 Corinthians 11:11–12; Acts 2:17-18; and Galatians 3:13, 28; 5:1.[8] According to those believers, Scripture permits women to serve as pastors, elders, and deacons, not because that is the socially acceptable thing to do, but because the Bible teaches it.

FEAR FACTOR

William Chafe writes that the women's movement of the late 60s and 70s frightened many Americans, not just Christians, because it sought to destroy the fabric of the traditional family. This was particularly so regarding its aggressive campaign to have Congress pass an Equal Rights Amendment (ERA), something that sounded extremist to much of the country. Those who had no difficulty supporting the principle of equal pay for equal work, or the ability of women to pursue whatever jobs or careers best suited their individual strengths and talents, nevertheless blanched at a feminist insistence that women serve in combat next to men, share unisex public bathrooms, or live in coed dorm rooms. Nor did they go for the designation "Ms." at first, which feminists created in place of the marital-status-defining "Miss" and "Mrs." It seemed to middle America that those feminists were really after the demise of the family and a blending of the sexes into a state of bland androgyny, as well as greater allowance for abortion, promiscuity, and homosexuality. It is ironic that in the 1950s, most people considered feminism to be "anti-American," but the "church-based civil rights struggle" of the 50s and 60s opened avenues to other social reformers, lending them a mantle of respectability.[9]

According to William Chafe, "the ERA ran into a solid wall of opposition. With conservative Republican Phyllis Schlafly in the lead, the anti-ERA coalition . . . brilliantly organized women and men throughout the country around issues of defending the family and preserving separation between the sexes."[10] Joining Schlafly in her pro-family cause were a number of other Christian leaders who formed entertainment companies and organizations to promote a biblically oriented outlook on marriage, dating, and parenting. In the 1960s, Pat Robertson created *The 700 Club* television program, which went into national syndication in 1974; three years later, he launched the Christian Broadcasting Network, and that morphed into the Family Channel in 1988. Other Christian broadcasting outlets also emerged on local, regional, and national levels, including The Trinity Broadcasting Network (1973), and the Roman Catholic Eternal Word Television Network (1980).

In 1977, psychologist James Dobson, a professor of pediatrics at the University of Southern California School of Medicine, published *Dare to Discipline* in which he took permissive child-rearing techniques to the woodshed. Instead, he urged mothers and fathers to exercise benevolent, though firm, authority over their children. He raised the ire of many contemporary parenting experts by saying that when children are willfully disobedient, they should be spanked, provided the parent is in control of his or her own emotions. Dobson founded Focus on the Family the same year as his book's publication "To cooperate with the Holy Spirit in sharing the Gospel of Jesus Christ with as many people as possible by nurturing and defending the God-ordained institution of the family and promoting biblical truths worldwide."[11]

That same year, a Methodist pastor who was disgusted with the content of much television programming challenged his church to participate in a "Turn the TV Off Week." The campaign garnered so much attention that Don Wildmon used it as a springboard to create the National Federation for Decency, which he renamed the American Family Association a decade later, along with American Family Radio, in 1991. His pro-family movement scored a number of "wins," including convincing 7-Eleven stores to stop selling *Playboy* magazine, filing a flurry of complaints against Howard Stern's radio program, and organizing boycotts of Disney for promoting "pro-homosexual practices."[12]

Around the same time, in 1979, Beverly LaHaye began her own association to help preserve the traditional American family. Known as Concerned Women for America, it exists to fight, as her website puts it, "the culture war." According to CWFA's Vision Statement, "the organization's goal is for women and like-minded men, from all walks of life, to come together and restore the family to its traditional purpose and thereby allow each member of the family to realize their God-given potential and be more responsible citizens."[13] CWFA regularly marshals its base to support or oppose legislation that would prove damaging to the family, including pro-abortion policies. It also speaks out against objectionable entertainment and judges who interpret the law in ways that hurt the traditional family.

Christian, pro-family issues also motivated the Reverend Jerry Falwell of the Thomas Road Baptist Church and Liberty University to establish the Moral Majority in 1979. According to Falwell, "God burdened my heart to mobilize religious conservatives around a pro-life, pro-family, strong national defense and pro-Israel platform, designed to return America to her Judeo-Christian heritage."[14] The name itself indicated a belief that the vast number of Americans disagreed with the feminist, secular schema presented by the media and the American academic community. Falwell summarized the initial efforts of his movement to save the nation's families:

> During Moral Majority's heyday, we registered millions of new voters and reactivated millions more. More than 100,000 pastors,

priests and rabbis and nearly seven million families joined hands and hearts to reclaim America for God. Many historians believe the result was the election of Ronald Reagan in 1980 and the genesis of what the media calls the "Religious Right."[15]

Toward the end of his life, Falwell said he was still trying to "successfully complete my 'salt of the earth ministry.'" "America is worth saving," he said. "Our children and children's children will hold us accountable if we fail."[16]

Many conservative Christian individuals got involved in efforts large and small to call attention to the harm being done to the family, and to reverse the slide, maintaining that the nation's overall health depended on the well-being of its families. Focus on the Family's "Guiding Principles" summarize the overall evangelical position: regarding marriage, it is a permanent relationship between a man and woman based on "a sacred covenant designed by God to model the love of Christ for His people and to serve both the public and private good as the basic block of human civilization."[17] Furthermore, "Christians are called to defend and protect God's marriage design and to minister in Christ's name to those who suffer the consequences of its brokenness."[18] Regarding children, they "are a heritage from God and a blessing from His hand."[19] They are not meant to be "choices" that adults make at pregnancy to determine whether or not to let them come into the world at all. Along with abortion, Focus on the Family promotes the overall "sanctity of human life" for "the preborn, the aged, the mentally disabled, those deemed unattractive, the physically challenged, and every other condition in which humanness is experienced from the single cell stage of development to natural death. Christians are therefore called to defend, protect, and value all human life."[20]

THE LEAST OF THESE

Joan E. Boydell may not be as nationally recognizable as Beverly LaHaye or James Dobson, but she, and thousands of other Christians like her, have been working to save the lives of unborn children since the legalization of abortion. She says, "I got involved because the issue stirred me. I could bear only two children, and it disturbed me to see others destroying children and suffering themselves as a result. Most of all, God called me to it."[21] The Pennsylvania woman directed the Amnion Crisis Pregnancy Center from 1989 until her retirement two decades later. A professional licensed counselor, she currently acts as a consultant for Care Net, a network of more than 1,100 crisis pregnancy centers that lend practical and emotional help to women experiencing unanticipated pregnancies. Boydell has counseled many pregnant and possibly pregnant women with the goal of encouraging them to choose life. She has also "trained many others to counsel and teach in pregnancy centers and churches," hoping "to touch others with a deep understanding of God's care and design for life from conception to through natural death."[22]

When the *Roe v. Wade* Supreme Court decision legalized abortion, Christian churches and their members responded in a variety of ways. The mainline denominations divided into factions for and against the ruling, which created considerable friction within their ranks. Boydell believes "evangelical Christians were asleep when *Roe v. Wade* was passed" but that "Catholics were much more aware and energized."[23] She also thinks that a "slowly growing awakening" occurred when Dr. C. Everett Koop and Francis Schaeffer published *Whatever Happened to the Human Race?* in 1983.

Most mainline churches have now taken official pro-choice positions along a continuum from guarded tolerance of the procedure in extreme or "last resort" cases (the official Anglican Church, Evangelical Lutheran Church, and United Methodist Church stances) to strongly supporting a woman's "right to choose." For example, the United Church of Christ officially supports the National Abortion and Reproductive Rights Action League. The Presbyterian Church U.S.A. has strong constituencies on both sides of the issue and publicly "encourages an atmosphere of open debate and mutual respect for a variety of opinions."[24] For the most part, evangelical Protestant denominations and independent churches, along with Mennonites, Brethren, the Lutheran Church Missouri Synod, and the Wisconsin Evangelical Lutheran Synod are pro-life. The Roman Catholic Church took a firm pro-life side in the 1968 encyclical *Humanae Vitae* maintaining that "the first right of the human person is his life."[25]

At the heart of the pro-life church movement are countless people who volunteer to counsel and help women dealing with unexpected pregnancies. They encourage those individuals to have their babies, and they help the mothers either pursue adoption or lead them to resources that will help them to care for their children. *Time* magazine attributes such efforts to a lessening of abortions in America in recent years saying, "The quiet campaign for women's hearts and minds, conducted in thousands of crisis pregnancy centers around the country, on billboards, phone banks and websites, is having an effect."[26] The publication even referred to those centers as the "calm, kind, nonjudgmental" face of the pro-life movement.[27]

ALICE DOESN'T LIVE HERE ANYMORE

In 1999, when Christian singer Amy Grant divorced her husband, then remarried, she became *persona non grata* in some church circles. Many radio stations refused to play her music, Christian magazines stopped writing about her career, and "disillusioned fans turned their backs on her. It was open season on Amy Grant," according to writer Mark Moring.[28] The story line was similar for Sandi Patty, another Christian singer who divorced in 1992. Ending one's marriage has become more commonplace in Christian churches since then, so that when notable public figures such as Kim Hill or Sheila Walsh call it quits today, they often maintain a loyal following and experience barely a blip in their careers. John H. Riggall, a pastor in the Bible Fellowship Church, began his ministerial career in 1942 and has watched the evangelical wing of Christianity in particular experience profound changes, including the way in which divorce is handled. In his early years in the pulpit, "divorce was not accepted, and the divorced person was looked down upon. That person was not allowed to teach a Sunday school class or perform any other spiritual subject in the church. A divorced man could not become an ordained minister in the Bible Fellowship Church."[29]

A decade ago, a national study not only jolted the Christian community, it also provided fodder for its detractors. The Barna Research Group surveyed just under four thousand Americans and discovered that 34 percent of those belonging to independent Christian churches had been divorced, compared to 25 percent for the overall population. Baptists, who represented several different denominations as well as unaffiliated churches, weighed in at 29 percent, with Pentecostals at 28 percent. The only groups that divorced less than the general public were Presbyterians (23 percent), Roman Catholics (21 percent), and Lutherans (21 percent). (Atheists and agnostics came in at 21 percent as well.)[30]

Many commentators questioned Barna's findings, including sociologist David Popenoe of Rutgers University, who cited 1980s statistics that showed "people who are religious tend to have lower divorce rates, especially if both husband and wife are religious. . . . It just stands to reason that the bond of religion is protective of marriage."[31] Dr. Nancy T. Ammerman of Hartford Seminary said that most Americans see themselves as Christians, but "that does not mean that they go to church" or "even know anything about" the denomination with which they identify."[32]

Even if Barna's data was flawed, his findings still provided some reason to think that Christian marriages weren't significantly more resilient than those of non-Christians. Christian commentator Cal Thomas says that the lack of uniqueness in Christian marriages is hurting the church's witness:

> From the statistics I read (George Barna, Gallup) it appears that divorce in Christian families is no different from non-Christian ones. How can we be a compelling witness that to live as believers makes a difference when our families are splitting up like the world? I think what is missing is a sense of disciplined biblical literacy. Too many believers are into the "feelings" culture

and as such are subject to the lure of the prince of the world who speaks to us in the language of feelings. He whispers, "You have a 'right' to happiness," not an obligation to honor your marriage vows. So, if your spouse isn't making you "happy," you have the right (even an obligation some would say) to divorce him or her. This is the virus that has invaded the church and only the fear of God (which fewer pastors preach in an era of seeker-friendliness) can keep it out.[33]

Sylvia Eagono, a director of Christian education at a Presbyterian church, regularly counsels people caught up in marital discord. She says, "We are such a throw-away society today. People move to new areas, change jobs, and look for excitement and the thrill of a new challenge at all turns. Daily routine of life and marriage require hard work. Today, if it's hard, too many people move on to something else. We lack that old 'stick-to-it-iveness.'"[34] She suggests that to help reduce divorces among Christians, churches should "teach regularly about the covenant of marriage" as well as to "present a realistic picture of the challenges of married life versus that presented by the media and the world."[35]

In spite of the sad fact that Christian husbands, wives, and children have been touched deeply by divorce in this present culture, there is a way in which the Church sometimes strongly upholds marriage. Many years ago Eagano endured an eight-year separation from a husband who did not share her Christian faith. She says that although her church stands firmly against the sundering of marriage, she also discovered how it upholds those who are suffering in marriage. It was a place "where people loved me for myself."[36]

Unlike the public reception that greeted news of Sandi Patty and Amy Grant's divorces, other Christian celebrities in more recent years have been shown more mercy and grace than shock and exclusion. One of them, singer Kim Hill, says that she encountered God's abundant grace during her own divorce, as well as a new opportunity for ministry. "It was in a place of complete 'brokenness' that . . . she learned the true meaning of God's love," according to a CBN interview. She says, "I think this simple message is so needed for people to hear. "[37]

BABY GENIUSES

In the 1990s, First Lady Hillary Clinton wrote a bestselling book, *It Takes a Village,* which many pundits lauded because in it she proclaimed that for children to be raised right, they needed to be nurtured by an entire community, not just their parents. Some critics denounced her philosophy, however, maintaining that little ones learn best from their parents, who must bear primary responsibility for them. Before the advent of the modern women's movement, society considered it anathema to take young children away from their mothers and put them into organized group care outside of the family. Today many Americans see day care as a right for working mothers. Likewise, for stay-at-home moms there is tremendous pressure to put their very young children into preschool as soon as possible.

The present culture is often one in which childhood is rushed instead of relaxed and carefree, and in which day care and preschools do the jobs that parents used to do almost exclusively, including teaching, socializing, and helping children bond with other people. Very early on they learn to be part of a public group, to conform to its pattern, and to become independent of their parents. Some "schools" advertise that they teach children from "six months to six years," and an enormous number of activities are available for toddlers, from sports to music to art to karate. Churches have joined the early education bandwagon, maintaining that if children are to be taken out of the home early on, churches can at least provide superior care, as well as an opportunity to teach them and their parents about Christ.

Educators in the past encouraged parents not to send their sons to kindergarten before they were ready for that kind of structure, that they often lacked developmental maturity for the classroom. How then, can any child of two or three—let alone six weeks to six years—be ready for formal learning? Moreover, the culture's cry for children to conform to the societal blueprint often leaves them feeling like a cog. One pediatrician told the parents of a four-year-old to put him in preschool so he didn't grow up thinking he was "the center of the universe." They replied, "He'll get that lesson soon enough from the world. He's not going to learn it from us."

Another area in which Christians have been mirroring society in raising children is by exposing very young ones to electronic entertainment, mainly videos and television. An entire industry is dedicated to creating videos and TV shows for infants and toddlers under the supposition that such material will turn children into geniuses. Christians have followed the leaders of this movement in creating their own series of entertainment for that age group in spite of cautionary messages from the American Academy of Pediatrics. That organization, and many others, has studied the effects on brain development and behavior of TV-watching children, and the overall outcome is negative. Viewing can lead to aggressive behavior, a zombielike state in which kids don't relate to other people, poor communication skills, a need to be entertained rather than to learn to play independently, hyperactivity, and obesity.

Christians, however, have not just been cultural consumers, they have also provided leadership and innovation in family matters. Churches and parachurch organizations sponsor marriage and parenting seminars, as well as programs for children that encourage intellectual and spiritual growth, including Pioneer Clubs and AWANA. Christian leaders have also stepped to the plate in producing family-friendly, Christ-centered motion pictures that have captivated the viewing public, including in recent years *Fireproof*, *Facing the Giants*, and *The Wager*. Christian publishing houses have continued excellent traditions of creating books, music, and creative supplies that encourage individuals and the corporate life of the church. Furthermore, Christian schools have offered parents an alternative to secular public schools where freedom of religious expression is often discouraged, sometimes forbidden.

One particular area of Christian education has ushered in an

American cultural trend—homeschooling. When it first commenced sometime during the societal mayhem of the late 60s and early 70s, the popular consensus was that homeschooling was the domain of a kook fringe. However, educational reformers Charles E. Silberman and John Holt, who wrote during that time, were doubtful that public schools could properly instruct young Americans.[38] Holt started the magazine *Growing Without Schooling* in 1977 that promoted the new movement, and Dr. Raymond and Dorothy Moore also wrote extensively about early childhood education, questioning "the wisdom of conventional schooling with a focus on the harm that can be created by rushing children prematurely into the existing school regimen."[39]

Homeschooling advocates emphasized that their vision was actually an age-old custom, that "government-sponsored schools (were) the variant . . . at least until the middle of the nineteenth century. Until then, the mostly agrarian American society lived a family-centered lifestyle; education happened at home."[40] That began to change, "over the objections of many teachers, parents, and (the) public press" in the 1850s when Massachusetts passed a "compulsory attendance law" and as the industrial revolution commenced.[41] Modern homeschooling gained true momentum in the 1980s as support groups sprang up for parents and children who left bricks and mortar establishments, and as states began making allowances for the "new" way of educating children. When, in the 1980s, tax laws burdened many small Christian schools to the point that they closed, that resulted in "a large second wave of homeschooling, joining earlier homeschoolers and boosting the numbers to record highs. Christian curriculum providers . . . followed the money and easily courted the new market of homeschooling parents."[42]

Today, those who teach their children at home come from a broad spectrum of beliefs and traditions. Parents do it because they want to be closer to their kids, they don't want to subject them to the dangers and temptations at many public schools, and they believe they can give their kids a better, more individual education at home that incorporates and respects their family's religious practices. The Internet has greatly contributed to the homeschooling experience, and parents can tap into large, supportive networks, including particular online schools that come in public as well as private varieties. Likewise, there are many homeschooling co-ops in which parents share their areas of expertise with other families, conduct field trips, and do other intramural activities.

WE'RE NOT IN KANSAS ANYMORE

At no time in history has it been easy or uncomplicated to maintain a traditional family, including those eras in which the church set the tone for society. Peter Nelson, a Baptist pastor in Pennsylvania, has ministered for almost twenty years during a time in which the institutional church "has not been the arbiter of American life."[43] He says,

> I see a wide range of attitudes and feelings (among Christians), from anger and resentment that secular people dare to snub or ignore the church, to wistful chagrin that yearns for the "good old days" when the culture propped up the values and customs of the church, to (misguided) sorrow that the church has somehow failed to keep its place of cultural influence in our world.[44]

Nelson and countless other believers like him wish that Christians would see "how the new hour provides a positive opportunity to live in such a way that they stand out and stand apart from the general culture—how this current situation—under God's providence—opens new doors for witness and creates new ways to help pursue the purity of the church."[45]

Chapter 18

THE MOST EXCELLENT WAY

A family is a formation center for human relationships. The family is the place where the deep understanding that people are significant, important, worthwhile, with a purpose in life, should be learned at an early age. The family is the place where children should learn that human beings have been made in the image of God and are therefore very special in the universe.[1]

ONE OF THE BENEFITS of being a theologically trained historian is having the ability to see events and trends, as well as belief structures and patterns, within the context of spirituality, in my case, biblically oriented spirituality. I have been able to detect how Americans from other eras did marriage and family well, how and where they struggled, and what enabled those who flourished to do so. I have discovered that there is a certain winsomeness about families who follow the teachings of Jesus, especially as He

calls people to love others as we love ourselves, to the point of sacrifice (Matthew 9:19; 1 Corinthians 13). In the household of faith
such people exhibit the fruit of the Spirit (Galatians 5:22–23),
including a couple who lovingly nurture grandchildren, volunteer in
many capacities at church, and travel thousands of miles to rebuild
homes devastated by Hurricane Katrina. There's the husband and
wife who homeschool and go on short-term mission trips with their
kids and another Christian family with three children and a live-in
grandparent who are pursuing international adoption so they can
pour the love of Christ into one more soul. Countless American
Christians shed their light on a darkened society, even as they
season it with the countercultural salt of gospel living. Most are
unknown to those outside their communities, while others, like
Francis and Edith Schaeffer, gained an international following.

When Francis was a pastor in western Pennsylvania and Edith
stayed at home to begin raising their four children, she often took
valuable time from her days to feed homeless men who came to the
"manse" requesting a simple cup of coffee and "maybe some bread."[2]
"Wait outside," she would say. "I'll fix something for you." She writes,
"It was too dangerous to invite such a stranger in, alone with small
children, but it would have been wrong to send him away.[3] Into her
kitchen she would go to prepare hot coffee, leftover homemade
soup, two thick sandwiches cut into triangles so they would look
nicer, then place everything on a tray with a small flower bouquet
picked by her children in addition to a pocket edition of John's
gospel. The recipients never could believe that this family had made
such a fuss over them, Edith said, people of no account by the wider
world's standards. But Francis and Edith Schaeffer taught their children to care not only for each other, but for those outside their
family as if they were doing it for Jesus Himself. She says that doing
for others even provided for her "a kind of outlet for (my own) creativity," the "opportunity to do something directly for the Lord, with
love of Him uppermost."[4]

Francis eventually sensed God's leading to "a higher level of
giving, working, and sacrifice," and he took his thoughts to his wife

and children because it would have to be a "family commitment."[5] Catherine Marshall wrote of them, "As the spiritual head of his home, Francis Schaeffer laid out before his wife Edith and their children all the alternatives. The decision was unanimous—they would say yes to God's call."[6] As a result, this Christian family moved to Switzerland and they established the legendary L'Abri community where they used their gifts of hospitality and teaching to minister to those seeking God, "to exhibit in some poor fashion the love of God and the holiness of God simultaneously in the whole of life."[7]

Whether a Christian family is known to many or few, certain distinctions ought to characterize it, among them a spirit of deference and sacrifice as they follow Paul's admonition to "be imitators of God" . . . and "dearly loved children (who) live a life of love, just as Christ loved us and gave himself up for us as a fragrant offering and sacrifice to God" (Ephesians 5:1–2). Families under His lordship should "show proper respect to everyone" (1 Peter 2:17a) as they stand in His grace (Romans 5:2) and learn to deal with each other's broken places. They "spur one another on toward love and good deeds" (Hebrews 10:24), helping develop each other's faith, character, and giftedness. Crowning their life together is the kind of giving, empathic, other-oriented love of which Paul wrote in 1 Corinthians 12, what he called "the most excellent way." Such love always protects, always trusts, always hopes, always perseveres. It never fails. (1 Corinthians 13:7–8a)

That is the essence of the Christian model. So how does a family follow it, reflecting the love of the Savior?

FIRST COMES LOVE

In the Mitford series by author Jan Karon, the orderly world of bachelor Episcopal priest Timothy Kavanagh faces total disruption when Cynthia Coppersmith moves next door to the parsonage. As they develop a deep friendship, they must come to terms with the prospect of love and marriage, and Cynthia, a children's book author, addresses the issue of physical intimacy. At that time she is actually far away from Mitford, North Carolina, in Manhattan, working to complete her latest book. In a letter to Father Tim, she invites him to visit, saying,

> You would have lots of privacy, for this is a very large apart-
> ment—and I promise I will not seduce you. Since we've never
> discussed it, I want to say that I really do believe in doing things
> the old-fashioned way when it comes to love. I do love you very
> dearly and want everything to be right and simple and good,
> and yes, pleasing to God. This is why I'm willing to wait for the
> kind of intimacy that most people favor having as soon as
> they've shaken hands.[8]

Father Tim responds, "It is amazing that you and I share the same ideal for sexual intimacy, which, needless to say, the world finds exceedingly outdated."[9]

This exchange demonstrates how single Christian women and men who honor the Lord are swimming upstream. The truth is that it has never been easy for people to follow Christ. Kari Torjesen Malcolm writes, "At every point in history the church is and has been caught in the tension between Christianity and culture. Jesus faced this problem as much as we do, for he was 'tempted in every way, just as we are' (Hebrews 4:15). The example of Jesus challenges us not to conform to culture or go against it, but to transform it."[10] Elisabeth Elliot concurs: "In the Christian community it's always been a temptation from the time of the New Testament to be con-formed to the world."[11]

As a college student at Wheaton, Elliot lived in the post–World War II years when the overall culture emphasized the importance of virginity. She writes, "A woman knew that she possessed a price-less treasure, her virginity. She guarded it jealously for the man who would pay a price for it—commitment to marriage with her and her alone."[12] Although that part was clear, she wondered how to follow Christ's pattern, not the world's, for finding a mate since the culture did emphasize "falling in love," the supremacy of romantic feelings over thoughtful choices, and heavy-duty kissing.

During her junior year, Elizabeth Howard became acquainted with Jim Elliot, her brother Dave's friend, a young man who was a leader in the Foreign Missions Fellowship and a standout wrestler. When Elliot came home with them for the Christmas holidays Elisabeth says, "The more Jim talked, the more I saw that he fitted the picture of what I hoped for in a husband . . . he loved God. That was the supreme dynamic of his life. Nothing else mattered much by comparison."[13] Slowly, the two became close friends whose admiration blossomed into full-fledged love, but the timing wasn't right for them to become a couple, she says, because they weren't ready for marriage. It was, rather, a time to concentrate on their respective training for the mission field; in fact, they weren't even certain if God meant them to marry at all, that they might be called to remain single in His service. During the following five years, they experienced a spiritual "sifting" individually in their walk with Christ, as well as in their relationship. They guarded closely any physical expressions when they were together out of a desire for holiness, personal purity, and mutual respect; they didn't want to cause each other to stumble.

Elliot has handed down what they learned, timeless principles, in her book *Passion and Purity*, where she emphasizes that her celibate singleness was not a matter of grinning and bearing it. "Real holiness can't possibly be miserable and long-faced," she says. "*Holiness* means 'wholeness.' Comes from the same root as *hale*—you know, hale and hearty. Healthy. Fulfilled."[14] She depended on God's promise in Psalm 32:8–11 (NEB):

> I will teach you, and guide you in the way you should go. I will keep you under my eye. Do not behave like horse or mule, unreasoning creatures, whose course must be checked with bit and bridle. Many are the torments of the ungodly; but unfailing love enfolds him who trusts in the Lord. Rejoice in the Lord and be glad.

Elliot's "chief concern" for today's single Christians is that they "consider the authority of Christ over human passion and set their hearts on purity."[15] She understands, of course, that "purity comes at a high price."[16] We do not live among a people that values innocence above infatuation. Sex is "commonplace," she observes, and it becomes, therefore, "dull and a bore."

It's available anywhere, everywhere, to everybody who is looking for it. Nothing is kept in reserve. No pleasures are saved for the wedding night, let alone for the bride and groom exclusively. Friends who run a honeymoon resort . . . have told me that they must announce new activities and recreation at every meal. "We don't want them to get bored and leave. You see, they've had it all before the honeymoon."[17]

Elliot encourages the unmarried not to "be among the marked-down goods on the bargain table, cheap because they'd been pawed over. Crowds collect there. It is only the few who will pay full price."[18] Similarly, she believes that

unless a man is prepared to ask a woman to be his wife, what right has he to claim her exclusive attention? Unless she has been asked to marry him, why would a sensible woman promise any man her exclusive attention? If, when the time has come for a commitment, he is not man enough to ask her to marry him, she should give him no reason to presume that she belongs to him.[19]

Shortly after presidential candidate John McCain named Alaska Governor Sarah Palin his running mate, she disclosed that her teenage daughter had become pregnant. A staunch pro-life and abstinence advocate, Palin was the recipient of nasty comments from critics who charged, "No one can bridle youthful passion." "If you have to teach abstinence at all, at least give them a condom just in case!" Ours is a culture that assumes young men and women cannot control themselves, that dating, hooking up, and living together are the best ways to advance toward marriage or cohabitation. Joshua Harris says, "The world takes us to a silver screen on which flickering images of passion and romance play, and as we watch, the world says, 'This is love.' God takes us to the foot of a tree on which a naked and bloodied man hangs and says, '*This* is love.'"[20]

As a young man dedicated to Christ, Harris decided that the dating scene, even among many Christians, emphasized "the fulfillment of self," but he chose to seek "the glory of God and the good of others."[21] He resists the notion that love is something people can't control, that it is all based on feelings and whims that can change abruptly. Rather, love doesn't make us "behave irresponsibly"; instead it seeks the highest and best for the beloved, as well as God's glory.[22]

In his journey, Harris discovered a major principle that became the cornerstone of his bestselling book *I Kissed Dating Good-Bye*, that "intimacy costs commitment. If I'm not in a position to pay in the cold, hard cash of commitment, I have no business going shopping for my future mate."[23] He determined to spend "the season before marriage preparing to be a godly . . . husband," a young man who regarded singleness as "an unparalleled opportunity for undistracted devotion to God."[24]

Harris urges single Christian men, instead of "acting like hunters" or thieves with girls, to see themselves "as warriors standing guard over them."[25] In the same way, he advises women to "keep your brothers from being led astray by (the wayward woman's— Proverbs 7:26) charms. Please be aware," he says, "how easily your actions and glances can stir up lust in a guy's mind."[26] He promotes "biblical friendships" between the sexes, as opposed to dating in the contemporary sense, to spur each other to godliness.[27] Romans 12:10 says, "Be devoted to one another in brotherly love. Honor one another above yourselves."

Many people have asked Harris, if dating doesn't prepare people for marriage, what does? Like Elliot, he sees the single years as a season of preparation and training. "I believe that God has given me a mother and a sister in order to practice understanding and honoring women," he writes. "If I can't love and serve my mother and sister today, what makes me think I'll be ready to love and serve a wife in the future?"[28] Elliot also says that other, often older, Christians, can play a key role in helping singles prepare for marriage, as well as to introduce them to prospective mates. "God's purpose from the very beginning, I believe, is that . . . wise people, somebody else should have a part in bringing two people together . . . to make young people available to each other."[29] She asserts that young people do well to gather in the homes of established Christian couples, in service to the church, and in group activities where they can observe one another and get to know each other better in a more relaxed setting than the often artificial ambience of dating.

THEN COMES MARRIAGE

Former Asbury College President Dennis Kinlaw has written of God's relationship with humans: "Our story began with the wedding of Adam and Eve, and it ends with the marriage supper of the Lamb."[30] He believes the Bible uses marriage, the most intimate of all relationships, "as a symbol of that greater, deeper, and more intimate relationship we are to have with God." In fact, he says, "Human marriage, human parenthood, and childhood are all metaphors of that other eternal relationship."[31] What, then, does marriage look like in God's eyes? Genesis 1:26–28 says that at creation, God made humans in His own image, male and female, and that He designed the woman to be a partner suitable for the man. Together they were to be, according to the Reverend Stan Key, "One man. One woman. In a holy covenant of love that excludes all rivals. For life."[32] Theirs was to be an "other-oriented" love, a relationship whose source could only be God Himself, the Giver, of life both here and hereafter.[33] Key says, "God's design is that our deepest longings for companionship will be met in the male-female intimacy made possible in the covenant of marriage."[34]

Of course, human history took a bad turn when Adam and Eve

violated the trust that God had established between them, and since then, couples have had to deal with the consequences of the fall. God did not abandon the first couple to their sin, however. Instead, He promised to send One who would crush their enemy and restore that which had been broken (see Genesis 3:15). So intimate would be the bond between Christ and those He rescued that it would be like marriage. His church, composed of His followers, would be His bride, and at the end of history, there would be a wedding so fabulous that it would render the most elaborate human affair downright shabby. Key says, "All human history will culminate in that glorious celebration of love. God's intent is that every human wedding on earth would be a prefiguring of *that* ultimate and final wedding."[35]

In the meantime, God calls His people to live differently. A common image of marriage is that a man and woman enter it in raptures of romantic zeal (or resigned boredom), children come (if they aren't there already), and the couple gets caught up in the never-ending press of careers, housework, and child rearing activities. The spark flickers, then fades; they get on each other's nerves. They resemble a couple in a teaser for a TV show in which the husband told his spouse he wasn't comfortable with something she was about to do. She answers quietly, "I had no idea you felt that way." As the man begins to relax over her placid response, her demeanor abruptly shifts, and she sneers, "Now that we had that flashback to the 50s, get out of my face!"[36] Christians, however, understand that according to God's design, marriage isn't about "making me happy"; rather, through the everydayness of it, partners help each other become more Christlike as the Holy Spirit enables them to imitate His spirit of devotion, loyalty, honor, and sacrifice. That is what marital love is all about. Edith Schaeffer says, "Love isn't just a kind of soft feeling. . . . Love isn't just happines in ideal situations with everything going according to daydreams of family life or married life or parent-child closeness and confidences. Love has *work* to do! Hard and sacrificial work."[37] She goes on to say that while human love will never be perfect this side of eternity, "it is meant to be worked at through the years, and it is meant to portray something within the family of the love of God for His Family. Family . . . (is a) formation center for human relationships—worth fighting for, worth calling a career, worth the dignity of hard work."[38]

In the husband-wife connection, "love is the basic ingredient,"[39] love that Paul discusses in 1 Corinthians 13—it exhibits qualities of character that are unattainable apart from God's transforming work—patience with each other's faults, lack of envy or competition, a curbing of the tongue when rudeness or sarcasm seem the best option, a refusal to gloat over our spouse's stumblings, a willingness to put the other person first. Rather than trying to get the best of them, we strive to bring out the best *in* them. That kind of love develops over time, within the exclusive permanency of marriage. Those relationships "do not just spring up without someone working at it, someone who is not putting himself or herself first," says Schaeffer.[40] She appeals to women to set aside the world's entreaty "to have 'time to be themselves' or 'time for fulfilling careers,'" believing that this message is "overworked."[41] Instead, she urges Christian women to find joy, even satisfaction, in the things that the rest of society considers unimportant, mundane, even a threat to the condition of women. In her own life, Schaeffer used such commonplace tasks as cooking and serving meals to enhance her family's lives and in so doing, found personal pleasure as well. She considered her work as vital and as significant any career. She says,

> Being challenged by what a difference her cooking and her way of serving is going to make in the family life gives a woman an opportunity to approach this with the feeling of painting a picture or writing a symphony. To blend together a family group, to help human beings of five, ten, fifteen and sixty years of age to live in communication with each other and to develop into a "family unit" with constantly growing appreciation of each other and of the "unit" by really working at it, in many different areas, but among others in the area of food preparation, is to do that which surely can compare with blending oils in a painting or writing notes for a symphony. The cook in the home has the

opportunity to be doing something very real in the area of making good human relationships.[42]

Feminists have portrayed family life so very differently, as a place of captivity, but the result is that many women have ended up serving a different "master," when the workplace becomes an idol. But in discovering one's identity first and foremost in Christ, says Kari Torjesen Malcolm, a woman finds the key to herself. A few generations ago, the culture said identity came from husbands and children. Now it says, "Careers!" However,

> if women search for their identity in roles, they make idols of those roles, of their careers, their homes, their children or husbands. None of these things and none of these roles can given women what they are searching for. It is only on the narrow path up the mountain, only in a first-love relationship with Jesus Christ that a woman will find what she seeks.[43]

She also rejects the idea that a wife serves her husband first, then God, and the man serves God for both of them, believing that "such a patriarchal pattern becomes dangerous when submission to this system replaces submission to the lordship of Christ."[44] Ephesians 5:21 calls on husbands and wives to "submit to one another out of reverence for Christ." Paul doesn't just require the woman to yield to her husband, but "husbands to be servants of their wives as Christ was a servant to the church in the act of washing the disciples' feet," Malcolm says.[45] Furthermore, "Paul wants the love of husbands for their wives to be as untarnished as Christ's love for the church."[46] A husband's primary responsibility is to love his wife in such a way as to promote her holiness, the well-being of her very soul (Ephesians 5:25–27).

In following this radically different way of loving, husbands and wives hold their marriages in honor (Hebrews 13:4), put off their old selves (Ephesians 4:22–24), honor each other (Romans 12:10), and love as sacrificially as God loves us (1 John 4:10–11). Francis Foulkes has said, "Love that is totally unselfish . . . that strives for the high-est good of the one loved . . . has as its standard and model the love of Christ for his church. 'It means not only a practical concern for the welfare of the other, but a continual readiness to subordinate one's own pleasure and advantage for the benefit of the other.' "[47] As Joshua Harris puts it, "God wants to use the fire of marriage not only to comfort us, but also to refine and cleanse us from our self-ishness and sin."[48]

One of the finest examples of that kind of love is found in the story of Dr. J. Robertson McQuilkin, who became president of Columbia International University in 1968 and served it, along with his wife, Muriel, for many years. In the late 1980s, Mrs. McQuilkin developed Alzheimer's, and her condition steadily deteriorated until it began to affect her husband's work. McQuilkin decided to resign from his duties to assume her full-time care, and his announce-ment to the CIU community has rung ever since with the profound clarity of biblical love. He explained that when he was with Muriel, she seemed "almost happy," but whenever he was not there, she became deeply fearful, so his choice to resign and take care of her was "simple and clear."[49]

He continued:

> It's not only that I promised "in sickness and in health, 'til death do us part," and I'm a man of my word. But . . . it's the only fair thing. She sacrificed for me for forty years to make my life pos-sible. . . so if I cared for her for forty years, I'd still be in her debt. However, there's much more. It's not that I *have to* but that I *get to*. I love her very dearly. She's a delight. And it's a great honor to care for such a wonderful person.[50]

THEN COMES THE BABY CARRIAGE

Children are a blessing from God, and those who enjoy bring-ing them up to godly manhood or womanhood have both a great responsibility as well as a wonderful privilege. Our culture gives a far more ambivalent message; it's okay to destroy the life of an unborn child if he or she might "burden" the parents, and even when a child does come into the world, he or she must not interfere with the mother or father's career—especially not the mother's. It is preferable, therefore, to remove a child from the home as early in life as possible and let the "village" take over. Once again, however, Christian families are not to follow the pattern of this world.

James Dobson speaks a lot about the impact of the laissez-faire parenting that the rest of American society has advocated since the 1950s, how it teaches children that they are in charge and fosters a consequent spirit of disrespect and rebellion. The Bible is clear that parents are to be in authority over their children, that little ones are to "obey your parents in the Lord, for this is right. 'Honor your father and mother'—which is the first commandment with a promise—'that it may go well with you and that you may enjoy long life on the earth'" (Ephesians 6:1–3). As children keep their father's commands and obey their mother's teaching (Proverbs 6:20), they learn to function within a caring, protective, loving environment, and they discover that they belong to a family, including to the God who created them for a specific and good purpose. Careful discipline teaches children that God holds them accountable for their actions, that they are not in this world for themselves. It enables children to harness the sin that infects the soul of every human, to learn empathy, self-control, boundaries, and confidence.

On the other hand, parents also need to maintain their own self-control when they discipline their children and to rein in any impulse simply to dominate—they are not to be dictators but shepherds. Nor are they to exasperate or cause their children to become disheartened (Ephesians 6:4; Colossians 3:21), but to provide encouragement and a steady presence that provides a safe place for children to discover their uniqueness.

Christian parenthood reflects the fatherhood of God toward His children—"How great is the love the Father has lavished on us, that we should be called children of God! And that is what we are!" (1 John 3:1a). Dennis Kinlaw says, "What a great thing it is to know that, behind all the perplexing processes of the universe, there is our Father. When the early Christians formally declared their belief in God, the first thing they said was, 'I believe in the Father.'"[51] Even as parents strive to reflect the Father's model of loving, guiding, and disciplining to their children, the effort will not be flawless; we cannot expect perfection. Edith Schaeffer says, "Children should learn very early that we are all sinners and we all fall into times of misbehaving."[52] As families grow together, they create a "place where loyalty, dependability, trustworthiness, compassion, sensitivity to others, thoughtfulness, and unselfishness are supposed to have their roots."[53]

Families need time together to foster the kind of environment in which true love can develop; that requires far more of parents than society's mantra of "quality time." It means, according to Shaeffer,

> the comfort of a little pot of tea, some cookies or toast, or a cup of coffee and some cheese and crackers, or a glass of milk and some fruit—just when (someone) was feeling "down" in the midst of a project—then knows how to do those same things for someone else. A family is the place where this kind of care should be so frequently given that it becomes natural to think of the needs of other people.[54]

Christian parents also need to be mindful that their job is to teach their children how to follow God's plan for their lives, and to be prepared for that plan not necessarily to conform to what they might desire. Dennis Kinlaw tells the story of E. Stanley Jones, who in college felt called to become a missionary. He wrote to his mother about it, and she objected—she was alone, a widow, why would God take away her son, whom she expected to take care of her? Jones persisted, although the conflict tore at his heart, and he told her, "Mother, it is not that I love you less. It is simply that I must put Christ first. He will not release me from the call that He has placed upon my life."[55] She accused him of being unfaithful to her, but slowly she came around and repented of putting her trust more in her son than in God. Much later in his life Jones wrote, "I honored my mother on that occasion, even though I disobeyed her, because there is One higher than an earthly parent. That is the true Parent, God the Father. I had to obey Him."[56]

OUTLANDISH ODDITIES

In his comments on 1 Corinthians 13, Joshua Harris says that Paul wrote his masterpiece about the Christian version of love in a place that had "elevated sex to a religious pursuit."[57] He compared the apostle's correspondence to having a contemporary believer write "a letter on family values to Hollywood."[58] Living in ways that go against cultural norms has always challenged those who follow a scriptural pattern for life, for marriage, and for family. History bears witness to this, as far back as the fifth century A.D., a time when, according to Thomas Cahill, the world of "reasonable men . . . was finished."[59] Not unlike the impressive United States of America for most of its history, the Roman Empire was huge, prosperous, and exerted great influence on the rest of the world. "That Rome should ever fall was unthinkable to Romans: its foundations were unassailable, sturdily sunk in a storied past and steadily built on for eleven centuries and more."[60]

Cahill says that "for many decades (Romans) scarcely noticed what was happening."[61] And yet, it began a period of steady decline around the period when killing Christians in the arena became a national pastime. At the point when the Visigoth King Alaric sacked the imperial city itself in 410, the Romans had lost everything, "titles, property, way of life, learning—especially learning. A world in chaos is not a world in which books are copied and libraries maintained."[62]

In the aftermath of the devastation, male and female Irish monastic communities sprang up in the far reaches of the Western world, just beyond the empire's boundaries, where Christians created learning centers that they flung open to all people. In them, scribes copied surviving classical manuscripts, along with sacred texts. Shortly after the death of St. Patrick, "all the great continental libraries had vanished . . . (and) Ireland, at peace and furiously copying, thus stood in the position of becoming Europe's publisher."[63] Realizing the decimated state of Europe, many Irish monks traveled there to spread God's Word and shed His light. Cahill says, without them "there would have perished in the west not only literacy but all the habits of mind that encourage thought. And when Islam began its medieval expansion, it would have encountered scant resistance to its plans—just scattered tribes of animists, ready for a new identity."[64]

Cahill paints a colorful picture of those intrepid people, with "books, many unseen in Europe for centuries . . . tied to their waists as signs of triumph . . . In the bays and alleys of their exile, they reestablished literacy and breathed new life into the exhausted literary culture of Europe. And that," he concludes, "is how the Irish saved civilization."[65] It would never have occurred to the proud Romans, he says, "that the building blocks of their world would be saved by outlandish oddities from a land so marginal that the Romans had not bothered to conquer it," but without the Church, "European civilization would have been impossible."[66]

HOW THE SAINTS SAVE CIVILIZATION

Joshua Harris writes, "In the midst of the harangue from the world, God's quiet message of true love still speaks to those who choose to listen."[67] The 1 Corinthians 13 way of sacrificial love, so beautifully expressed in the everydayness of family life, has prevailed through all the ages. It is timeless—"The grass withers and the flowers fall, but the word of our God stands forever" (Isaiah 40:8)—while Rome and Corinth belong to the ash heap of history.

According to Thomas Cahill, "If our (present) civilization is to be saved—forget about our civilization, which as (St.) Patrick would say, may pass 'in a moment like a cloud or smoke that is scattered by the wind'—if we are to be saved, it will not be by Romans but by saints."[68]

Notes

Introduction: State of the Union

1. Julie Jordan, "First Look: Ellen and Portia's Wedding Album," *People*, August 19, 2008, http://www.people.com/people/article/0,,20220057,00.html.

2. "Lindsay Lohan Finally Admits Gay Love Affair With Samantha Ronson," *Daily Mirror*, July 7, 2008, http://www.mirror.co.uk/celebs/3am/2008/07/07/lindsay-lohan-finally-admits-gay-love-affair-with-sam-ronson-115875-20635350/.

3. "Clay Aiken Comes Out: 'Yes, I'm Gay,'" *MSNBC*, September 24, 2008, http://www.msnbc.msn.com/id/26859859.

4. "Memorable Quotes for *You've Got Mail* (1998)," *IMDb*, http://www.imdb.com /title/tt0128853/quotes.

5. Wikipedia, "The Bridges of Madison County," http://en.wikipedia.org/w/index. php?title=The_Bridges_of_Madison_County&oldid=232796286.

6. *10 Commandments with Adrian Snell*, DVD, 2005.

7. William Harms, "Marriage Wanes as American Families Enter New Century, University of Chicago Research Shows," University of Chicago News Office, November 24, 1999, http://www-news.uchicago.edu/releases/99/991124.family.shtml.

Chapter One: The English Colonies

1. Lee Miller, *Roanoke: Solving the Mystery of the Lost Colony* (New York: Arcade Publishing, 2001).

2. David B. Quinn and Alison M. Quinn, *The First Colonists: Documents on the Planting of the First English Settlements in North America, 1584–1590* (Raleigh, NC: North Carolina Department of Cultural Resources Division of Archives and History, 1982), 16.

3. John D. Neville for the National Park Service, "Roanoke Revisted, Heritage Revisited Program, The John White Colony," *Fort Raleigh National Historic Site, Manteo*, NC, http://www.nps.gov/fora/forteachers/the-john-white-colony.htm.

4. Peter Marshall and David Manuel, *The Light and the Glory* (Grand Rapids, MI: Fleming H. Revell, 1977), 83.

5. Ibid.

6. Ibid., 84.

7. Gail Collins, *American Women: 400 Years of Dolls, Drudges, Helpmates, and Heroines* (New York: HarperCollins, 2003), 3–4.

8. Charles E. Hatch Jr., *The First Seventeen Years: Virginia, 1607–1624* (Charlottesville, VA: University Press of Virginia, 1957), 7.

9. Ibid., 10.

10. Collins, 6.

11. Ibid., 12–13.

12. Ibid., 15.

13. Ibid.

14. "Women on the Mayflower," Mayflowerhistory.com, www.MayflowerHistory.com /History/women.php.

15. Collins, 24.

16. Wikipedia, "Priscilla Alden," http://en.wikipedia.org/w/index.php?title=Priscilla_ Alden&oldid=262572753.

Chapter Two: "Down the Rivers, o'er the Prairies"

1. James Axtell, ed., *The Indian Peoples of Eastern America: A Documentary History of the Sexes* (New York: Oxford University Press, 1981), 22.

2. Gary B. Nash, *Red, White, and Black* (Englewood Cliffs, NJ: Prentice-Hall, Inc., 1974), 9.

3. Ibid.

4. Ibid., 10.

5. Ibid., 20.

6. Axtell, 7.

7. Nash, 23.

8. Axtell, 35–36.

9. "Native American: Courtship and Marriage," Augustana College Library, Special Collections, "Courtship and Marriage" excerpt from "The Black Hawk Watch Tower" by John Henry Hauberg, Driffill Printing, 1927, 18; John Henry Hauberg papers, MSS 27, box 39, folder 5, http://www.augustana.edu/library/Special Collections/naent.html#e.

10. Axtell, 90.

11. Rebecca Price Janney, *Great Women in American History* (Camp Hill, PA: Horizon-Books, 1996), 182–83.

Chapter Three: For God and Gold

1. L. S. Stavrianos, *The World Since 1500: A Global History* (Englewood Cliffs, NJ: Prentice Hall, 1988), 411.

2. John Huxtable Elliott, *Empires of the Atlantic World: Britain and Spain in America, 1492–1830* (New Haven, CT: Yale University Press, 2007), 156.

3. Ibid., 82.

4. Ibid.

5. Ibid.

6. Ibid.

7. Rosemary Radford Ruether and Rosemary Skinner Keller, *Women and Religion in America: Volume 2, The Colonial and Revolutionary Periods, A Documentary History* (San Francisco: Harper & Row, 1983), 49.

8. Ibid., 44–45.

9. Ibid., 45.

10. Wikipedia, "Los Angeles Pobladores," http//www.en.wikipedia.org/wiki/Los_Pobladores.

11. "Founding Families of El Pueblo De La Reina Los Angeles, of 1781," Ancestral Heritage Association, http//www.lospobladores.org/archive1.htm#Founding%20Families.

12. Richard M. Ketchum, ed., *American Heritage Illustrated History of the United States: Volume 1, The New World* (Great Neck, NY: Choice Publishing, 1988), 46.

13. Ruether and Keller, 84.

14. Wikipedia, "History of New Orleans," http//www.wikipedia.org/w/index.php?title=History_of_New_Orleans&oldid=260613929.

15. Ibid.

16. "Marie-Therese Bourgeois Chouteau (Madame Chouteau)," *The Lewis and Clark Journey of Discovery, National Park Service*, http://www.nps.gov/archive/jeff/lewisclark2/circa1804/StLouis/BlockInfo/Block33BMadameChouteau.htm.

17. Ketchum, 64.

18. Ibid., 65–66.

Chapter Four: With the Girls Be Handy

1. David Freeman Hawke, *Everyday Life in Early America* (New York: Harper & Row, 1988), 67.

2. Ibid.

3. Ibid., 57.

4. Gail Collins, *American Women: 400 Years of Dolls, Drudges, Helpmates, and Heroines* (New York: HarperCollins, 2003), 60.

5. Ibid., 58.

6. Ibid., 58–59.

7. Hawke, 59.

8. Benjamin Franklin, *The Autobiography of Benjamin Franklin* (New York: The Modern Library, 1981), 7.

9. Hawke, 150.

10. Ibid., 171.

11. Ibid., 168.

12. Collins, 61.

13. Hawke, 72.

14. Ibid.

15. Ibid, 65.

16. Collins, 54.

17. Ibid.

18. Ibid.

19. Ibid.

20. Hawke, 93.

21. Collins, 75.

22. Ibid.

23. Ibid.

24. Ibid., 74.

25. Ibid.

26. Paul F. Boller, *Presidential Wives: An Anecdotal History* (New York: Oxford University Press, 1988), 25.

27. Ibid., 29.

28. Hawke, 129.

29. Collins, 48–49.

30. Hawke, 68.

31. Collins, 51.

32. Ibid., 64.

33. Ibid.

34. Ibid., 71.

35. Cokie Roberts, *Founding Mothers: The Women Who Raised Our Nation* (New York: William Morrow, 2004), 25.

36. Ibid., 36.

37. Ibid.

38. Ibid.

39. Rebecca Price Janney, *Great Women in American History* (Camp Hill, PA: Horizon Books, 1996) 7–8.

40. Ibid., 8.

41. Roberts, 84.

42. Boller, 19.

43. Ibid., 15.

44. Ibid., 34.

45. Ibid.

46. Edwin Morris Betts and James Adam Bear Jr., *The Family Letters of Thomas Jefferson* (Charlottesville, VA: The University Press of Virginia, 1966), 5.

47. Ibid., 8.

48. Ibid., 151.

49. Ibid., 10.

50. "Thomas Jefferson and Sally Hemings: A Brief Account," *Monticello Plantation*, www.monticello.org/plantation/hemingscontro/hemings-jefferson_contro.html.

51. Ibid.

52. Collins, 65.

53. Peter Lillback, *George Washington's Sacred Fire* (Bryn Mawr, PA: Providence Forum Press, 2006), 366.

Chapter Five: Jumping the Broom

1. Rebecca Price Janney, *Harriet Tubman* (Minneapolis: Bethany House Publishers, 1999), 234.

2. Ibid., 41.

3. Gail Collins, *Women in America: 400 Years of Dolls, Drudges, Helpmates, and Heroines* (New York: Harper Collins, 2003), 147.

4. Eugene Genovese, *Roll, Jordan Roll: The World the Slaves Made* (New York: Vintage Books, 1976), 469.

5. Collins, 147.

6. Ibid.

7. Ibid.

8. Ibid.

9. Ibid., 154.

10. Gary B. Nash, *Red, White, and Black* (Englewood Cliffs, NJ: Prentice-Hall, Inc., 1974), 210–11.

11. Ibid., 207.

12. Genovese, 464.

13. Ibid., 468.

14. Ibid., 473.

15. Ibid., 474.

16. Collins, 145–46.

17. Genovese, 466.

18. Ibid., 476.

19. Ibid.

20. Ibid., 478.

21. Collins, 150.

22. Ibid.

23. Genovese, 481.

24. Ibid.

25. Ibid.

26. Collins, 150.

27. Ibid., 151.

28. Ibid.

29. Ibid., 153.

30. Ibid., 145.

31. Spartacus Educational, "Slave Marriages," http://www.spartacus.schoolnet.co.uk/USASmarriage.htm.

32. Collins, 145.

33. Ibid.

34. Nash, 208.

35. Ibid., 208–9.

36. Genovese, 415.

37. Ibid., 419.

38. Ibid., 416.

39. Ibid., 428–29.

40. Ibid., 427.

41. Nash, 209.

Chapter Six: The Victorian Ideal

1. James Parton et al, *Eminent Women of the Age* (Hartford, CT: S. M. Betts & Co., 1869), 415.

2. Ibid., 43–31.

3. Ibid, 431.

4. Wikipedia, "Victorian Morality," http://en.wikipedia.org/w/index.php?title=Victorian_morality&oldid=267202061.

5. Ibid.

6. Ibid.

7. Ibid.

8. Eugene D. Genovese, *Roll, Jordan, Roll: The World the Slaves Made* (New York: Vintage, 1976), 424.

9. Wikipedia, "Victorian America,"   http://www.en.wikipedia.org/w/index.php?title=Victorian_America&oldid+274979008.

10. Lisa Niles, "Sarah Josepha Hale," University of Central Oklahoma, http://www.womenwriters.net/domesticgoddess/hale1.html, 03.

11. Ibid.

12. Ibid.

13. Melissa Moore, "Women's History Then and Now: A Feminist Overview of the Last 2 Centuries; Marriage," http://www.cwrl.utexas.edu~ulrich/femhist/marriage.shtml.

14. Joan D. Hedrick, *Harriet Beecher Stowe: A Life.* (New York: Oxford University Press, 1994), 374.

15. Nancy Rosin, "Victoriana: Collecting Victorian Expressions of Love," http://www.Victoriana.com/Valentines/expressionsoflove.htm, 07.

16. Ibid.

17. Ibid.

18. Ibid.

19. Heather Palmer, "Dating in the Victorian Age: 'The Unsuitable Suitor of 1879,'" http://www.Victoriana.com/library/suitor.html.

20. Ibid.

21. Hedrick, 372.

22. "Familiarities Among Relations," http://www.Victoriana.com/library/doors /cousins.html.

23. Ibid.

24. Ibid.

25. Moore, ibid.

26. Moore, ibid.

27. Ibid.

28. Hedrick, 196.

29. Wikipedia, "Victorian Literature," http://www.wikipedia.org/wiki/Victorian_ Literature.

30. www.victoriaspast.com/ChildrenofVicParents/revisitthepast.html.

31. Ibid.

32. Wikipedia, "Victorian Literature," ibid.

33. Ibid.

Chapter Seven: Extreme Makeovers

1. Sydney E. Ahlstrom, *A Religious History of the American People* (New Haven, CT and London: Yale University Press, 1972), 491.

2. Ibid.

3. Ibid.

4. J. C. Furnas, *The Americans: A Social History of the United States, 1587–1914* (New York: G.P. Putnam's Sons, 1969), 495.

5. Ahlstrom, 492.

6. Ibid., 494.

7. Furnas, 497.

8. Raymond Lee Muncy, *Sex and Marriage in Utopian Communities* (Baltimore: Penguin Books, Inc., 1973), 19–20.

9. Furnas, 497.

10. Ibid., 499.

11. Ibid., 497.

12. Ahlstrom, 495.

13. Muncy, 33.

14. Rebecca Price Janney, *Who Goes There? A Cultural History of Heaven and Hell* (Chicago: Moody Publishers, 2009), 62.

15. Muncy, 198.

16. Connie King, "Portraits of American Women Writers That Appeared in Print Before 1861, Frances Wright," http//:www.librarycompany.org/women/ portraits/wright.htm, 05.

17. Wikipedia, "Joseph Smith, Jr.," http://en.wikipedia.org/wiki/Joseph_Smith,_Jr.

18. Muncy, 122.

19. Vern Anderson, *Salt Lake Tribune, The Associated Press*, 12.13.97, Page C1, untitled, http://www.lds.-mormon.com/12117.shtml.

20. *The More Good Foundation*, "Temple of the Church of Jesus Christ of Latter-day

Saints, 'Mormon Celestial Marriage,'" http://www.ldschurchtemples.com /mormon/marriage/.

21. Ibid.

22. Ibid.

23. Todd Compton, *In Sacred Loneliness: The Plural Wives of Joseph Smith*-Book review, http://www.lds.-mormon.com/isl.shtml.

24. Ibid.

25. Ibid.

26. Marlyn Klee-Hartzell, "'Mingling the Sexes': The Gendered Organization of Work at the Oneida Community," http://libwww.syr.edu/digital/collections/c/ Courier/#Klee.

27. Muncy, 160.

28. Ibid., 162.

29. Ibid., 167.

30. Ahlstrom, 499.

31. Muncy, 167.

32. Randall Hillebrand, "The Oneida Community," New York History Net, http://www. nyhistory.com/central/oneida.htm.

33. Muncy, 175.

34. Ibid.

35. Ibid., 178.

36. Wikipedia, "Oneida Community," http://en.wikipedia.org/wiki/Oneida_Community, March 8, 2009.

37. Ibid.

Chapter Eight: Of Bloomers and Revivalists

1. Kary Torjesen Malcolm, *Women at the Crossroads* (Downers Grove, IL: InterVarsity Press, 1982), 120–21.

2. Rebecca Price Janney, *Great Women in American History* (Camp Hill, PA: Horizon Books, 1996), 211.

3. Joan D. Hedrick, *Harriet Beecher Stowe: A Life* (New York: Oxford University Press, 1994), 196.

4. John A. Garraty and Robert A. McCaughey, *The American Nation: A History of the United States* (New York: Harper & Row, Publishers, 1987), 308.

5. Janney, *Great Women in American History*, 280.

6. Ibid., 273.

7. Ibid.

8. Rebecca Price Janney, *A Study of How the Role of Women in the American Protestant Church and Society through the Centuries Bears Upon the Faithfulness of Contemporary Evangelical Women*, a doctoral dissertation submitted to the faculty of Biblical Theological Seminary, May, 2000.

9. Nancy Hardesty, *Your Daughters Shall Prophesy: Revivalism and Feminism in the Age of Finney* (Brooklyn: Carlson Publishing, 1991),127.

10. Gail Collins, *Women in America: 400 Years of Dolls, Drudges, Helpmates, and Heroines* (New York: Harper Collins, 2003), 114.

11. Ibid.

12. Ibid.

13. Hardesty, 76.

14. Janney, Dissertation, 83.

15. Hardesty, 76.

16. Ibid.

17. Hardesty, 129–30.

18. Malcolm, 126.

19. J. C. Furnas, *The Americans: A Social History of the United States*, 1587–1914 (New York: G. P. Putnam's Sons, 1969), 492.

20. Ibid., 493.

21. Ibid, 643.

22. Ibid., 644.

23. Ibid.

24. "Charles Dana Gibson and the Gibson Girls," http://www.livelyroots.com /things/gibsongirl.htm.

25. Wikipedia, "Gibson Girl," http://en.wikipedia.org/wiki/Gibson_Girl.

26. Garraty, McCaughey, *The American Nation: A History of the United States*, 728.

Chapter Nine: Beside the Golden Door

1. John A. Garraty and Robert A. McCaughey, *The American Nation: A History of the United States* (New York: Harper & Row, Publishers, 1987), 546.

2. Ibid., 295.

3. Ibid.

4. Ibid.

5. Ibid., 381.

6. Ibid.

7. Ibid., 382.

8. Ibid.

9. Ibid., 384.

10. Ibid., 547.

11. Ibid., 548.

12. J. C. Furnas, *The Americans: A Social History of the United States*, 1587–1914 (New York: G. P. Putnam's Sons, 1969), 492.

13. Ibid.

14. Julie Byrne, "Roman Catholics and Immigration in Nineteenth-Century America," *National Humanities Center*, Department of Religion, Duke University, http:// nationalhumanitiescenter.org/tserve/nineteen/nkeyinfo/nromcath.htm.

15. Ibid.

16. Furnas, 837.

17. Ibid.

18. Byrne, ibid.

19. Ibid.

20. Ibid.

21. Furnas, 843.

22. Ibid., 844.

23. "The Saranoff Family Embraces America," *The Library of Congress, The Memory Learning page*, http://loc.gov/learn///features/timeline/progress/immigrnt/saranoff.html.

24. Ibid.

25. Irving Howe, *World of Our Fathers: The Journey of the East European Jews to America and the Life They Found and Made* (New York: Simon and Schuster, 1976), 171.

26. Ibid.

27. Ibid., 172.

28. Ibid.

29. Ibid., 173.

30. Ibid., 172.

31. Ibid., 173.

32. Ibid.

33. Ibid.

34. Ibid.

35. Ibid.

36. Eloise Paananen and George Tsui, "The Chinese in America," *WorldandI.com— American Waves*, http://www.worldandi.com/subscribers/americanwavesdetail.asp?num=12325.

37. Ibid.

38. Ibid.

Chapter Ten: See the USA

1. John A. Garraty and Robert A. McCaughey, *The American Nation: A History of the United States* (New York: Harper & Row, Publishers, 1987), 249.

2. Janet Davidson and Michael Sweeney, *On the Move: Transportation and the American Story* (Washington, D.C.: The Smithsonian Institute, 2001), 30.

3. Ibid.

4. Robert G. Athearn, *American Heritage Illustrated History of the United States Volume 5: Young America* (New York: Choice Publishing, Inc., 1988), 421.

5. Davidson and Sweeney, 29.

6. Garraty and McCaughey, 300.

7. Ibid.

8. Ibid.

9. Ibid.

10. Athearn, 441.

11. Ibid., 455.

12. Garraty and McCaughey, 389–90, 392.

13. Davidson and Sweeney, 47.

14. Ibid., 48.

15. Ibid., 74.

16. Bonnie Lilienfeld, "Chicago, The Transit Metropolis: The 1890s–1920s: Transit Shapes the City," *National Museum of American History*, http://americanhistory.si.edu/onthemove.themes/story_45_1.html.

17. J. C. Furnas, *The Americans: A Social History of the United States*, 1587–1914 (New York: G. P. Putnam's Sons, 1969), 809.

18. Ibid.

19. Ibid.

20. Ibid., 808.

21. James Kirby Martin, et.al., *A Concise History of America and its People* (New York: HarperCollins College Publishers, 1995), 622.

22. Ibid.

23. Ibid., 621.

24. Ibid.

25. Ibid.

26. Ibid., 622.

27. Davidson and Sweeney, 167.

28. Martin, 622.

29. Ibid.

30. Ibid.

31. Davidson and Sweeney, 167.

32. Ibid., 172.

33. Ibid., 141.

34. Martin, 624.

35. "1955 Ford Country Squire Station Wagon," *Smithsonian National Museum of American History*, Kenneth E. Behring Center, http://americanhistory.si.edu/collections/object.cfm?key=35&objkey=167.

36. Ibid.

37. Inga Saffron, "Changing Skyline: Modernist Gems of the Northeast," *The Philadelphia Inquirer*, E1, April 24, 2009.

38. Samuel Eliot Morison and Henry Steele Commager, *The Growth of the American Republic, Vol. 1* (New York: Oxford University Press, 1962), 921.

39. Ibid.

40. Ibid., 925.

41. Ibid., 928.

42. Ibid., 929.

Chapter Eleven: Through The Darkness of The Night

1. Rebecca Price Janney, *Great Stories in American History* (Camp Hill, PA: Horizon Books, 1998), 112.

2. Sydney E. Ahlstrom, *A Religious History of the American People* (New Haven, CT and London: Yale University Press, 1972), 881.

3. Ibid.

4. Leon F. Litwack, Winthrop D. Jordan, et al., *The United States: Becoming a World Power*, vol. II (Englewood Cliffs, NJ: Prentice-Hall, Inc., 1987), 579.

5. Woodrow Wilson, Address to the Senate, September 30, 1918, http://www.public.iastate.edu/~aslagell/SpCm416/WoodrowWilsonsuff.html.

6. "WWI Patriotism, Politics and Women," *Something About Everything Military*, http://www.jcs-group.com/military/ushome/1917patriotism.html.

7. Ibid.

8. Litwack and Jordan, 583.

9. Ibid., 581.

10. John Mack Faragher, Mari Jo Buhle, Daniel Czitrom, Susan H. Armitage, *Out of Many: A History of the American People* (Englewood Cliffs, NJ: Prentice Hall, 1995), 465.

11. Ibid., 466.

12. Ibid.

13. Ahlstrom, 920.

14. Ibid.

15. Ibid.

16. Digital History, "Explorations: Children and the Great Depression," http://www.digitalhistory.uh.edu/learning_history/children_depression/depression_children_menu.cfm.

17. Ibid.

18. "Everyday Life During the Great Depression," *The Great Depression*, http://drake.marin.k12.ca.us/academics/comacad/decades%2000/1930s/The%Great%20.

19. Ibid.

20. Faragher et.al. 473.

21. Litwack and Jordan, 638.

22. Ibid., 645.

23. "Great Depression," *Britannica Online Encyclopedia*, http://www.britannica.com/Ebchecked/topic/243118/Great-Depression.

24. Litwack and Jordan, 675.

25. Stanley K. Schultz, "World War II: The Impact at Home," University of Wisconsin-Madison, American History 102: Civil War to the Present, http://us.history.wisc.edu/hist102/lectures/lecture21.html.

26. Litwack and Jordan, 678.

27. Ibid.

28. Ibid., 679.

29. William H. Chafe, *The Paradox of Change: American Women in the 20th Century* (New York: Oxford University Press, 1991), 130.

30. Ibid.

31. Ibid.

32. Ibid.

33. Ibid., 131.

34. Ibid., 142.

35. Ibid.

36. Ibid.

37. Ibid.

38. Ibid., 133.

39. Ibid.

40. Litwack and Jordan, 679.

Chapter Twelve: Planet Hollywood

1. Leon F. Litwack, Winthrop D. Jordan, et al., *The United States: Becoming a World Power*, vol. II (Englewood Cliffs, NJ: Prentice-Hall, Inc., 1987), 611.

2. Wikipedia, "Cinema of the United States," http://en.wikipedia.org/wiki/Cinema_of_the_United_States.

3. Tim Dirks, "Sexual or Erotic Films," *AMC Filmsite*, http://www.filmsite.org/sexual-films.html.

4. Ibid.

5. Ibid.

6. Litwack and Jordan, 612.

7. John Mack Faragher, Mari Jo Buhle, Daniel Czitrom, Susan H. Armitage, *Out of Many: A History of the American People* (Englewood Cliffs, NJ: Prentice Hall, 1995), 447.

8. Ibid., 448.

9. Ibid.

10. Ibid.

11. "Morality Clause for Films; Universal Will Cancel Engagements of Actors Who Forfeit Respect," September 22, 1921, Pg. 8, *The New York Times*, http://query.nytimes.com/gst/astract.html?res=9A02E0DC123EEE3ABC4A51DFBF66838A639EDE.

12. Litwack and Jordan, 612.

13. Dirks, ibid.

14. Ibid.

15. Ibid.

16. Ibid.

17. Ibid.

18. Ibid.

19. Ibid.

20. Wikipedia, "Cinema of the United States," ibid.

21. "Motion Picture Production Code," http://en.wikipedia.org/wiki/Hays_Code.

22. Ibid.

23. Ibid.

24. Ibid.

25. "Religions Legion of Decency," Monday, June 11, 1934, *Time.com*, http://www.time.com/time/magazine/article/0,9171,762190-1,00.html.

26. "National Legion of Decency," http://en.wikipedia.org/wiki/National_Legion_of_Decency.

27. Ibid.

28. Ibid.

29. "Cinema of the United States," ibid.

30. Ibid.

31. Litwack and Jordan, 615.

32. "The Payne Fund Studies," http://www.angelfire.com/journal/worldtour99/payne fund.html.

33. Ibid.

34. Ibid.

35. Ibid.

36. "American Films About Children Before World War II," *children+apos;sFilms* http://www.film reference.com/encyclopedia/Academy-Awards-Crime-Films/Children-s-Films= AMERICAN=FILMS=ABOUT=CHILDRENBEFORE=WORLD=WAR=II.html.

37. Ibid.

38. "Shirley Temple," http://en.wikipedia.org/wiki/Shirley_Temple.

39. "American Films About Children," ibid.

40. "Shirley Temple," ibid.

41. Ibid.

42. Kathy Merlock Jackson, E-mail interview with the author, May 18, 2009.

43. Ibid.

44. Ibid.

45. Ibid.

46. Ibid.

47. "Ginger Rogers and Fred Astaire," 'Top Hat,' (1935)," Reel Classics http://www.reel classics.com/Teams/Fred&Ginger/fred&ginger4.htm.

48. Wheeler W. Dixon, *American Cinema of the 1940s: Themes and Variations* (Piscataway, NJ: Rutgers University Press, 2005), 30.

49. Ibid., 29.

50. Jackson, ibid.

51. Tim Dirks e-mail interview with the author, May 13, 2009.

52. Dixon, 73.

53. Samuel Eliot Morison and Henry Steele Commager, *The Growth of the American Republic, Vol. 1* (New York: Oxford University Press, 1962), 658.

Chapter Thirteen: Happy Days: The 1950s

1. Donald Spoto, *Notorious* (New York: DaCapo Press, 2001), 292.

2. Ibid., 293.

3. Wikipedia, "Ingrid Bergman,"' http://en.wikipedia.org/wiki/Ingrid_Bergman.

4. David Halberstam, *The Fifties* (New York: Villard Books, 1993), x.

5. Tom Brokaw, *The Greatest Generation* (New York: Randon House, 1998), inside cover.

6. Ibid., 232.

7. Ibid., 231.

8. Ibid., 231–32.

9. Ibid., 239.

10. Ibid.

11. Halberstam, 134.

12. Ibid.

13. Ibid., 142.

14. Ibid., 140.

15. Doris Kearns Goodwin, *Wait Till Next Year* (New York: Touchstone, 1997), 53.

16. Ibid., 52.

17. Ibid., 20.

18. Peggy Noonan, *Patriotic Grace: What It Is and Why We Need It Now* (New York: Collins, 2008), 103–104.

19. "People & Events: Mrs. America: Women's Roles in the 1950s"; *American Experience, The Pill*, www.pbs.org/wgbh/amex/pill/peopleevents/p_mrs.html.

20. William H. Chafe, *The Paradox of Change: American Women in the 20th Century* (New York: Oxford University Press, 1991), 157.

21. Ibid.

22. "People & Events" ibid.

23. Rebecca Price Janney, *A Study of How the Role of Women in the American Protestant Church and Society through the Centuries Bears Upon the Faithfulness of Contemporary Evangelical Women,* a doctoral dissertation submitted to the faculty of Biblical Theological Seminary, May, 2000, 90.

24. "People & Events," ibid.

25. Ibid.

26. Gail Collins, *American Women: 400 Years of Dolls, Drudges, Helpmates, and Heroines* (New York: HarperCollins, 2003), 404.

27. Ibid.

28. PBS, "The Pill," Ibid.

29. Ibid.

30. The Dr. Spock Company, 2004, "Dr. Benjamin Spock, 1903–1998," http://www.drspock.com/about/drbenjaminspock/0,1781,,00.html.

31. Ibid.

32. Ibid.

33. "Dr. Benjamin Spock Comments on Spanking (1989)," http://www.nospank.net/spock2.htm.

34. Ibid.
35. David Halberstam, *The Fifties* (New York: Villard Books, 1993), 473.
36. Ibid.
37. Ibid., 474.
38. Ibid.
39. Ibid., 475.
40. Ibid., 476.
41. Ibid., 478.
42. Ibid., 479.
43. Ibid., 197.
44. Ibid., 198-99.
45. Ibid.
46. Ibid., 199.
47. Ibid., 200.
48. Ibid.
49. Ibid., center photo pages.
50. Ibid., 508.
51. Ibid., 509.
52. Ibid.
53. Ibid., 509–10.
54. Ibid., 510.
55. Ibid. 511.
56. Ibid., 201.

Chapter Fourteen: Mutiny in the Bounty

1. Wikipedia, "Beatnik," http://en.wikipedia.org/wiki/Beatniks.
2. David Halberstam, *The Fifties* (New York: Villard Books, 1993), 299.
3. Ibid.
4. Ibid.
5. Ibid., 300.
6. Ibid.
7. Ibid., 479.
8. Ibid., 295.
9. Ibid., 301.
10. Wikipedia, ibid.
11. Ibid.
12. Halberstam, 307.
13. Ibid.
14. Ibid.
15. Gail Collins, *American Women: 400 Years of Dolls, Drudges, Helpmates, and Heroines* (New York: HarperCollins, 2003), 410.

16. William H. Chafe, *The Paradox of Change: American Women in the 20th Century* (New York: Oxford University Press, 1991), 196.

17. Ibid, 197.

18. Ibid.

19. Ibid., 196.

20. Collins, 426.

21. Ibid.

22. Ibid., 427.

23. Chafe, 194.

24. Rebecca Price Janney, *A Study of How the Role of Women in the American Protestant Church and Society through the Centuries Bears Upon the Faithfulness of Contemporary Evangelical Women,* a doctoral dissertation submitted to the faculty of Biblical Theological Seminary, May, 2000, 92–93.

25. Chafe, 195.

26. Ibid.

27. Ibid., 196.

28. Ibid., 197.

29. Ibid., 200.

30. Ibid.

31. Ibid., 200.

32. Ibid.

33. Ibid.

34. Collins, 429.

35. Charles R. Morris, *A Time of Passion: America 1960*–1980 (New York: Penguin Books, 1984), 75.

36. Ibid., 82.

37. Ibid., 84.

38. Ibid., 87.

39. Ibid.

40. Ibid., 113.

41. Ibid., 114.

42. Ibid., 128.

43. Collins, 428.

44. Ibid.

45. Ibid.

46. Ibid., 431.

47. Ibid.

48. Ibid., 427.

49. Ibid., 427–28.

50. Charles Schulz, "A Charlie Brown Christmas," United Features Syndicate and Coca Cola for CBS, 1965.

Chapter Fifteen: What's Love Got to Do with It?

1. David Halberstam, *The Fifties* (New York: Villard Books, 1993), 195–96.
2. Ibid., 196.
3. Ibid.
4. Wikipedia, "Smothers Brothers," http://en.wikipedia.org/wiki/Smothers_Brothers.
5. Wikipedia, "Rowan & Martin's Laugh-In," http://en.wikipedia.org/wiki/Rowan_%26 _Martin%27s_Laugh-In.
6. Ibid.
7. Wikipedia, "All in the Family," http://en.wikipedia.org/wiki/All_in_the_Family.
8. Roger Streitmatter quoted in "Madonna" (entertainer)," http://en.wikipedia.org/ wiki/Mdonna_entertainer.

Chapter Sixteen: We Are Family

1. Walter Scott, *Parade*, "Personality Parade," July 12, 2009, 2.
2. William Harms, "Marriages Decline, Divorces Climb as Families Evolve into 21st Century," *The University of Chicago Chronicle*, December 2, 1999, vol. 19, no. 6, http://chronicle.uchicago.edu/991202/families.shtml.
3. "50 Million Children Lived with Married Parents in 2007," July 28, 2008, Tom Edwards, U.S. Census Bureau, http://www.census.gov/Press-Release/www.releases /archives/marital_status_living_arrange. . .
4. Harms, ibid.
5. Ibid.
6. "Marriage Statistics," *Chicagoland Marriage Resource Center*, http://www.chicago landmarriage.org/marriage_statistics.htm.
7. Harms, ibid.
8. Tricia Goyer, *Generation NeXt Marriage: A Couple's Guide to Keeping it Together* (Colorado Springs: Multnomah, 2008), 25.
9. Ibid., 2.
10. Tom Edwards, "Most People Make Only One Trip Down the Aisle, But First Marriages Shorter," *Census Bureau Reports*, September 19, 2007, http://www.census. gov/Press-Release/www/releases/archives/marital_status_living_arrange.
11. "Blended Family Statistics," *Willing Stepfamilies: Helping Blended Families Succeed*, http://www.winningstepfamilies.com/BlendedFamilyStatistics.html.
12. Karen Troccoli, "Modern Love," *Family Circle*, April 11, 2009, 42–44.
13. Ibid.
14. Ibid.
15. Ibid.
16. Ibid.
17. Sherrie Schneider and Ellen Fein, *The Rules*, http://www.therulesbook.com/.
18. Ibid.
19. *"The Rules II," Large Print Reviews, 2001–2009*, http://www.largeprintreviews.com /0446606219.html.
20. Leslie Bennetts, "The New Push for Quality Child Care," *Parade*, July 19, 2009, 4–5.
21. Suzanne Venker, *7 Myths of Working Mothers: Why Children and (Most) Careers*

Just Don't Mix (Dallas: Spence Publishing Company, 2004), 4.

22. Ibid.

23. Meghan Rabbitt, "Juggling Your Kids and Job," August 2009, *Parents*, 98–102.

24. Venker, 76.

25. Ibid., 26, 56.

26. Ibid., 153.

27. Ibid., 162.

28. Edwards, *Census*, ibid.

29. Venker, 159.

30. Ibid., 153.

31. Ibid., 154.

32. Dianne Hales, "Raising Kids in an R-Rated Culture," http://www.parents.com/fun/entertainment/movies/raising-kids-in-an-r-rated-culture.

33. Ibid.

34. Ibid.

35. Ibid.

36. Ibid.

37. "Sex and Media Tips," 2005, Common Sense Media, http://www.commonsensemedia.org/sex-and-media-tips.

38. Ibid.

39. Venker, 100.

40. Ibid., 81, 104.

41. Ibid., 94.

42. Ibid., 75.

43. Ibid., 75–76.

44. Ibid., 80.

45. Ibid., 108.

46. "How Many Abortions Performed Since 1973?" *National Right to Life Political Action Committee*, http://www.nrlc.org/news/2000/NRL02/how.html.

47. Carrie Gordon Earll, "What We Did Not Know: The Aftermath of Thirty Years of Legal Abortion," *Focus on the Family's Issue Analysis*, http://www.citizenlink.org/FOSI/bioethics/abortion/A000001338.cfm.

48. Susan W. Enouen, PE, "Down Syndrome and Abortion," *Physicians For Life.org*, http://www.physiciansforlife.org/content/view/1301/26/.

49. The Mayo Clinic Staff, "Infertility: Definition," *MayoClinic.com*, http://www.mayoclinic.com/health/infertility/ds00310.

50. Marlo Schlesky, e-mail interview with the author, July 17, 2009.

51. Ray Fowler, "Statistics on Living Together Before Marriage," April 18, 2008, *Ray Fowler.org*, http://www.rayfowler.org/2008/04/18/statistics-on-living-together-before-marriage.

52. Michael Foust, "'Living Together' Before Marriage a Statistical Risk," March 26, 2008, *Baptist Press*, http://www.baptistpress.net/bpnews.asp?id=27699.

53. Ibid.

54. Ibid.

55. "Sociological Reasons *Not* to Live Together," from All About Cohabitating Before Marriage, *Leadership U*, http://www.leaderu.com/critical/cohabitation-socio.html.

56. Ibid.

57. Ibid.

58. Ibid.

59. Arianne Cohen, "Two Women, Two Babies, One Family," *Real Simple*, http://www.realsimple.com/worl-life/family/kids-parentings/two-women-two-babies-one-family=00000000012723/index.html.

60. "Don't Ruin My Gay Wedding," *Tyra*, June 24, 2009.

61. Mikaya Heart, "Gay or Not, Marriage Limiting," *The Philadelphia Inquirer,* June 7, 2009, C5.

62. Ibid.

63. Venker, 149.

64. Ibid., 141.

65. Ibid.

Chapter Seventeen: Follow the Leader

1. Janet Porter, "Anita Bryant Was Right," *WorldNetDaily*, March 11, 2008, http://www.wnd.com/index.php?fa=PAGE.view=pageId58600.

2. Ibid.

3. Sylvia Dooling, e-mail interview with the author, August 5, 2009.

4. Ibid.

5. Ibid.

6. Victor Paul Furnish, *The Moral Teaching of Paul* (Nashville: Abingdon, 1979), 14.

7. Rebecca Price Janney, *A Study of How the Role of Women in the American Protestant Church and Society through the Centuries Bears Upon the Faithfulness of Contemporary Evangelical Women*, a doctoral dissertation submitted to the faculty of Biblical Theological Seminary, May, 2000, 40–41.

8. Ibid.

9. William H. Chafe, *The Paradox of Change: American Women in the 20th Century* (New York: Oxford University Press, 1991), 200.

10. Ibid., 219.

11. "Focus on the Family Mission Statement," *Focus on the Family*, http://www.focuson thefamily.com/about_us.aspx.

12. "Don Wildmon," *NNDB Tracking the Entire World*, The Notable Names Datebase, http://www.nndb.com/people/201/000062015/.

13. "Mrs. Beverly LaHaye," *CWK*, http://gideon.cwfa.org/articledisplay.asp?id=2114&department=CWA&categoryid=.

14. Jerry Falwell, "What We Are All About: The Four-Pronged TMMC Platform," *The Moral Majority Coalition*, http://www.moralmajority.us/index.php?option=com_content&task=view&id=12&Itemid=.

15. Ibid.

16. Ibid.

17. "Guiding Principles," *Focus on the Family*, http://www.Focusonthefamily.com/about_us.aspx.

18. Ibid.

19. Ibid.

20. Ibid.

21. Joan E. Boydell, E-mail interview with the author, July 31, 2009.

22. Ibid.

23. Ibid.

24. Wikipedia, "Christianity and Abortion," http://en.wikipedia.org/wiki/Christianity_and_abortion#Anglican_Church.

25. Ibid.

26. "About Care Net," *Time* Magazine, January 21, 2008, *Care Net*, http://www.care-net.org/aboutus/.

27. Ibid.

28. Mark Moring, "Simply Complicated," ChristianMusicToday.com, posted 8/25/2003, http://www.christianitytoday.com/music/interviews/2003/amygrant-0803.html.

29. John H. Riggall, e-mail interview with the author, August 13, 2009.

30. Christine Wicker, "Dumbfounded by Divorce: Survey inspires debate over why faith isn't a bigger factor in marriage," 2000, *The Dallas Morning News*, http://www.adherents.com/largecom/baptist_divorce.html.

31. Ibid.

32. Ibid.

33. Cal Thomas, Facebook interview with the author, August 1, 2009.

34. Sylvia Eagono, e-mail interview with the author, July 29, 2009.

35. Ibid.

36. Ibid.

37. Lori D'Augostine, "Kim Hill: How God Loves the Broken," *CBNMusic.com*, http://www.cbn.com/cbnmusic/interviews/lda_kimhill042807.aspx.

38. "A Brief History of American Homeschooling," excerpted from Linda Dobson, *Homeschoolers' Success Stories: 15 Adults and 12 Young People Share the Impact That Homeschooling Has Made on Their Lives* (Roseville, CA: Prima Publishing, 2000), SynergyField.com, http://www.synergyfield.com/history.asp.

39. Ibid.

40. Ibid.

41. Ibid.

42. Ibid.

43. Peter Nelson, e-mail interview with the author, July 22, 2009.

44. Ibid.

45. Ibid.

Chapter Eighteen: The Most Excellent Way

1. Edith Schaeffer, *The Art of Life* (Westchester, IL: Crossway Books, 1987), 53.

2. Edith Schaeffer, *The Hidden Art of Homemaking: Creative Ideas for Enriching Everyday Life* (Wheaton, IL: Tyndale House Publishers, 1971), 28.

3. Ibid., 128–29.

4. Ibid., 130–31.

5. Edith Schaeffer, *The Art of Life*, 8–9.

6. Ibid., 8.

7. Ibid., 10.

8. Jan Karon, *A Light in the Window* (New York: Penguin Books, 1995),160, 162.

9. Ibid.

10. Kari Torjesen Malcolm, *Women at the Crossroads* (Downers Grove, IL: InterVarsity Press, 1982), 27.

11. Elisabeth Elliot, "Dating Activities—Are They Wrong?" *Family Life Today* radio broadcast, September 3, 2009.

12. Elisabeth Elliot, *Passion and Purity: Learning to Bring Your Love Life Under Christ's Control* (Grand Rapids, MI: Revell, 1984), 22.

13. Ibid., 35.

14. Ibid., 43.

15. Ibid., 14.

16. Ibid., 66.

17. Ibid., 147.

18. Ibid., 129.

19. Ibid., 154.

20. Joshua Harris, *I Kissed Dating Good-Bye* (Colorado Springs: Multnomah, 1997), 67.

21. Ibid., 10.

22. Ibid., 68.

23. Ibid., 78.

24. Ibid., 79, 80.

25. Ibid., 98.

26. Ibid., 99.

27. Ibid., 131.

28. Ibid., 157.

29. Elliot, "Dating Activities."

30. Dennis F. Kinlaw, *We Live as Christ: The Christian Message in a New Century* (Nappanee, IN: OMS International, 2001), 20.

31. Ibid., 22.

32. Stanley Key, sermon, "Marriage Matters," Loudonville Community Church, Loudonville, NY, June 17, 2007.

33. Kinlaw, 39.

34. Key, ibid.

35. Ibid.

36. Rebecca Price Janney, *A Study of How the Role of Women in the American Protestant Church and Society through the Centuries Bears Upon the Faithfulness of Contemporary Evangelical Women,* a doctoral dissertation submitted to the faculty of Biblical Theological Seminary, May, 2000, 96–97.

37. Schaeffer, *The Hidden Art of Homemaking*, 58.

38. Ibid.

39. Ibid.

40. Ibid., 153–54.

41. Ibid.

42. Ibid., 125.

43. Malcolm, 23.

44. Ibid., 161.

45. Ibid, 164.

46. Ibid.

47. Francis Foulkes, *Ephesians Tyndale New Testament Commentaries* (Grand Rapids: William B. Eerdmans Publishing Company, 1989), 165.

48. Harris, 170.

49. "J. Robertson McQuilkin," *Columbia International University*, http://www.ciu.edu/faculty/bio_short.php?id=129.

50. Ibid.

51. Kinlaw, 50.

52. Schaeffer, *Act of Life*, 53.

53. Ibid., 57.

54. Ibid.

55. Kinlaw, 50.

56. Ibid.

57. Harris, 63.

58. Ibid.

59. Thomas Cahill, *How the Irish Saved Civilization* (New York: Doubleday, 1995), 4.

60. Ibid., 12.

61. Ibid., 14.

62. Ibid., 35.

63. Ibid., 181, 183.

64. Ibid., 194.

65. Ibid., 196.

66. Ibid., 4, 5.

67. Harris, 63–64.

68. Cahill, 218.

WHO GOES THERE?

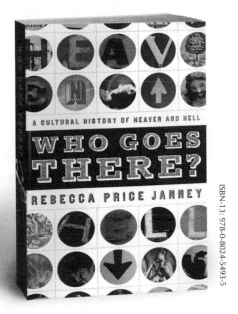

ISBN-13: 978-0-8024-5493-5

Princess Diana, John Ritter, Saddam Hussein, Mother Teresa, Chris Farley . . . Does it seem reasonable to guess where each of these people ended up after they died? While it is comforting to suppose that everyone who's "good" goes to a better place when they die, and everyone who's "bad" doesn't, on what is that hope based? To adequately understand how these thoughts influence us today, Rebecca Price Janney goes back to the colonization and founding of the United States. From the Great Awakening to the American Revolution, through the tumultuous 19th century, and all the way past two world wars and a technological revolution, *Who Goes There?* pieces together a thoughtful narrative of American beliefs about the afterlife.

www.MoodyPublishers.com